Greenwich Readers

Education & Training for Life

Equality, Participation and Inclusive Learning

This Reader is one of a series designed to support teachers and trainers in the post-compulsory sector of education. It will be of value to those who are working in colleges of further and higher education, sixth form colleges, adult and community education institutes, training units, and institutions of specific vocational preparation in the health service, the police service and the armed forces. The topics have been selected to represent a wide view of currently important issues and, by providing appropriate material for critical reflection on professional practice, the book will meet the needs of experienced teachers and trainers as well as those in the earlier stages of their careers.

In addition to such general use, the volume is one component of an integrated Certificate in Education/Postgraduate Certificate in Education course offered by the School of Post-Compulsory Education and Training at the University of Greenwich. Further information on this and other programmes of study and related academic services may be obtained from:

School of PCET
University of Greenwich
30 Park Row
London SE10 9LS

telephone: 020 8331 9230
fax: 020 8331 9235
e-mail: pcet@gre.ac.uk
www.gre.ac.uk

The planned range of titles in this series is as follows:

- Adult Learners, Key Skills & the Post-16 Curriculum
- Equality, Participation & Inclusive Learning
- Flexible Learning & ICT
- Language, Communication & Learning
- Perspectives on Learning
- Planning Teaching & Assessing Learning
- Professionalism, Policies & Values
- Supporting Students

Enquiries about the current availability of these publications should be addressed to the School Office at the above address.

Tony Lewis
Series Editor

Equality, Participation and Inclusive Learning

A Reader

Maude Gould
&
Ann Lahiff

Published in 2000 by Greenwich University Press and prepared for publication by:

Procurement and Business Services Department
University of Greenwich
Woolwich University Campus
Wellington Street
London SE18 6PF

ISBN 1 86166 077 4

Cover designed by Pete Birkett

Text design and layout by Christine Murray

In the majority of cases the contents of the readings and extracts in this volume have been reproduced as they appear in the publications from which they have been taken.

Every effort has been made to trace all the copyright holders, but if any have inadvertently been overlooked the publishers will be pleased to make the necessary arrangements at the earliest opportunity.

University of Greenwich, a charity and a company limited by guarantee, registered in England (reg no 986729). Registered Office: 30 Park Row, Greenwich, London SE10 9LS.

Contents

Introduction   xi

Part One – Conceptual and Legal Frameworks   1

1.   The Concept of Equality   3
      Jim Tarrant

2.   Equality and the Law   9
      Ann Lahiff

Part Two – Social Dimensions of Inequality   29

3.   Disability   33
      John Tomlinson

4.   Race and Ethnicity   41
      Trevor Leahong

5.   Sex and Gender   59
      Ann Lahiff

6.   Sexuality   73
      Jane Andrews

7.   Social Class   89
      Ann Lahiff

8.   Age   97
      Ann Lahiff

Part Three – The Development of Inclusive Provision   101

9.   The Background to Furthering Opportunities in FE   103
      David Johnstone

10.   The Role of Resource Centres in the Development of Inclusive   109
      Learning
      David Johnstone

11.   Students with Special Needs   117
      Mary Warnock

12. Equal Opportunities for All?   125
    John Fish

13. Checklist for Disability Statements   127
    Deborah Cooper

14. Inclusive Learning   131
    John Tomlinson

15. The Tomlinson Committee   137
    Lani Florian

16. Beyond the 'Inclusionist' Debate   141
    Liz Maudsley & Lesley Dee

Part Four – The Experience of Students and Teachers   147

17. The Learning Age   149
    John Lawton

18. Towards Exclusion   153
    Deborah Weymont

19. Adult Appropriateness and Students with Learning Difficulties   159
    Hilary Beverley

20. Only Connect: a Curriculum for Personal Development and Social Inclusion   163
    Bryan Merton

21. Accessing Further Education: Views and Experiences of Students   167
    Joyce Harrison

22. Specific Learning Difficulties in Maths: a Guide for Teachers and Tutors   177
    Nicola Martin

23. Inclusive Practices in Higher Education   181
    Jenny Corbett & Sue Ralph

24. Improving Transition for Students with Disabilities and Dyslexia from Further Education to Higher Education   185
    Viv Parker & Marion West

Acknowledgements

Acknowledgement is made for permission to reproduce the extracts quoted:

Bagilhole B & Woodward H (1995) 'An occupational hazard warning: academic life can seriously damage your health. An investigation of sexual harassment of women academics in a UK university' *British Journal of Sociology of Education* (Taylor & Francis Ltd, PO Box 25, Abingdon, OX14 3UE) 16 (1), pp37–40

Beverley H (1997) 'Adult appropriateness and students with learning difficulties' *Adults Learning* June, pp237–274

Bilton T, Bonnett K, Jones P, Skinner D, Stanworth M & Webster A (1996) *Introductory sociology* 3rd edn Macmillan, pp138–9; 202; 342

Blumenfield WJ & Raymond D (1988) 'A discussion about differences: the left-handed analogy' in *Looking at gay and lesbian life* Beacon Press, pp23–33

Commission for Racial Equality/Equal Opportunities Commission (1995) *Further education and equality – a manager's guide* CRE/EOC, pp8–10; 13; 14

Cooper D (1996) 'Checklist for FE disability statements' *The Skill Journal* November, pp8–11

Corbett J & Ralph S (1997) 'Inclusive practices in higher education: an example of imaginative provision by Stuart Olesker' *The Skill Journal* December, pp26–29

Farish M, McPake J, Powney J & Weiner G (1995) *Equal opportunities in colleges and universities: towards better practices* Society for Research into Higher Education/Open University Press, pp1–6

Fish J (1985) *Equal opportunities for all? (Fish Report)* Inner London Education Authority, pp205–208

Florian L (1997) 'The Tomlinson Committee' *British Journal of Special Education* 24 (1) March, pp7–12

Further Education Funding Council (1996) *Inclusive learning: principles and recommendations. A summary of the findings of the learning difficulties and/or disabilities committee (Tomlinson Report)* FEFC, pp2–11

Further Education Funding Council (1997) *How to widen participation – a guide to good practice* FEFC, pp40–44

Further Education Unit (1988) *Staff development for a multicultural society (RP 390) Booklet 1, Introductory Module: Appendix* FEU/Further Education Development Agency, pp89–94

Harrison J (1996) 'Accessing further education: views and experiences of FE students with learning difficulties and/or disabilities' *British Journal of Special Education* 23(4) December, pp187–197

Hinde J (1998) 'Cash for female participation' *The Guardian* 11.5.98

HMSO (1978) *Special educational needs Report of the committee of enquiry into the education of handicapped children and young people (Warnock Report)* HMSO, pp170–177

Johnstone D (1995) *Further opportunities: learning difficulties and disabilities in further education* Cassell, pp1–11

Johnstone D (1997) 'The role of resource centres in the development of inclusive learning' *The Skill Journal* December, pp22–26

Lawton J (1998) 'The learning age' *Adults Learning* April, pp19–22

Martin N (1997) 'Specific learning difficulties in maths: a guide for teachers and tutors' *Skill* March, pp39–41

Maudsley L & Dee L (1995) 'Beyond the "inclusionist" debate' in *Redefining the future: perspectives on students with learning difficulties and disabilities in FE* Institute of Education, pp79–88

Merton B (1998) 'Only connect: a curriculum for personal development and social inclusion' *Adults Learning* March, pp12–15

Mitsos E & Browne K (1998) 'Gender differences in education: the underachievement of boys' *Sociology Review* 8 (1) September, pp27–31

Parker V & Marion West M (1996) 'Improving transition for students with disabilities and dyslexia from further education to higher education: a report of an HEFCE-funded project' *Journal of Access Studies* 11, pp227–240

Powney J, Hamilton S & Weiner G (1997) *Higher education and equality: a guide* CRE/EOC, pp7; 13–16

Reid I (1997) 'An anti-classist checklist for literature and other media' *Sociology Review* 6 (3) February, pp32–33

Skellington R (ed) (1996) *Race in Britain today* 2nd edn Sage/Open University Press, pp13–16; 246–247

Skill (1996) *Skill's guide to the Disability Discrimination Act 1995: a guide for colleges, universities, education authorities and training providers* National Bureau for Students with Disabilities, pp4–22

The Stationery Office (1997) *HE in the learning society: report of the national committee of inquiry into higher education (Dearing Report)*, Section 3: 'Alternative students and widening participation'

Tomlinson J (1997) 'The findings and recommendations of the Further Education Funding Council Learning Difficulties and/or Disabilities Committee's report: Inclusive Learning' *The Skill Journal* March, pp29–32

Twitchin J (ed) (1988) *The black and white media book* Trentham Books, p32

Winch C (1996) 'Equality, quality and diversity' *Journal of Philosophy of Education* 30 (1), pp114–115

Worsley R (1998) 'Broken promises' *The Guardian* 4.11.98

The School of Post-Compulsory Education and Training

The School of PCET, as it is known, has its origin in Garnett College in London, one of three institutions set up by the Ministry of Education in the late 1940s for the initial training of technical college lecturers. After many developments and organisational changes over the past 50 years, its future within the University of Greenwich will be from a campus on the banks of the River Thames in Christopher Wren's former Royal Naval College.

The School's services and students, though, are not only locally based, but nationwide and international. PCET is a leader in distance provision for lecturers, trainers, administrators and other support staff from all sectors of post-school provision, as well as from the public services and voluntary and commercial training organisations. It has associated centres in various parts of the United Kingdom, and there are projects in China, South Africa and Russia, and leadership of research and information networks within the European Union.

We aim, in both our teaching and our research, to relate professional practice to learning theory and current policy issues. This permeates all of the School's programmes – from initial training on Cert Ed/PGCE programmes, through professional development at BA/BSc and Masters levels and the work of our Training and Development Office, to our portfolio of short courses and bespoke in-house provision. There is a thriving group of research students, and the School has been at the forefront of innovation in computer mediated communication. We provide a comprehensive service for further, higher and adult education, helping people to help others learn through life.

Ian McNay
Head of School

Maude Gould divides her time between working in the Open Learning Centre at a further education college and running the BA/BSc Education and Training at the University of Greenwich. Previously, she taught for many years in a variety of institutions before becoming staff development co-ordinator at an inner London college.

Ann Lahiff worked for a number of years in colleges of FE in London before joining Greenwich, where she is currently programme leader for the MA and MSc degrees in the School of PCET. Her principal teaching areas are the Sociology of Education, Equality Issues and Educational Research Methods, and her research interests lie in the impact of computer-mediated-communication on teaching and learning and the development of CMC as a research tool.

Introduction

A commitment to equality of opportunity in the public domain has long been required by national and European legislation, and for a number of years now most providers in the post-school sector have produced equal opportunities policies designed to achieve equity, improve access and widen participation. Making the case for equality may, therefore, seem a little dated. 'Surely', you will say, 'we are all equal now.'

Such a view, however, can hardly be confirmed by observation of the institutions around us. For instance, whilst it is true that some social groups are afforded a measure of protection against discrimination (e.g. through the Sex Discrimination Act 1975, the Race Relations Act 1976, the Disability Discrimination Act 1995) current legislation offers no specific protection at all to others (gay men and lesbians for example, and the over 50s). In addition, much of the discussion around post-compulsory education and training policy in the late 1990s and into the new century arises from the recognition that there are still considerable differences between social groups with respect to their participation and/or achievement rates. Consequently, whatever area of post-16 education and training practitioners find themselves working in, they are urged to 'widen participation' and search out 'alternative students'.

As a prelude to the scrutiny of such policies and practice, it is important that we consider some of the fundamental concepts – in particular those of equality and justice – that underpin the legislation, the equal opportunities policies and the widening participation initiatives. Implications for practice need to be examined too. For instance, we have to ask ourselves whether our activities may reinforce potentially discriminatory behaviour. The assumption here is that good *professional* practice demands good practice in the promotion of equality of opportunity. We must believe that it is not enough just to talk about equality; it has to be demonstrated to be part of the culture of our institutions, and it has to lead to an increase in participation rates and individual success.

Progress seems to have been made in some areas over the past twenty years. For example, a survey carried out in 1985 by Skill: the National Bureau for Students with Disabilities found that there were approximately 40,000 young people and adults with learning difficulties and disabilities receiving some kind of education or training in or through public sector and independent further and higher education colleges (excluding the then universities) in England (see Stowell, 1988). This was five times the number at the time of the Warnock Report in 1978. In 1996, the mapping exercise carried out for the Tomlinson Report located 126,500 students with learning difficulties and disabilities in colleges funded by the FEFCE (Further Education Funding Council for England). This is over five per cent of all students in these institutions.

But the growth in numbers has not been reflected in a corresponding increase in the breadth of curriculum opportunity. Students with learning difficulties and disabilities continue to be placed predominantly on learning programmes designed specifically for them, rather than working and studying alongside their peers and contemporaries. And for a variety of reasons students from minority ethnic groups are under-represented in the national provision.

This Reader is made up of a collection of journal and newspaper articles, extracts from books and official documents, together with specially written materials, which have been selected in order to provide an opportunity to explore the themes identified above. The first two parts of the text (*Conceptual and Legal Frameworks* and *Social Dimensions of Inequality*) comprise a review of general issues associated with the search to increase participation in post-school provision for members of hitherto under-represented groups in society. The second half (*The Development of Inclusive Provision* and *The Experience of Students and Teachers*) addresses in more detail the progressive expansion of access to main-line education and training for those with learning difficulties and disabilities.

Many of the contributions have bibliographies and suggestions for further reading, so that specific areas of interest can be followed up and studied in greater detail.

Maude Gould & Ann Lahiff
May 2000

Reference

Stowell R (1988) 'The student population in further education' *The Vocational Aspect of Education* 40 (107), pp101-104

Part One – Conceptual and Legal Frameworks

This first Part has two sections, offering:

- a preliminary analysis of definitions and basic concepts

- a consideration of the principal legal issues which lie behind our institutional policies and everyday behaviour.

Section 1 (*The Concept of Equality*) is informed by those philosophical discussions which arise when the idea of equality is explored. The aim of this section is to provide an introduction to the concept of equality and a consideration of it in relation to other notions such as freedom, liberty and democracy. The section thus provides a background to the discussions of legislation and of education and training policy which follow.

The second section (*Equality and the Law*) presents extracts from documents which outline key legislation in the area of equality, specifically the Sex Discrimination Act (1975), the Race Relations Act (1976) and the Disability Discrimination Act (1995). The legal framework is considered particularly in relation to the provision of education and training in the post-compulsory sector. The emphasis here is on how education and training providers have responded to these legal obligations, and the section reviews a range of positions institutions have taken in relation to the promotion of equality. It asks what understandings of the concept of equality underpin these positions and what obligations institutions and practitioners have towards promoting good practice.

It is in the nature of things that the process of consultation, legislation and implementation of policy progresses rapidly over time, especially after a change of government. We recommend that you keep up to date with events via the Internet. Some of the websites that you might find useful in your study of equal opportunities issues are:

www.cre.gov.uk	Commission for Racial Equality
www.dfee.gov.uk	Department for Education and Employment
www.disinhe.ac.uk	Disability and Information Systems in HE
www.eoc.org.uk	Equal Opportunities Commission
www.feda.ac.uk	Further Education Development Agency
www.skill.org.uk	Skill: National Bureau for Students with Disabilities

1. The Concept of Equality

Jim Tarrant

The concept of equality is a highly contentious one. Initially, this may seem surprising, since equality is surely a familiar and universally approved notion: we have laws and policies concerned with enforcing equality; we share equally between children; we expect to be treated in much the same way as our colleagues. However, it is not so easy to defend equality *as a concept*.

Descriptive equality

For example, if we examine people in detail, they do not appear equal in any obvious way. Some are taller than others, some have money and possessions and some do not, some are highly intelligent – however measured – and others are not. The philosopher Aristotle in the 4th century BC, argued that human beings were distinguished from other living creatures not by birth and growth, nor by their senses, but by their *reason*.

> *The mere act of living is not peculiar to man – we find it even in the vegetable kingdom – and what we are looking for is something peculiar to him. We must therefore exclude from our definition the life that manifests itself in mere nurture and growth. A step higher should come the life that is confined to experiencing sensations. But that we see is shared by horses, cows, and the brute creation as a whole. We are left, then, with a life concerning which we can make two statements. First, it belongs to the rational part of man. Secondly, it finds expression in actions. The rational part may be either active or passive: passive in so far as it follows the dictates of reason, active in so far as it possesses and exercises the power of reasoning.*
>
> (Thomson, 1953: 38)

But Aristotle's insistence that it is the power of reasoning that distinguishes human beings from other animals does not seem to agree with any descriptive account of humankind. What seems, instead, to be the case is that people can and do differ markedly from one another in their capacity for reason. Indeed, in the case of newly-born infants, or brain-damaged adults, it might be the case that an animal would have to be judged more 'intelligent' than the human being. The reliance on rationality, however, has had remarkable persistence. In the 18th century, the American Constitution roundly declared all men [sic] to be created equal. But this can hardly count as an accurate description of human beings; there are readily observable differences between people. In fact, the declaration that all are born equal sounds much more like an article of faith than a statement of fact, and we may, of course, dissent from it.

Normative equality

At this point, one might wonder how it is that we have any concept of equality at all. Surely, something so at variance with descriptive accounts of human beings would not have survived. From a philosophical point of view, there are at least two reasons why the concept has proved useful and acceptable. First, philosophers, following the 18th century Scottish philosopher David Hume, distinguish between what is *known as fact* and what is *judged to be of value* (see for example Hume, 1911). So far in our discussion of equality we have been dealing with the language of *fact*. That is, we have considered the descriptive properties of human beings: their height, reason and intelligence. However, we should bear in mind that equality is also addressed in a different way. Consider the slogans: 'we ought to treat people equally', 'the right thing to do is to treat people equally', 'we should treat one another equally'. All of these slogans are what we call *value-loaded*. Language which uses terms such as *ought, right, should*, is what philosophers call value language. It does not describe, it prescribes, or recommends, that is to say, it is *normative*. Talk about equality, then, may best be understood as talk prescribing or recommending a certain course of action, in this case to treat people equally. Such talk does not rest upon a description of people; it is not trying to describe facts about human beings. We may, of course, disagree with a person's values, but we would not be able to settle the argument simply by reference to a description or a statement of fact.

However, equality talk is not merely value-loaded talk. It also has what philosophers call a *positive connotation*. Many terms that we use are highly emotive and may have either positive or negative overtones. For example, in our current society competition seems to have a positive ethos for many people. Similarly, equality may have a positive ethos for most of us. This means that we virtually want to express our approval when we hear the word used. Of course, the emotive aspect of equality does not settle everything about the use of the term. You and I may both have a positive attitude to equality, but have quite different views about how far, and in what ways, equality should be implemented.

Equality and liberty

There has traditionally been much *agreement* about the positive ethos of equality and much *disagreement* about how far and to what extent it might be implemented in society. The reason for this lies in the fact that equality is part of a wider family of concepts which are also highly emotive and contentious. Let us take the concept of freedom as an example. In the early nineteenth century, the debate on banning the slave trade reached its climax to calls of freedom from the public gallery. You may think these cries were from former slaves, or relatives of slaves, but they were not. In fact, the calls for freedom came from the slave *traders* who wanted the right to continue their trade. This notion of freedom as the right to be left alone (except for slaves!) has been very important in Britain and has had its supporters in America. The American philosopher Robert Nozick (1993), believes that taxation amounts to enforced slavery. In his opinion, to tax me is to interfere with my freedom. However, for other philosophers, interference with the freedom of some is necessary to secure the well being of others. Here, the freedom to be left alone hampers the provision of basic needs, or more, to others.

Anyone who believes in the right to freedom as non-interference, will see a conflict between liberty and equality. My liberty may be under threat from your desire to improve your quality of life. How much liberty is perceived to be under threat from equality depends on how far a state goes to promote positive measures to secure equality. Suppose a state decides we should all be equal with respect to a minimum quality of life, set high with provisions of material needs. The state is then committed to transfer resources from those with a high quality of life, to those with a lower quality of life. In that way, equality can be seen as interference with freedom, and gives us a conflict of values. How we decide between such a conflict depends on a wider 'form of life' to which we are committed.

Equality and education

Not all conflict between liberty and equality need have such a monetary overtone. Consider the position of equality in education. In the past, this has often been addressed as *equality of opportunity*, which has entailed giving everyone access to education on an equal footing, for example, ensuring that all are allowed to take competitive examinations at the age of eleven. However, whilst equality of opportunity insists on access by all to instruction and assessment in education, it says nothing about providing for equal advantage within that system. The provision for all to take equal advantage of the educational system would require some interference with the notion of liberty. For example, children whose homes do not have the advantage of middle class discourse and books might be given extra classes to ensure they were in the same position as middle class children.

I hope you can see that such an understanding of equality is much more controversial than equality of opportunity. Some of the issues are apparent in the following extract from Winch (1996) on diversity, egalitarianism and the nature of justice:

Procedural and social justice

If a group of individuals are alike in a relevant respect, then they should be treated as alike in that respect. For example, if two individuals have each been accused of a crime, then they should both be accorded the same investigative and legal procedures to determine innocence or guilt. An essential attribute of justice is that individuals alike in the relevant respect should have the same criteria of judgement applied to them. Notice that this does not mean that they should necessarily be given exactly the same *treatment*. We often say, for example, not just that a punishment should fit the crime but that it should be just to the individual, taking into account his circumstances and history. In many cases this will entail that the sentences given to different individuals for the same type of crime will differ. The principle under which they are sentenced, and to which all are subject, is that the punishment should fit the crime *taking into account the history and circumstances of the particular individual.*

To take another example, if the principle operating in education is that all students should sit an examination in order to gain a qualification, then it is a requirement of procedural justice that they all sit it under the same conditions of difficulty. In practice this will mean that most will sit the examination under the same conditions, but others, who are not well or who are disabled, for example, will sit it under different conditions in order to ensure that the degree of difficulty is not greater for them than for anyone else...

Continued...

Equality of *outcome* is a principle of equality that asserts that the endpoint of a process ought to be the same for everyone who goes through it. For example, the outcome of the work of a hospital after a year might be that all post-operational patients recovered after six weeks, irrespective of the seriousness of the surgical procedures applied to them. More to the point, perhaps, the outcome of an educational process might be that all pupils on a certain course gained the same grades in their examinations. The concept of equality of *opportunity* frequently arouses some confusion. This is because it is susceptible to different interpretations. There are those who adhere to a *liberal* interpretation whereby it is thought of as no more than procedural justice. Radical interpretations of the concept, however, see it as more concerned with equality of outcome. So, for example, it might be maintained that a certain outcome, whereby one group receives proportionally less of a certain good, say, higher education, than another, means that the opportunities of its members to take part in higher education must have been fewer than those applying in groups with a higher proportion of entrants...

(Winch, 1996: 114–115)

However, it is not simply the early years sectors of education that can involve controversy over equality. In further and adult education, provision often exists to promote gender equality. This can range from an equal ratio of males and females in appointments to institutional guidelines for ways in which teaching staff and students address one another. Again, this can cause tensions. For example, an institution with a gender policy on employment may, within the parameters of existing legislation, promote positive discrimination on behalf of its female appointments to management.

In the face of these examples, we need to return to the notion of a form of life. Equality, I said, had much to do with our values, and our values are basic to a form of life. Our values are basic moral notions; things we think of as good and right. At one time, philosophers argued for objective values; good, for example, was something about which we could be right or wrong. Recent philosophers have been against such an understanding of values. However, our adoption of values such as equality, is influenced by a number of factors. For one thing, there are legislative issues to take account of. Whatever our values, we may be constrained by legal requirements. I mentioned an institutional policy which can favour positive discrimination for women in employment; the institution may be constrained to the extent to which it can adopt positive discrimination. There is also the matter of consistency.

Suppose someone adopted a positive stance on equality favouring institutional rules about positive discrimination, yet also championed negative freedom. In such a case, we might well question how their position was consistent.

Equality and democracy

There is also an issue about the form of life in relation to an educational institution in a democracy. Consider the following brief passage from Tarrant (1989):

There are undoubtedly differences between elitists, pluralists, and moral democrats, both about values and political institutions. Elitists want minimum participation in politics by the electorate, confining it to a choice between competing parties at election time. To them, democracy is merely a political method, by which government is periodically subject to renewal or change. Pluralists are concerned with countervailing centres of power to match the state, rather than simply periodic elections, which they regard as an insufficient check to government. The meaning of democracy here is a society with a multiplicity of autonomous groups, in which the state is only one association. Moral democrats hold that democracy fundamentally presupposes individual autonomy, a necessary condition of which would be the opportunity for participation in social and political institutions, and the provision of an adequate moral and political education.

What remains evident as common is the possibility of changing the government of society. At minimum, in the elitist's model, this involves elections at which rival parties stand for office. There may be means of changing governments other than at elections, but I find them difficult to conceive of, if it be allowed that the choice to be made by society is between rival parties. Without the possibility of a change to a rival government, there seems to be no democracy. Elections would then be an empirically necessary condition of a democracy and a firm indication that if this institution were missing, the political system concerned would not be a democracy.

(Tarrant, 1989: 22)

If democracy entails alternative points of view about the sort of society we live in, then, insofar as education reflects the values of democracy, it, too, ought to afford the same scope to consideration of alternative points of view. But in such a case, it is vital that we extend equal consideration to others. At the centre of democratic education should be the whole issue of debate on what counts as a worthwhile society. In practice, governments fail to commit themselves to such ideas. Nevertheless, what they do commit themselves to is the hearing of other points of view, in the legislature and in the media. The most important principle operative here is respect for persons. When we allow another person to venture a different point of view, we extend respect through that procedure.

In other words, the principle operative here, in education, is equality of *respect*. This means, that whatever a person's gender or race or nationality or age, we extend to them the respect of the same hearing that we ask for ourselves.

References and further reading

Baker J (1990) *Arguing for equality* Verso
Cole M (1989) *Education for equality: some guidelines for good practice* Routledge
Hume D (1911) *A treatise of human nature* Dent
Nozick R (1993) *The nature of rationality* Princeton
Radcliffe Richards J (1994) *The sceptical feminist* Penguin
Saunders P (1989) 'The question of equality' *Social Studies Review* November

Singer P (1993) *Practical ethics* Cambridge University Press (especially Chapter 2)

Tarrant JM (1989) *Democracy and education* Gower Press

Thomson JAK (1953) *The Ethics of Aristotle* Penguin

Warburton N (1995) *Philosophy: the basics* Routledge (especially Chapter 3)

Winch C (1996) 'Equality, quality and diversity' *Journal of Philosophy of Education* 30 (1)

2. Equality and the Law

Ann Lahiff

The policy context for a consideration of the concept and practice of equality in organisations of education and training is provided by the framework of legislation over the past twenty-five years. In the absence of any significant addressing of equality issues in the specifically educational legislation, three Acts are of particular relevance: the Sex Discrimination Act 1975 (and 1986); the Race Relations Act 1976; and the Disability Discrimination Act 1995. Relevant provisions of the Acts are set out below.

Legislation for sex and race equality

The first two readings for this section are from a joint publication by the Commission for Racial Equality (CRE) and the Equal Opportunities Commission (EOC), dealing with legislation in relation to sex and race as it applies to institutions of further education since the Further and Higher Education Act of 1992.

The first of the extracts concerns the Sex Discrimination Act 1975 and the Race Relations Act 1976. The references, in brackets, refer to the specific sections and paragraphs of those Acts.

Relevant provisions of the Sex Discrimination Act 1975 and the Race Relations Act 1976

Colleges in the further education sector are brought under the Sex Discrimination Act 1975 and the Race Relations Act 1976 by paragraphs 75 to 88 of schedule 8 to the Further and Higher Education Act 1992.

The Acts define three main types of discrimination:

Direct discrimination occurs when a person is treated less favourably than others on grounds of sex or race. The Race Relations Act defines 'racial grounds' as race, colour or nationality (including citizenship), and ethnic or national origins (RRA s1(1)(a); SDA s1(a)(1)).

Indirect discrimination occurs when a rule or condition or requirement which applies equally to everyone has a disproportionately adverse effect on people from a particular racial group, or either sex, and there is no objective justification for the rule (RRA s1(1)(b), s28; SDA s1(b)(1), s37).

Victimisation occurs when a person is discriminated against for taking action under the Race Relations Act or the Sex Discrimination Act, or for supporting such action by another (RRA s2; SDA s4(1)).

Instructions or pressure to discriminate
Both Acts make it unlawful to bring pressure on a person, or to instruct them, to discriminate on grounds of sex or race; or to aid another to discriminate unlawfully

Continued...

(RRA s30, s31, s33; SDA s39, s40, s42). Vicarious liability also covers the acts of agents (RRA s32; SDA s41).

Discriminatory advertisements

It is unlawful under both Acts to publish an advertisement that is discriminatory on grounds of race, or seen to be discriminatory (RRA s29; SDA s38).

Discrimination in education provision

It is unlawful under both Acts to discriminate:

in recruiting students or providing access to benefits, facilities and services (RRA s17; SDA s22)

in providing vocational training (RRA s13; SDA s14)

in conferring vocational or professional qualifications (RRA s12; SDA s13).

Positive action

It is lawful under both Acts to provide training and special encouragement for people of a particular racial group, or either sex, who have been under-represented in certain occupations or grades during the previous 12 months (RRA s37, s38; SDA s47). It is also lawful to address any special educational, training or welfare needs identified for a specific racial group (RRA s35).

Other discrimination

Colleges must comply with those parts of both Acts that relate to discrimination in employment. They must also observe the general prohibitions against discrimination in access or 'indirect access' to goods, facilities and services they provide (RRA s20, s40; SDA s29, s50). 'Indirect access' would apply to the actions of agents providing services as contractors or franchisees.

(CRE/EOC, 1995: 9)

The guide stresses the responsibilities of Governors in FEFC-funded institutions with regard to race and sex discrimination. These duties are outlined in more detail in the next extract.

Institutional responsibilities

The college governing body is responsible for ensuring that no unlawful discrimination on grounds of race or sex occurs in the college. Chapter 17 of the FEFC's *Guide to Governors* sets out the Council's expectations of colleges in relation to equal opportunities.

The governing body should note that an employer is liable for any discriminatory act by an employee in the course of his or her employment. The fact that a discriminatory act was done without the employer's knowledge or consent provides no defence in law, unless the employer can show that all reasonably practicable steps had been taken to prevent such discrimination; for example, through staff training,

Continued...

briefings, codes of conduct, guides on good practice and regular monitoring by ethnic group and sex...

Both the CRE and EOC can investigate allegations of discrimination and publish their findings. They can also assist individuals to bring complaints of discrimination before a county court (or sheriff court in Scotland); employment complaints are heard in industrial tribunals. Both Commissions also promote good equal opportunities practice, and seek to work in partnership with a wide range of agencies in fulfilling their duties.

Advice is available from both the EOC and CRE on measures to prevent discrimination. Both Commissions have published detailed codes of practice for employers:

Code of Practice for the elimination of racial discrimination and the promotion of equality of opportunity in employment (CRE)

Guidelines for Equal Opportunities Employers: Code of Practice for the elimination of discrimination on the grounds of sex and marriage and the promotion of equality and opportunity in employment (EOC).

These codes have statutory force, which means that failure to follow their recommendations can be cited as evidence in a case of discrimination brought against an employer. The CRE has also published a *Code of Practice for education.*

(CRE/EOC, 1995: 8)

Another publication sponsored by the CRE and EOC (together with the Committee of Vice Chancellors and Principals) focuses specifically upon higher education. It indicates the expectations that the Commissions have of the educational institutions with regard to disability issues as well as to race and sex.

Unlawful discrimination in HE

It is the responsibility of higher education institutions to ensure that no unlawful discrimination on grounds of race, sex or disability occurs in the institution. This applies to the institution as an 'employer' as well as a 'service provider', with certain exceptions in the case of the Disability Discrimination Act (1995)...

The Commission for Racial Equality (CRE) and the Equal Opportunities Commission (EOC) expect institutions to:

- take responsibility for promoting equal opportunities
- ensure that institutional procedures, policies and actions comply with the Race Relations Act and the Sex Discrimination Act, and are not unlawfully discriminatory
- take positive action, when appropriate, to redress any unjustified disparities by ethnic group or sex in the fields of education and employment.

(Powney *et al.* 1997: 7)

You will note that the responsibility that any educational institution has to its *employees* as well as to those who use its services (e.g. *students* and *trainees*) is clarified in this extract.

The CRE, CVCP and EOC recommend that colleges and universities should develop sets of detailed performance indicators in order to 'provide evidence to those outside the institution that equality of opportunity is taken seriously'. They make suggestions as to appropriate categories, as follows:

- the institution's response and range of provision
- boards, committees and the executive
- students' recruitment, guidance and support
- teaching and the promotion of learning
- staff recruitment, support and career development
- research and quality assurance

(Powney *et al.* 1997: 17–20)

Disability and the law

A relatively new area covered by legislation is that of disability. In the extracts below from a set of guidelines published by Skill – the National Bureau for Students with Disabilities – it will be clear that the legislation stops short of the protection offered to people on the grounds of race or sex.

The Skill document acts as a guide to the Disability Discrimination Act. It is designed for staff in colleges, universities, education authorities and for training providers. It covers the main areas of the Act, but concentrates on the Act's impact on education. All references to the Disability Discrimination Act 1995 are given in square brackets, e.g. [Part II, Section 6]. I have included extended extracts because of the newness of the legislation and its impact on colleges and training providers and because of the number of exceptions that are made in the legislation.

Disability Discrimination Act 1995 – implications for education

The Disability Discrimination Act 1995 became law in November 1995. The Act is a measure to reduce discrimination against disabled people. It is the most comprehensive anti-discrimination legislation for disabled people to date, but it does not amount to comprehensive civil rights legislation; there are situations in which disabled people can still legally be discriminated against. Parts of the Act [came] into force around the end of 1996, but it will be several years before the entire Act is fully implemented.

Education appears twice in the Act; once in the goods, facilities and services section where educational provision is excluded; and again in the section devoted to education, which requires educational establishments to provide information about their facilities and services for disabled people.

Continued...

Educational establishments and training providers also have to adhere to other relevant sections, particularly the employment and the goods, facilities and services sections of the Act...

What the Act does

The Disability Discrimination Act aims to tackle discrimination in:

* employment
* goods, facilities and services
* the sale and letting of premises.

The Act creates the National Disability Council (in England, Wales and Scotland) and the Northern Ireland Disability Council. These councils advise the Government on how to reduce and eliminate disability discrimination and help the Government interpret the Act. The National Advisory Council on Employment of People with Disabilities (NACEPD) continues to advise the Government on employment issues.

The Act also amends education legislation, and requires colleges and universities to provide more information about their facilities and services for disabled people. In addition, the Act gives the Government new powers to set standards of accessibility in new public transport vehicles.

Definition of disability

The Act states that a person has a disability:

if he [sic] *has a physical or mental impairment which has a substantial and long-term adverse effect on his ability to carry out normal day-to-day activities*

[Part I, Section 1]

This definition includes:

* physical disabilities
* mental impairments
* sensory impairments
* severe disfigurement
* progressive conditions which have an effect, however small, on day-to-day activities, but are expected to become substantial
* people who have a history of disability (e.g. a person recovering from a mental illness).

The disability must have substantial, long-term effects on day-to-day activities and have lasted, or be expected to last, 12 months. The Secretary of State issued guidance on the definition of disability in July 1996. The guidance will help to determine whether or not a person has a disability under the definition in the Act.

The definition of disability in the Act is different from definitions in previous legislation. However, any person who has been registered as disabled between January 1995 and 2 December 1996 will not have to prove they meet the new definition of disability for three years.

Continued...

The definition of learning difficulty and/or disability in the Further and Higher Education Act 1992, which is different from the definition used in the Act, will continue to exist alongside this definition.

Employment provisions

... The main employment provisions are:

- treating a disabled person less favourably than a non-disabled person without good reason is unlawful
- reasonable adjustments must be made to working conditions or the workplace to help a disabled person do a job
- a complaint of discrimination may be presented to an industrial tribunal.

Unlawful discrimination

Employers may not discriminate in:

- recruitment and retention arrangements
- promotions and transfers
- training and development
- working conditions
- employee benefits, e.g. bonuses and social clubs
- the dismissal process...

The legislation makes it quite clear that only *reasonable* adjustments need to be made [to workplaces so that they are accessible]; they do not amount to positive discrimination...

Changes to current law

Changes have been made to current employment law which [came] into effect on 2 December 1996:

- disabled people no longer need to register [as disabled].

Quota Designated Employment Schemes have been abolished. The quota system has existed since 1944. It imposed upon employers with 20 or more employees a duty to have a percentage (at least 3%) of registered disabled people in their workforce.

Educational establishments

All educational establishments, as employers, must comply with all of the employment parts of the Act...

Exceptions

There are occasions where discrimination by service providers might be justified:

- when health and safety would be seriously endangered
- when the disabled person cannot understand the contract
- when the service provider would otherwise be unable to provide a service
- when providing the same service to the disabled person would mean a higher charge...

Continued...

Education

There is one major exemption to what is included as a service. Education which is:

- funded
- secured, or
- provided at an establishment which is funded by a relevant body.

The relevant bodies are:

- schools
- a local education authority in England and Wales
- an education authority in Scotland
- the Funding Agency for Schools
- the Schools Funding Council for Wales
- further education funding councils in England and Wales
- higher education funding councils in England and Wales, the Scottish Higher Education Funding Council
- the Teacher Training Agency
- a voluntary organisation, or
- a body of a prescribed kind.

Education taking place in school and much, but not all, of the activity in colleges and universities is therefore exempt. Educational establishments will not have to make their educational services accessible. Education providers do have other responsibilities, details of which are in the next section. If an educational establishment offers non-educational provision to the general public such as a theatre, conference facilities, or holiday accommodation these services are not exempt from the goods, facilities and services section in the same way as educational provision. Institutions providing these services will have to ensure that the services comply with the provisions. Students' unions, catering facilities, training, careers services, sports facilities and student accommodation are all considered to be non-educational for this purpose...

Disability statements in further education

Local education authorities (LEAs) in England and Wales have new duties in relation to their further education provision: to publish disability statements.

Further education colleges in England and Wales

The Further and Higher Education Act 1992 has been amended so that the funding councils in England and Wales must require colleges to publish disability statements. These statements relate to the provision made by further education colleges with respect to disabled people. Specialist (non-sector) colleges are not required to submit disability statements, but may do so if they wish.

Statements are designed to help students with disabilities to make informed choices about further education. The Government issued regulations in July 1996 outlining what disability statements must contain.

Continued...

Statements must include:

- information about policies
- names of members of staff responsible for students with disabilities
- admissions arrangements
- educational facilities and support
- complaints and appeals procedure
- examination arrangements
- welfare and counselling arrangements
- physical access to educational and other facilities.

The DfEE published guidance for colleges in England and Wales in September 1996 about producing disability statements.

Scotland and Northern Ireland

There is no current legal requirement for colleges in Scotland or Northern Ireland to produce disability statements... Scottish colleges will be asked to include statements on students with learning difficulties in their Development Plans, as a condition of grant with effect from 1997/98.

In Northern Ireland the Education and Library Boards directly fund further education institutions. Boards have a duty to take the needs of disabled students into account when providing educational facilities. The structure of further education is changing in Northern Ireland, and colleges may have to produce statements as a result of these changes.

Higher education – overview

Two sections of the Disability Discrimination Act 1995 affect the Further and Higher Education Acts with regard to higher education. Section 30 affects the working of the higher education funding councils in England and Wales and Section 31 affects the Scottish Higher Education Funding Council (SHEFC). The provisions of both are the same. They impose two duties on the higher education funding councils.

The first duty is, when carrying out their functions, to have regard to the requirements of disabled people. This is a duty similar to that already held by the FEFCs under the Further and Higher Education Act 1992... It requires the councils to consider the impact that all their activities, including funding and quality assessment, will have on disabled people.

The Act does not apply to higher education institutions in Northern Ireland. The Northern Ireland Department of Education directly funds institutions in Northern Ireland.

SHEFC responded to the duty to have regard to the requirements of disabled people by setting up the Chief Executive's Disability Advisory Group.

Continued...

The Higher Education Funding Council for England (HEFCE) has responded to the duty as well, by setting up the Specific Learning Difficulty and Disability Advisory Group. It is deciding on:

- how disability is reflected in the activity of the funding council
- the content of disability statements.

Disability statements

The second duty given to the funding councils is to require institutions to publish disability statements. In debate the Minister said that the statements are to contain information about the provision of 'facilities for education and research' at each institution for disabled people. Institutions must produce statements in order to receive funding...

Statements are intended to give a clear and accurate outline of the level of provision and accessibility in an institution. The law does not require institutions to change their provision, simply to state what policies and provision exist. The Government intends statements to be of use to prospective students and to the funding councils, but not to be an exhaustive account of every detail of provision.

England and Wales

In May 1996 the funding councils in England and Wales issued requests for disability statements. Institutions in England were asked to supply statements by 10 January 1997. Institutions in Wales were asked to supply statements by 30 September 1996.

Scotland

In February 1996 SHEFC issued a consultation paper containing a proposed specification for disability statements. SHEFC funded institutions are invited to submit, but not publish, draft disability statements later in 1996. Institutions will be offered feedback on the content of their draft statements. After this exercise the council will publish a circular specifying what statements must contain and when they must be published. It is likely that statements will have to be published by spring 1997...

All three funding councils state the purpose of disability statements is to:

- inform students of the provision that is available
- inform the funding councils of the nature and extent of the provision.

SHEFC includes a third purpose, to provide an opportunity for institutions to share information on good practice.

The funding councils have asked for disability statements to be structured under three headings:

- existing policy
- existing provision
- future activities and future policy development.

(Skill, 1996: 4–22)

Implementation of legislation

These then are the legal requirements that institutions, their managers and other practitioners must observe. However, studies have shown that there are a range of responses made to the legal responsibilities set. Some institutions can be seen simply to abide by their legal duties whilst others may be as concerned with the *spirit* of the legislation as the duties they have imposed on them by the legislation. The three readings that follow provide an opportunity to consider a range of such responses.

The next one is from the CRE/EOC *Manager's guide*, quoted from earlier. Whilst the guide emphasises the legal requirements, it additionally provides not only a set of 'good practice' guidelines, but also a rationale for an active approach to the promotion of equal opportunity practice. It, too, draws attention to the importance of performance indicators.

The extract begins with the 'quality case for equality' and, though it is aimed at FE College managers, it is readily transferable to all post-16 establishments. In today's financially aware institutions, an emphasis on the cost of potentially *discriminatory* practices does not go unheard. The link with performance indicators may also be particularly relevant to institutions held accountable to external funding agencies.

Guidelines for good practice

Providing equality of opportunity enables further education colleges to ensure they provide good quality services for everyone.

Enhancing customer satisfaction
Providing a high standard of educational service which meets the needs of all sections of the local community is likely to increase student satisfaction with the college. A good equal opportunities policy will help managers to ensure that the college meets the various learning needs of men and women from all racial groups.

Deepening community roots
Close and full involvement in the college of men and women from all ethnic groups will help strengthen and deepen its roots in the local community.

Meeting students' needs
Further education colleges that understand and meet the needs of students from all ethnic groups, and both sexes, will be more successful in recruiting and retaining students.

Becoming an employer of choice
Human talent is a critical competitive resource, and each college needs to develop the reputation and practice that will attract the very best job applicants from all backgrounds.

Enhancing partnership
A further education college that is respected by all in the community will attract partnerships from a variety of agencies, such as local authorities, Training and Enterprise Councils and private sector employers.

Continued...

Avoiding the costs of discrimination

Racial and sexual discrimination is expensive. It costs money, undermines staff morale and reputation, and makes the college unattractive to students. Industrial tribunals are no longer constrained by limits on the compensation they can award victims of discrimination. Adverse publicity from such cases, or from a CRE or EOC formal investigation of alleged discrimination by the college, or both, may be an additional, expensive liability...

Equality performance indicators

The council is aware that colleges have been developing performance indicators for internal management purposes, both individually and collaboratively, and expects that colleges will wish to use more detailed performance indicators to supplement the indicators proposed by the council. The effectiveness of the use of performance indicators contributes to the assessment of a college's quality assurance system, and is taken into account by the inspectorate in assigning a grade for this aspect of work.

(FEFC, 1994 Measuring achievement Circular 94/12)

The CRE and the EOC believe that equality of opportunity is a sufficiently important component of quality to merit a specific set of performance indicators. As the FEFC makes clear above, colleges may develop their own supplementary indicators.

We suggest below a number of equality performance indicators... Colleges may wish to use the full set of indicators, or only a selection of them; they may decide to adapt all or some of them, or to create others. Whichever option they choose, the CRE and EOC recommend that a set of equality indicators should be developed and used, incorporating target levels, or timetabled improvements in performance, or both.

Suggested equality performance indicators:

- The college has an effective equality monitoring system, which measures progress towards its equality objectives.
- Staff can demonstrate good understanding of the main equal opportunity issues, and have clear responsibilities for implementing the college's policy.
- Student surveys demonstrate good understanding of the college's equal opportunity policy and procedures.
- External 'stakeholder' surveys show good awareness of the college's equal opportunity commitment and relevant policies.
- New services cater for both sexes and all ethnic groups in the local community.
- College publicity and marketing materials establish the college as an equality standard setter.
- Among new client groups being targeted and recruited, both sexes and all ethnic groups in the local community are fairly represented.
- Participation rates for ethnic minorities and women in selected programme areas show increases.

Continued...

- Drop-out rates for all groups are lower; with corresponding savings in the costs of falling student numbers.

- The range of employers providing work experience placements, including businesses led by women and people from ethnic minorities, increases over a defined period.

- Levels of student and staff absenteeism, including absenteeism among women and ethnic minorities, consistently decrease.

- Grievances and complaints, including those from women and ethnic minority students, decrease over a specified period.

(CRE/EOC, 1996: 10,13,14)

The next extract outlines what the CRE and EOC consider an institutional equal opportunities policy should look like. It emphasises the point that if real change is considered desirable, a policy on its own without any action plan is meaningless. In this extract you may be reminded of the 'value positions' outlined in Section 1 of this Reader. The text has been written with higher education institutions in mind, but I have amended specific references so that you should be able to relate it to your own institutional context.

Institutional equal opportunities policies

A statement that an organisation is committed to equal opportunities will be meaningless unless backed by a clear and thorough policy, together with an action plan applicable to all areas of education: employment, recruitment, teaching, learning and assessment, curricula and research. Such a plan will include explicit arrangements for collecting and monitoring data and evaluation which in turn informs subsequent policies and development plans.

The institutions ... that are most successful at providing equal opportunities will be able to demonstrate:

- commitment to, and involvement in, equality initiatives at senior level and throughout the organisation
- plans providing for strategic development and improvement
- action (internal and external)
- ways of monitoring and evaluating outcomes and periodic review of policies.

These elements of a good equal opportunities policy are elaborated below.

Commitment
Institutions should be able to demonstrate the following:

- A written equal opportunities policy, linked clearly to the institution's strategic plan, its mission statement and charter, and informed by the Race Relations Act 1976, the Sex Discrimination Acts 1975 & 1986 and Disability Discrimination Act 1995.

Continued...

- Endorsement of the policy by senior management teams and the governing body and clear lines of responsibility and accountability for ensuring that the policy is put into effect.

- An established infra-structure with sufficient resources allocated to increase awareness of the policy and to support necessary training and advice. This is likely to involve a senior member of the top executive team having overall responsibility for examining issues of managing the equal opportunities policy; and also possibly a sub-committee of governors or a staff or student/staff committee with responsibility for examining issues of equality. Some institutions prefer that equal opportunities should not be the exclusive business of a sub-committee for equality issues but that these should be integrated into the business of all standing and ad hoc committees and workshops.

- Further delegation of responsibility may be through the appointment of equal opportunities co-ordinators responsible for aspects of implementing, monitoring and reviewing equal opportunities policies.

- Commitment to identifying priorities for action and developing appropriate plans for implementing the policy throughout the organisation.

Planning

The action plan will refer to issues and intended improvements to the ways in which equal opportunities are defined and applied in employment, education and research in the organisation... Education institutions are at different points in their development of equal opportunities policy making and practices and each action plan should, therefore, start from the current situation with realistic goals.

- The foundation of the plan should involve a description and audit of the current equal opportunities situation in the context of the organisation's goals and targets. At its fullest it would cover all aspects of:
  - recruitment, induction, support and career development of ... students
  - methods and content of learning and teaching
  - recruitment, employment, support, in-service training and career development of academic and support staff
  - external suppliers of goods and services
  - the management and governance of the organisation.

- Not all of these can be tackled at once and planning will involve establishing priorities and desired outcomes for improving equal opportunities in the organisation. Linked with these should be targets, timetables and time scales.

- An essential part of the plan is to clarify the role of senior management and other people and groups who are expected to be involved in equal opportunity development. Who are they and what are their individual and group responsibilities? What resources, time and training might they require to carry out the work effectively?

- For an ethos of equality to pervade the organisation, it is important to plan the process of consultation and involvement with the students and staff in the institution as well as with those in the wider community who will be affected by the plans.

Continued...

- Outsiders may in turn influence decisions in relation to equal opportunities. For example, in choosing between contractors offering services, colleges and universities will need to balance carefully their equal opportunities requirement with other quality factors and price.

- The action plan should include methods of confirming and assessing progress. Targets set should be related to local census, employment and other relevant data and reflected in equality performance indicators... Advice on setting targets is given in the CRE's *A measure of equality* (1991), and the EOC's *Monitoring, positive action, targeting* (1995).

- Action plans should be given a high public profile within and outside the institution, with regular communication and publicity to ensure awareness among current staff and student members of the institution; potential students or staff; suppliers of goods and services; and other recognised consultative platforms likely to reach the broader public.

Action – internal

Priorities and action plans to improve equal opportunities will be determined by each ... institution. In relation to its priorities the institution should be able to show that:

- Data are collected and used to review the relationships between ethnicity, gender and disability and, for example, student and staff applications, recruitment and progression; student distribution by course, achievement rates and retention rates; staff distribution in terms of grades and pay, full-time and part-time, permanent and temporary and other conditions of service...

- Targets and priorities are set for training in the implementation of equal opportunities. Governing bodies, managers, personnel, administrative and support staff, academic and research staff, student welfare service staff should all have equal opportunities training.

- Each aspect of the institution's activities takes account of equal opportunities which are underwritten by governors and managers in terms of formal policy.

Action – external

Colleges ... are affected by other business, political, social and research communities; they also have an impact on those communities. As educational organisations, they should take a lead in demonstrating good equal opportunities practices and show for example that:

- Work placements for students and staff are supportive of students' needs and that these are carefully monitored including in relation to equal opportunities.

- Regular consultations take place with a full range of outside organisations concerned with issues related to gender, ethnic minority groups and other groups representing those with disabilities and special needs. Advice on equal opportunities can be sought from outside agencies, such as local racial equality councils, the CRE, the EOC and the ... funding and quality assurance bodies.

- The organisation projects itself in the community as an equal opportunity institution and one that sees the enriching effects of diversity among students and staff.

Continued...

- The institution's commitment to equal opportunities is always made explicit in contacts with outside organisations including professional accrediting bodies, research councils, government agencies, other sponsors and contractors. Information and marketing material is provided in community languages, when appropriate.

- In the case of formal working relationships with another institution (such as franchise programmes/Access partner institutions), the college or university ensures that there is agreement on the principles of equal opportunities and on the appropriate procedures to be followed in the case of any alleged breach of, for example, the harassment policy where the alleged harasser was not in his, or her, own institution.

Outcomes

- proportional gender and ethnic representation at all levels and across all aspects of the institution's activities including subject interests, research, composition (and chairing) of committees, services and facilities;

- evidence that conditions of service, staff development and promotion opportunities do not discriminate against certain groups or individuals;

- diversity in the student population and consistently high levels of student retention and attainment;

- ways in which curricula and methods of learning and teaching support the needs of the full range of students;

- enhanced reputation locally, nationally and internationally for teaching and research;

- buoyant application rates from students and staff and increasing levels of student satisfaction and high staff morale;

- full and attractive presentation internally and to the external media about the aims and achievements of equal opportunities in the university or college;

- employers offering a wide range of work experience and pre-employment opportunities;

- grievances and complaints dealt with satisfactorily.

(adapted from Powney *et al.* 1997: 13–16)

With specific regard to the Disability Discrimination Act 1995, Skill notes that during the passage of legislation, the Minister responsible in the Lords made it clear that colleges have 'responsibilities' towards the students they accept. Quoting the debate documented in Hansard, Lord Henley argued: 'Once accepted by a college, students will be entitled to expect that they will enjoy the access and support necessary to pursue their studies' (Lord Henley, 18 July 1995, Lords Hansard col 246, cited in Skill, 1996: 18).

Clearly this emphasises the *spirit* of the legislation rather than simply the actual legal position. Whilst the Government may expect colleges (and other training providers) to provide their students with the support 'necessary to pursue their studies', the extent to which this will be actually achieved, without comprehensive legislation, remains to be seen.

The final reading for this section is from the opening chapter of a text which reports a series of case studies conducted in colleges and universities in the UK. The chapter sets the scene by identifying the range of responses that institutions have made to the legal requirements. It ends with a reminder that understanding the policy response has much to do with the concept of equality to which institutions and individuals commit themselves.

---

25 years of progress?

There is now a considerable history of equal opportunities policy-making in Britain, arising out of the need for organisations to show their compliance with the equality legislation from the 1970s onwards, especially the Sex Discrimination Act passed in 1975 and the Race Relations Act passed a year later... The themes emerging from the equal opportunities policy literature suggest increased activity in the field of equal opportunities policy-making, though there is also a level of scepticism as to what it is possible to achieve...

Equal opportunities and policy-making

As already mentioned, effective equal opportunities policies and practices have begun to make inroads into organisational cultures, being perceived by some as significant indicators of quality (Jenkins & Solomos, 1989). Certainly, a polished, newly revised equal opportunities policy and mission statement seems to be a compulsory accessory for any modern education institution. In fact, according to Heward & Taylor (1993: 76) most universities have a long history of commitment to equal opportunities in the 'rhetoric of their charters', though there remains a wide gap between principle, practice and interpretation (or between 'rhetoric and reality', as Burton & Weiner (1993) put it) in the implementation of equal opportunity policies. What exactly are the policies being claimed in the name of equal opportunities? How do they relate to existing legislation? Jenkins & Solomos (1989) report that there is 'relative weakness' in interpretation of legal requirements, though the British government has so far deflected responsibility for tougher equality opportunity demands, say from the European Community's Social Chapter. It has thus been left to committed employers, professional associations and groupings, and individuals to develop workable strategies.

Understandably, therefore, developments have been patchy and the high expectations of early policy developments seem, to some extent, to have been dashed. Heward & Taylor (1993) argue that equal opportunities policies have had little effect on the position of women in higher education while Cockburn (1991) details the disappointment in the progress of equal opportunities in the 1980s felt by the respondents in her study of four large organisations with a formal commitment to positive action on sex equality. Cockburn suggests a number of reasons for this apparent failure:

Continued...

The law is too weak and difficult to use. Organisations taking positive action are too few and their goals and methods too limited. Organisations choose high profile, cost-free measures and neglect the more expensive changes that would improve things for a greater number of women. Policies adopted are seldom implemented. Implementation is not monitored. Non-compliance is not penalised, nor is co-operation rewarded.

(Cockburn, 1991: 215)

In addition, there has been much confusion about what equal opportunities actually means. In 1986, an investigation for the Commission for Racial Equality (CRE) found that 20 of the 42 universities involved in the study cited their charters as sufficient indication of their commitment. In a survey of 68 polytechnics and universities, Williams *et al.* (1989) found a similar ignorance and lack of clarity surrounding the notion of equal opportunities...

Studies have shown that different interpretations of policy have prioritised different aspects of inequality. Some institutions deem it sufficient to assert their commitment to equal opportunities through policy statements; others have developed detailed programmes of policy change. Significantly, both kinds of institution are likely to label themselves equal opportunities employers! Variations about which equal opportunities or 'minority' issues should be most highly prioritised within institutional policy-making have masked the fact that different groups are likely to want different things (Jewson & Mason, 1986; 1989). As Cockburn (1991: 45) found in her study: 'Black women and white, women with children and without, feminists and anti-feminists varied in their hopes and fears of the policy.'

Equality programmes have also tended to be specific to particular institutions and have arisen from specific histories and sets of problems. Thus, the two major organisational contexts affecting the implementation of (and obstruction to) equal opportunity initiatives are institutional and cultural.

[They] include structures, procedures and rules. Cultural impediments arise in discourse and interaction. They influence what men and women think and do. The two levels are interactive. Structures can be changed in the right cultural environment. But cultures predispose how people think and act.

(Cockburn, 1991: 45)

Despite the disappointment expressed about past efforts at equal opportunities policy-making, there has been evidence more recently that some colleges and universities have achieved substantial improvements in their equal opportunities policies and practices. For example, in Australia in the mid-1980s equal opportunities policies led to a significant rise in the number of women in senior positions in certain universities. Another more recent survey by the Commission of University Career Opportunity shows some progress in the UK but also considerable room for improvement.

Cottrell (1992) further suggests that the newer universities (ex-polytechnics) have had a greater commitment to equality issues citing those vice chancellors who were

Continued...

early signatories to the government-led Opportunity 2000, an initiative aimed at increasing the number of women in top jobs. And according to Anand (1992), ex-polytechnics are also better in terms of gender-fair representation on appointment panels and recruitment training...

Equal opportunities as expressed in policy has moved higher up the institutional agenda alongside government policies to increase and widen access to higher education. It is not at all surprising that the traditional university sector has sought to buttress its elite position in higher education through distancing itself from equal opportunities considerations.

Even where equal opportunities is adopted as an institutional issue, commitment can vary as to whether the policies addressed are long or short term. Short-term policy-making involves making quick responses to procedural issues: for example, institutions producing statements of intent and codes of practice without recognising the need for adequate resources to put policy into practice.

The longer agenda has a more ambitious aim of permanently transforming the dominant (male, white, middle-class) institutional culture (Cockburn, 1989).

Not surprisingly, the longer agenda has also been likely to attract more resistance. According to Cockburn's study of organisations, male employees erected institutional obstacles to the advancement of their women colleagues, fostering 'solidarity between men' at the cultural level in order to 'sexualise, threaten, marginalise, control and divide women' (Cockburn, 1989: 215).

On a more positive note, a study by Powney and Weiner (1992) which explored equality issues concerning female and Black and minority ethnic managers from a range of educational institutions found that, despite institutional variations, a number of sound and well-tried equal opportunities practices had been put into place, aimed at counteracting discrimination at different organisational levels. A continuum of institutional adoption of equal opportunities policies and practices was identified as follows:

1. Equal opportunities is a significant part of the ethos of the institution; for example, reflected in power structures and permeating all institutional activities *(ethos)*.
2. There is a genuine commitment to good equal opportunities practice *(commitment)*.
3. The institution is in the process of working towards equal opportunities *(predisposition)*.
4. There is some 'lip-service' given to equality issues *(lip-service)*.
5. There is no evidence of any real interest in equal opportunities issues *(none)*.

An institution with an ethos of equal opportunities is one where there is an awareness of the full range of obstacles barring individual progress and where every attempt has been made to remove such obstacles. For example, in the case of a further education college:

The stated ethos of the organisation is to create a supportive, comfortable, non-hostile place where black people could meet, organise and talk openly... There is a

Continued...

26

large percentage of black staff in the college, in excess of 30–40%... Black staff are represented at those [top tier] levels ... there are more black women than black men... There is a systematic staff monitoring process in the college which is explicit, public and open... The recruitment and selection process is systematically adhered to with black staff members sitting on the panel.

(Powney & Weiner, 1992: 29)

Also evident in the study was the comparatively greater progress made by smaller, lower status, educational institutions such as schools and further and adult education colleges, perhaps because of their relatively low status, their need to recruit from a wide range of groups in the community or their more intimate and student-oriented atmosphere. Additionally, the ex-polytechnics appeared to be moving more quickly on equality issues than the traditional university sector.

Gatekeepers of equal opportunities policies

One important feature of the spread of equal opportunities policies has been that women and Black senior staff are more likely to be allocated responsibility for equality issues... Thus, life is made more difficult for, say, women as ... managers because they are likely to become targets for those wishing to resist change, and also because of their very interest in equality issues, rendered peripheral to the most prestigious elements of academia...

In a UK study reported by Weiner (1993), Black managers (male and female) tended to have similar patterns of responsibility, often for both race and gender. A Black male college deputy suggested that such responsibilities further compromised his status...

It seems that high visibility can be the consequence either of having specific responsibility for equal opportunities and/or of being a woman and/or a member of a 'minority' institutional group in a senior position. And ... frequently the two come together to produce maximum visibility.

What do we mean by equal opportunities?

One of the problems with examining the effectiveness or otherwise of equal opportunities policy-making is that the term 'equal opportunities' itself is so elusive. It can be applied to a wide variety of contexts within educational institutions; for instance, to staff issues, curriculum, pedagogy, assessment, access and recruitment, priorities in funding, staff-student relations, the general work environment and so on.

Moreover, putting aside the fact that at various times equal opportunities has been used to address different kinds of educational or socio-economic inequality ('race', gender, class, disability, religion, ethnicity, sexual orientation, age), there are also distinct differences in its conceptualisation.

For some, achieving equality means enabling certain under-represented groups to attain their rightful place in the existing social, economic and political order; for others it means offering radical alternatives to an essentially biased social and political system.

(Weiner, 1986: 266)

Continued...

Bibliography

Anand P (1992) 'Equality faces an unknown hurdle' *Times Higher Education Supplement* 27 November

Burton L & Weiner G (1993) 'From rhetoric to reality: strategies for developing a social justice approach to educational decision-making' in I Siraj-Blatchford (ed) *Race, gender and the education of teachers* Open University Press

Cockburn C (1989) 'Equal opportunities: the long and short agenda' *Industrial Relations Journal* Autumn, pp213-25

Cockburn C (1991) *In the way of women: men's resistance to sex equality in organisations* Macmillan

Cottrell P (1992) 'Fairer university image' *Times Higher Education Supplement* 20 November

Heward C & Taylor P (1993) 'Effective and ineffective equal opportunities policies in higher education' *Critical Social Policy* 37, pp75-94

Jenkins R & Solomos J (eds) (1989) *Racism and equal opportunities policies in the 1980s* 2nd edn Cambridge University Press

Jewson N & Mason D (1986) 'The theory and practice of equal opportunities: liberal and radical approaches' *Sociological Review* 324, pp307–34

Jewson N & Mason D (1989) 'Monitoring equal opportunities policies: principles and practice' in R Jenkins & J Solomos (eds) *Racism and equal opportunities policies in the 1980s* 2nd edn Cambridge University Press

Powney J & Weiner G (1992) *Outside of the norm: equity and management in educational institutions* South Bank University

Weiner G (1986) 'Feminist education and equal opportunities' *British Journal of Sociology of Education* 7(3)

Weiner G (1993) 'A question of style or value? Contrasting perceptions of women as educational leaders' Paper presented at the Women in Leadership Conference, Perth, Australia, December

Williams J, Cocking J & Davies L (1989) *Words or deeds? A review of equal opportunities policies in higher education* Occasional paper, Commission for Racial Equality, London.

(Farish *et al.* 1995: 1–6)

References

CRE/EOC (1995) *Further education and equality: a manager's guide* Commission for Racial Equality/Equal Opportunities Commission

Farish M, McPake J, Powney J & Weiner G (1995) *Equal opportunities in colleges and universities: towards better practices* SRHE/OUP

Powney J, Hamilton S & Weiner G (1997) *Higher education and equality: a guide* Commission for Racial Equality/Equal Opportunities Commission/CVCP

Skill (1996) *Skill's guide to the Disability Discrimination Act 1995: a guide for colleges, universities, education authorities and training providers* Skill

Part Two – Social Dimensions of Inequality

In this Part we present a wider and more detailed exploration of the social aspects of each of the main areas of activity in which inequality of opportunity is manifest in our institutions. We offer the opportunity to analyse specific dimensions of inequality and consider ways in which these impact on our professional practice in education and training and on the experiences of our students and trainees within these institutions.

The dimensions presented include those that have been highlighted in the earlier discussion of the relevant legislation: race, sex and disability. In these areas there is a legal duty on practitioners and institutions to act in a non-discriminatory manner. Whilst it has been seen that practices vary in terms of the interpretation of the law – some institutions being more proactive than others – there is a formal, legal commitment to combat and seek to eliminate at least some of the discriminatory practices that might otherwise occur.

There are, however, other dimensions of inequality in our society which are not specifically covered by legislation – inequality in relation to social class for instance. Similarly, some social groups who are frequently discriminated against as a result of their sexuality or age do not generally have recourse to the law. In many respects a person's right to be treated fairly, irrespective of their sexuality or age, is still contested ground. These dimensions of inequality are therefore also included to enable practitioners in PCET to confront their own value-positions and to consider their practice, as well as the practices of their institutions, accordingly.

The emphasis throughout this Part is on an exploration of how our behaviour in 'classrooms' and institutions can either reinforce inequalities or advance the promotion of equality.

The following brief extract will set the scene.

> *Our individual lives – our autobiographies – inevitably build for us personal life histories that tell us why we are where we are in society. These stories tend to speak of inequality and our position in highly individualistic terms: we write CVs listing our biographical details, achievements and current position; we 'know' we are strong at some things but not at others, and that only by our efforts will we make anything of ourselves. In other words, inequality is not something to be explained or experienced collectively, for it only exists, if at all, as the advantages or disadvantages individuals have created for themselves.*

> *Occasionally, of course, a very different story of inequality is told, one that has not an individual but a collective narrator – a trades union defending its members' pay, a civil rights march demanding votes for blacks, a women's caucus declaring rights for their sisters around the world, a gay and lesbian rally against discrimination on grounds of sexuality. At times like these, people regard themselves as occupying a shared position, and construct a powerful sense of collective identity as members of a single economic class, or ethnic group, gender or sexual minority...*

> (Bilton *et al.* 1996: 138–139)

It is this collective dimension that is of particular concern to us and, whilst it is not possible to cover all aspects of inequality in society, those included here have been selected because of their particular relevance to post-compulsory education and training.

Section 3 (*Disability*) comprises a substantial extract from the introduction to the summary of the findings of the influential report of the FEFC committee of inquiry, chaired by John Tomlinson, set up to examine educational provision for school leavers and adults with learning difficulties and/or disabilities (FEFC, 1996: 2-11). Professor Tomlinson provides an overview of the context and history of the education and training of people with learning difficulties and/or disabilities, emphasises the need to raise standards of provision and participation rates, and reinforces the approach to 'inclusive' learning advocated in his committee's report.

In Section 4 (*Race and Ethnicity*) Trevor Leahong draws upon discussions in the literature to stress the point that change will not be forthcoming unless individual practitioners recognise the ways in which racism operates both at a structural and an organisational level. The debates arising from the McPherson Report show only too well how susceptible public institutions can be to the insidious progress of racism. The section offers a checklist for practitioners to consider implementing in their professional practice.

Section 5 (*Sex and Gender*) explores the patterns of gender inequality operating throughout post-compulsory education and training. Starting with a definition of terms, it explores the issues associated with 'differential attainment', highlighting the debate surrounding the underachievement of boys. The segregated curriculum is explored and its links to the segregated market identified. Practitioners are asked to consider what they can do to challenge stereotypes and to bring about change in their area of practice.

In Section(*Sexuality*) Jane Andrews suggests that if inclusivity is about responding to individual needs, then sexuality is an inclusiveness issue. Accounts of the experiences of gay and lesbian students and staff require all practitioners to examine their own values and prejudices; the use of the 'left-handed analogy' draws attention to significant aspects of 'being different'. Practical suggestions are offered as to the steps we can take to counter discriminatory practices in relation to sexuality.

In Section 7 (*Social Class*) we ask what bearing family background and circumstances can have on educational success and occupational choice at 16+, and whether practitioners need still to be concerned about it. In answer, the continuing correlation between social class and educational opportunity is firmly established. The commitment of practitioners to challenge common practices is considered as a pre-requisite to changing the structural and individual practices which still impede the life chances of a significant proportion of our young people.

But not only our young people. Section 8 (*Age*) addresses the last dimension of equality which still has no specific legislation to combat prejudice and assumption. The claims of those campaigning for protection against discrimination are presented here and, in the age of 'widening participation', it is argued that it is difficult to support any educational/social arguments against anti-discriminatory legislation on the grounds of age.

Reference

Bilton T, Bonnett K, Jones P, Skinner D, Stanworth M & Webster A (1996) *Introductory sociology* 3rd edn Macmillan

Further Education Funding Council (1996) *Inclusive learning: principles and recommendations. A summary of the findings of the learning difficulties and/or disabilities committee (Tomlinson Report)* FEFC

3.   Disability

John Tomlinson

Inclusive learning – the background

When I first entered educational administration, nearly 40 years ago, some of our citizens were deemed ineducable and never offered any formal educational opportunity or stimulus, seeing out their childhood and adult lives in families (who received little help or advice), in hospitals or in occupation centres (later called training centres). That regime was brought about by the terms of the *Mental Deficiency Act 1913*, and the attitude it betokened was altered in law only in 1970 (1980 in Northern Ireland) and then only so far as schoolchildren were concerned. Those who experienced that regime, at least for some of their lives, may still be as young as 30. If they are over 45, it will have covered what for other children would have been their whole experience of school. For those with disability or learning difficulty who *were* permitted to attend school, the starting-point was usually the description of their condition given by doctors. Whatever may have been the intentions of those passing the *Education Act 1944*, the effect was to define special educational need as springing from physical or mental disability. The formal process that was required in order that an LEA could 'ascertain' the need for special education often entailed resort to compulsory medical examination or the use of intelligence testing and invariably meant assigning the child to one of the statutory categories of handicap. It was not until 1959 that parents were given a right to appeal against the LEA's decision. Once ascertained as needing special education, children were for the most part taught in separate schools or classes. The term 'educationally sub-normal' remained in law until 1981. Such rigidities and perceptions perpetuated the isolation of children receiving special education, even though they were technically within the education system. However, attitudes and understanding were changing rapidly in the post-war years. In 1976 an Education Act declared that as far as practicable all children with special educational needs should be educated in ordinary schools. In 1978, the Warnock committee, in a landmark report, broke through with proposals to achieve this and much more which led to the *Education Act 1981*, now amended and extended by the Act of 1993. As a result, the lives and expectations of very many have been transformed. They include not only the children themselves, who have experienced a more sensitive and effective education, but also other children who have had the experience of working alongside them, and teachers, who had hitherto not worked in these ways; and not least, the families of the children and the organisations and services that collaborate with the education service.

Those working in further education need to remember this history and that our adult society contains at least three layers of experience. Depending on the period in which you grew up and the nature of your disability or learning difficulty, you may have been excluded altogether from education, included but isolated within it, or increasingly regarded as part of the whole work of the education service.

While these developments in attitudes towards children of school age were taking place, further education, in the post-war years, became a more recognised and vigorous part of the education service. It was thus better able, when called upon from the 1970s, to play a part in providing for older people with learning difficulties and/or disability. Section 41 of the Education Act 1944 had placed a duty on every local education authority to 'secure the provision for their area of adequate facilities for further education, that is to say, full-time and part-time education for persons over compulsory school age'. Growth was slow and achieved with difficulty. Immediately after the war, resources were concentrated on rebuilding and extending the school system. From the mid-1950s, governments began to emphasise the need for technical education and during the next 20 years building programmes were introduced and numbers grew dramatically so that in 1974 there were 335,000 full-time day students compared with 52,000 in 1953; and 727,000 part-time day students compared with 333,000 (Bristow, 1976). However, the general expectation was that students who entered further education courses would have the required minimum standard of educational achievement and be able to take the courses as offered. A survey of 1973, which did not include those with severe learning difficulties who had not been in the school system up to that time, found that only 10% of those leaving special schools entered further education. A further 9% entered special residential courses, an important reminder of the historical significance of specialist residential colleges and the foundations which supported them. Some 51% of those considered 'suitable' for further education were without any provision at all.

The impetus for change came from two directions. Some LEAs encouraged and funded provision, often spurred on by colleges themselves, by expert advisory staff and the experience of implementing the 1970 and 1981 Education Acts in schools. And the Manpower Services Commission, formed in 1974, promoted a series of youth training schemes as youth unemployment rose dramatically. Courses in basic education became a significant element in the programmes, as those with learning difficulties were increasingly disadvantaged in the changing labour markets. A survey of 1987 identified some 250 courses of this kind, in approximately half the colleges of further education in England (Stowell, 1987).

This, crudely summarised, was the situation at the passing of the *Further and Higher Education Act 1992* in which students with learning difficulties and/or disabilities are the only group of students specially mentioned. It not only places these students fully within the scope of further education, itself a powerful message, but also signifies the importance attached by government and parliament to provision for them. It is a landmark in the development of education policy. The Act says that the Further Education Funding Council 'shall have regard to the requirements of persons having learning difficulties' in the course of carrying out its general duties to provide full-time and part-time education.

'Have regard' is a relatively flexible duty in law and gives the Council room for the exercise of judgement as to what should be done for any individual according to circumstances. It is thus the starting-point of the Council's turning to the committee for advice and of the advice we now offer.

Our approach to learning

Central to all our thinking and recommendations is the approach towards learning, which we term 'inclusive learning', and which we want to see adopted everywhere. We argue for it because it will improve the education of those with learning difficulties, but believe it is also true that such an approach would benefit all and, indeed, represents the best approach to learning and teaching yet articulated. When we tested our approach in a number of colleges, that is what we were told. Put simply, we want to avoid a viewpoint which locates the difficulty or deficit with the student and focus instead on the capacity of the educational institution to understand and respond to the individual learner's requirement. This means we must move away from labelling the student and towards creating an appropriate educational environment; concentrate on understanding better how people learn so that they can better be helped to learn; and see people with disabilities and/or learning difficulties first and foremost as learners. It may sound simple, even obvious; but it has profound consequences. There is a world of difference between, on the one hand, offering courses of education and training and then giving some students who have learning difficulties additional human or physical aids to gain access to those courses, and, on the other hand, redesigning the very processes of learning, assessment and organisation so as to fit the objectives and learning styles of the students. But only the second philosophy can claim to be inclusive, to have as its central purpose the opening of opportunity to those whose disability means that they learn differently from others. It may mean introducing new content into courses, or it may mean differentiated access to the same content; or both.

Let it be clear that this approach does not involve glossing over disability or learning difficulty, still less pretending that given some change to the ways we teach they make no difference. Many individuals with disabilities and/or learning difficulties told us bluntly that we should not seek to minimise still less ignore the real difficulties or differences that a disability or learning difficulty can bring into a person's life. I recall vividly, for example, at one of the many conferences I have addressed since we started, a man who had been blind from birth telling me emphatically:

> I am blind, I have always been blind and always will be. I don't mind people knowing that: in fact I want them to know it. What I do not want is their pity or condescension. And what I do want is to be able to learn the same kinds of things as sighted people learn.

I have not forgotten. However, that instance and many others in the evidence we received only serve to re-emphasise that for a teacher the focus should not be on the disability itself but on what it means for the way that person can learn, or be helped to learn even more effectively.

Moreover, all students in further education bring with them a history of earlier educational experiences of more or less success in learning. That is especially true for those with disability or learning difficulty because of the history I have already outlined of our changing approaches to their education over the last 50 years. Since so much of the burden a disability or learning difficulty places on individuals is thus socially constructed – the result of attitudes and attributions by those who deem themselves without disability or able to learn normally – all the more reason for all those in education, governors, managers and teachers, to make their central concern the ways an individual learns and how they can be accommodated.

A key element in reconceptualising provision for students with learning difficulties is the recognition that their needs are cognate with those of all learners. Ensuring that all pupils or students make progress demands that teachers do not treat them uniformly, but differentiate their approaches according to the previous experience and varied learning styles of those pupils or students. Providing audio-tapes for a blind learner, amplification or photographs for a deaf person or simplified text for a hesitant reader are matters of degree rather than kind. Moreover, teachers have to select materials and methods appropriate to the subjects being taught: artists must encourage visual awareness and skill with colour, shape and texture, scientists must foster observation and an experimental approach, historians must learn how to use evidence from the past. Each domain of knowledge has its different procedures for examining the world, different tests for truth. Each student must learn the ways needed to proceed in the chosen study and adjust their learning styles accordingly. The task of teachers is always to effect a marriage between the requirements of particular subject-matter and the predispositions, stage of development and capacities of those who would learn. The wider the spectrum the greater the insight and ingenuity called for. We extend this view to the learning strategies adopted by people with disabilities and/or learning difficulties and their teachers.

One more thing needs to be said about this approach to learning, for the removal of doubt. Our concept of inclusive learning is not synonymous with integration. It is a larger and prior concept. The first step is to determine the best possible learning environment, given the individual student and learning task. Colleges told us, in evidence and when we tested this approach with a few, that this was increasingly their approach to all students. For those with a learning difficulty the resulting educational environment will often be in an integrated setting and, as in schools, increasingly so as the skills of teachers and capacities of the system grow. Sometimes it will be a mixture of the integrated and the discrete. And sometimes, as in the specialist residential colleges, it will be discrete provision. We envisage a system that is inclusive and that will require many mansions. Each element of the system will need to play its part: the teacher and learner; the institution or college; and the whole further education system. We acknowledge that this will require a degree of sector-wide and regional planning and collaboration so that scarce resources are best matched to estimated needs; and for this purpose the Council's regional committees and the colleges will need to co-operate and agree on sensible divisions of labour.

This is consonant with the proposal we also make that the time has come when colleges must share with the Council the legal duty to 'have regard' to the requirements of these students and thus assist in building a system that is 'sufficient' and 'adequate' for all who come forward. It also is realistic. Some colleges have made great strides over the last 10 years or so towards the inclusive approach. The different stages of development can be a basis for planning for the future, but in a way that can allow all who so wish to develop new capacities.

But there is also clear evidence that the quality of the provision made for these students is less good than that to be found in colleges generally. The work seldom features in college-wide systems of strategic planning, quality assurance or data collection and analysis. Few questions are asked about the purpose or relevance of what students with learning difficulties and/or disabilities are being asked to learn. Monitoring and evaluation of students' achievements is less common in this work than elsewhere and managers often lack awareness or understanding of what is required. We recognise fully that there is good provision with skilled teachers and knowledgeable managers, but remain concerned about the overall quality of provision nationally...

Increasing participation

An inclusive approach to the education of those with learning difficulties and/or disabilities has two aspects. The approach to learning just outlined would raise the quality of the educational experience of students in the colleges. But we must also find ways to increase participation and ensure that all who may want further education can be welcomed on terms they can accept. This means both trying to understand the underlying dynamic of current patterns of participation and creating ways to help the Council and colleges to know better how far they may be satisfying the potential demand. There is no escaping the fact that this requires clear definitions of who may be included in the phrase 'learning difficulties and/or disabilities'. A process that allows us to know in broad terms for how many we should be providing does not require the definitions that used to be attached to individuals once they are within education, and we have demonstrated that it is more effective to concentrate on providing the education environment needed to meet an individual's learning goals...

... [A] mapping exercise provided the best data now available about the number of students with learning difficulties in sector colleges (Meager *et al.* 1996). The figure is 131,000, roughly 5% of the total student population. This figure is about three times the number found by a survey in 1985, allowing for the addition of sixth form colleges to the sector since and remembering that our definitions were more fully thought through and the data collected more rigorously, thanks to the quality of the work by the researchers at the Institute for Employment Studies and the co-operation of the colleges. There is little difference between type of college in the average share per college of students, evidence that most colleges are strenuously seeking to extend their work in this field. There is, however, considerable variation between regions. In future, the individualised student record (ISR), if adapted in the ways we suggest, will allow both colleges and the Council to maintain statistics on a consistent basis so that for the first time, we shall have a reliable picture of how provision and participation may be changing over time.

Turning to the other question, of how many ought we to be providing for, it is far more difficult to make progress...

The data that are available, however, are thought-provoking. The 1991 census records just under 3,000 16 to 19 year olds with a limiting long-term illness living in communal establishments and a further 69,000 living in private households. This is considerably higher than the estimated 46,000 16 to 19 year olds with a disability estimated from the OPCS disability survey of 1995. The 1991 census records nearly 2 million aged 16 to 59 with a limiting long-term illness, while the labour force survey of 1993 gives a figure of just over 3 million based on answers to questions about health problems or disabilities which affect the kind of paid work the person can do. The general household survey (GHS) of 1992 gives the highest figure for 16 to 64 year olds with health problems, namely almost 6 million. This is likely to be due to the phrasing of the question in the GHS which relates to any long-standing illness, disability or infirmity that limits the activities of the respondent. The general impression seems inescapable: there must be many more who could benefit from education than the 130,000 now involved. The statistical instrument that we have had devised, if used by colleges in the future, should allow them to make useful estimates of the incidence of learning disabilities and/or difficulties in their area, as part of a strategic approach to needs analysis, itself one of the many approaches needed to widen access.

The student

Our proposals are rooted in the belief that students with learning difficulties should be helped towards adult status. This requires the achievement of autonomy, and a positive self-image realistically grounded in the capacity to live as independently as possible and contribute both to the economy and the community.

The case for providing further education for those with learning difficulties is fundamentally no different from that for providing it for anyone, just as the Warnock Report declared 20 years ago (HMSO, 1978: para. 1.4). Moreover, the economic case for improving educational opportunities for those with learning difficulties and/or disabilities should loom much larger in public policy than it has done hitherto. Involvement in productive economic activity of people of working age with disability is one half that of those without disability (40% compared with 83%). Two-fifths (41%) of disabled people of working age have no educational qualifications compared with under one-fifth (18%) of non-disabled people; but for those who are economically active the proportion is 26% (compared with 16% for non-disabled). The economic advantage of education for both individual and society is manifest. Yet, unemployment rates (on the International Labour Organisation definition) among people with disabilities are around two and a half times those for non-disabled people (21.6% compared with 9%), and this is about the same for both men and women (Sly *et al.* 1995, and Institute of Manpower Studies, 1995). There can be little doubt that many of our citizens are failing to contribute as they and society would wish because low educational opportunities have reinforced the difficulties presented by disability.

Quality: management; teaching and assessment; inspection

The part played by college governors and managers in colleges and services is one of the constant factors determining the quality of what the student receives. Evidence from all parts of further education confirms that unless senior management is knowledgeable, committed and energetic in the pursuit of creating a good service for students with learning difficulties, the work and dedication of middle management and teachers is diminished or frustrated. Likewise those holding departmental, faculty and similar senior but middle-range positions of responsibility must ensure that teachers are supported in making the provision intended by college plans. Their role is crucial also, and we were given evidence from many quarters that strong and sympathetic middle managers can help create the optimum conditions for learning and teaching.

It is clear beyond all doubt that those teaching students with learning difficulties bring a dedication and humanity to the task that is admirable and deeply appreciated by the students. To join a class or workshop session, or to observe an assessment or review is often to see a range of human understanding and giving and receiving (by both teacher and student) which is at a level of emotional intensity greater than the common modes of teaching require. Moreover, as those with disability and learning difficulty have increasingly become members of the 'ordinary' classroom or workshop, so both teachers and other students have had the humanising experience of these extended relationships and procedures in the pursuit of learning. Just as in the school system over the last 15 years, so increasingly in further education, the system and the experience of all in it has been enriched as those with disability have taken a full place and made a unique contribution.

However, the existing levels of training of teachers working with those with learning difficulties are not sufficient, taken overall, and urgently need improvement...

... It must not be forgotten that, whatever structural changes may be made or opportunities for staff development may be offered, the transformation we wish to promote is dependent ultimately on changes in attitudes and practices of staff which challenge many aspects of current thinking and organisation.

We are clear that a major, carefully planned and adequately funded programme of staff development supported by ear-marked national funding is essential. Its purpose will be not only to train the current cohorts of managers and teachers, but also to transform provision so that universities and others continue to offer teacher training and curriculum development of the highest order. We place the improvements needed in the training of managers equal in importance with that needed by teachers for the classrooms or workshops. And we place this total necessity for a nationally-planned and funded development of staff in our group of most essential and urgent recommendations...

Further Education Funding Council

... Whilst the sector is, we believe, complying with the law as it is written, a more generous interpretation is clearly needed in the light of changing conditions. The volume of provision is probably meeting demand as currently expressed, but there is clear evidence that many groups are under-represented, including adults with mental health difficulties, young people with emotional and behavioural difficulties and people of all ages with profound and multiple disabilities. For those who *are* taking part, the quality of provision is not good enough, and as a result student experience is too often unacceptably inferior. A combined effort to improve management, teaching, support systems and collaboration with other services is essential to build the framework for learning and the inclusive system we could now create...

The British ought to feel some pride in the approach they have made to the education beyond school of those with disabilities and/or learning difficulties. Without the structure of a formal constitution bestowing rights on individuals, we have yet found a powerful way in which to promote the enfranchisement of those with learning difficulties. During school age this is done through formal requirement for a statement, now backed up by a transition plan, and access to special education for up to about 20% of the age group as may be required by individuals from time to time.

In the USA, for example, a similar legal framework brings between 14 and 16% of the school population within reach of the Individual Education Plan. Beyond school in the USA, however, the individual has no rights under any education law. He or she must claim a right to 'reasonable accommodation' under laws to do with disability or rehabilitation. In the USA the system shifts its basis abruptly from paternalism relying on professional expertise during the compulsory school period to individualism, relying on the student's strength in the market, thereafter. And there is much concern in that country about the extent of exclusion from education, training and employment of adults with disabilities, considerable though the provision for those brought within scope may be in many respects. In England by contrast, the *Further and Higher Education Act 1992* required the Further Education Funding Council 'to have regard' to students with learning difficulties in all aspects of discharging its responsibilities. The more we have examined the implications that follow from this formulation, coupled with the requirement that further education should be 'adequate' and 'sufficient', the more we have come to appreciate how strong the foundations of an excellent further education service for such students are.

References

Bristow A (1976) *Inside the colleges of further education* HMSO

HMSO (1978) *Special educational needs. Report of the committee of enquiry into the education of handicapped children and young people (Warnock Report)* HMSO

Institute of Manpower Studies (1995) *Equality for employment targets: a consultative document*

Meager N, Evans C & Dench S (1996) *Mapping provision: the provision of and participation in further education by students with learning difficulties and/or disabilities: a report to the learning difficulties and/or disabilities committee* HMSO

Sly F, Duxbury R & Tillsley C (1995) *Disability and the labour market: findings from the labour force survey* HMSO

Stowell R (1987) *Catching up? Provision for students with special educational needs in further and higher education* NBHS/DES

4.   Race and Ethnicity

Trevor Leahong

The evidence provided by Richard Skellington (1996) indicates that both structural and institutional racism are present in the organisations of contemporary British society, as well as racist ideas and actions at the individual level. Educational institutions inevitably reflect the characteristics of the wider society but they have a special responsibility to bring about changes in attitudes and practice and have particular opportunities to do so. This can be achieved by increasing access, opportunities and levels of accomplishment for black and minority ethnic people and by challenging and changing racist and discriminatory attitudes and beliefs. This work needs to be done at all levels:

- individual staff and students' behaviour and awareness
- the curriculum, including content, resources and teaching/learning strategies
- the 'ethos' or atmosphere of the organisation, including its public image
- institutional procedures and practices.

Much work has been done over the past thirty years by Local Education Authorities (LEAs), but since the incorporation of colleges in the early 1990s it has largely been left to individual institutions to develop and implement policy and practice on equality issues. These issues (and particularly race equality) have, in many PCET institutions, become subsumed under the heading of 'quality', which has often diffused the focus, though policy and practice vary considerably across the sector. There is, therefore, a need for strong and practical initiatives from agencies with responsibility, power and influence in the post-compulsory sector as a whole, as well as more action at the institutional level. The funding councils now require the collection of data on students' ethnicity. It is important that this information is made available and is used by individual institutions to inform policy initiatives (and resources) and to monitor the effectiveness of their own implementation of policy.

The Further Education Unit has offered a number of definitions of key terms, which will help to clarify and inform discussion of these important issues.

Terms and concepts

Race

Historically, race as a concept has been used by scientists and others who attempted to categorise people on the basis of appearance and other inherited characteristics. Skin colour, hair colour and texture, eye colour and shape, and bone structure were emphasised. Nineteenth century writers on 'race' ... at the time of European colonial expansion developed a full-scale hierarchy of races, based on beliefs that other

Continued...

---

features such as physical strength, intelligence and moral and aesthetic qualities were biologically determined. Such beliefs fulfilled an important function in seeming to justify the so-called civilising mission which accompanied the struggle of European powers for territorial and economic domination of Africa and Asia. The apparent scientific basis was widely accepted until well into the twentieth century. The implications of the application of theories of race in certain countries became apparent. The biological theories on which early race theory was based have been discredited, and this has further contributed to the decline in the use of the concept in scientific discussion. Theories of 'race' facilitated the exploitation of black people by white; they were used to 'justify' slavery and the plunder of colonies.

Ethnicity

This term is used primarily to refer to the cluster of beliefs, attitudes and behaviours which distinguishes one's own social, 'racial' or cultural group from others. Ethnic differences do not therefore necessarily have associations with skin colour. Ethnicity is felt strongly by members of such groups, and can become particularly important as a means of maintaining identity and dignity when the group is in a minority or is facing hostility.

Racism

Racism is hard to define. The term has a recent history and has been used to refer to societies in which one 'racial' or cultural group is in a position of dominance which is used to keep another group in a position of subservience. Thus in European ex-colonial societies it refers in particular to the relations between the white majority and the immigrant population recruited to combat labour-shortages during the post-war boom, which have resulted in worse pay, social conditions and life-chances for the latter groups. Hence the shorthand formula: racism equals prejudice plus power, in the sense that it is the existence of power structures to support racist beliefs which differentiates racism from the inter-racial and inter-ethnic rivalries common in many societies. Racist beliefs range from positive and extreme biological theories of supremacy to unconscious assumptions of superiority.

In British discussions three levels of racism have sometimes been identified:

structural racism – in which, as a result of the economic and historical context of immigration, economic and social discrimination against black people is embedded in the structure of society (as evidenced in employment, housing, and education);

institutional racism – in which institutions, reflecting the structure of the society they serve, maintain a set of rules, procedures and practices which operate in such a way as to perpetuate discrimination against black people;

individual racism – in which the actions and attitudes (often unconscious) of individuals to black people support and sustain a broader social pattern of discrimination.

Anti-racism is used to describe the climate of thought and action which has grown up over the past generation determined to take action to eliminate racism as far as possible at all levels: structural, institutional and individual. Anti-racism attempts to

Continued...

build a multicultural society based on tolerance, justice and equality for all groups in that society. Anti-racism therefore goes beyond multiculturalism; it takes the view that the notion of Britain as a just multicultural society can be a reality for all groups only if racism in British society is recognised and tackled effectively.

Ethnocentrism

This term is used (especially in discussions of the curriculum) to describe the tendency to view events from the perspective of one's own culture. Other cultures tend to be undervalued and considered inferior, while one's own culture is regarded as superior. In curriculum studies, in addition to clear cases of ethnocentric approaches in subjects such as history and geography, evidence of prejudice has been put forward in mathematical, scientific and technological subjects – especially in the tendency to emphasise British or European discoveries, theories or achievements as against those of other cultures.

Multicultural society

The multicultural view of British society has been accepted since the late 1970s as being the only adequate description of that society. There is a 'weak' multicultural analysis which emphasises a unitary British culture but accepts the presence of other cultures and their right to maintain their religious and cultural traditions. A 'strong' form, in contrast, emphasises the equal status of all cultures, and accepts the implication that in a multicultural society the assumptions and cultural norms of the majority culture will come under question as much as those of minority cultures. The multicultural approach has been criticised on the grounds that it assumes that equality of status for cultures can exist in a society where racism and racial discrimination continue.

Racial discrimination

This has been defined for Britain in the 1976 Race Relations Act where two forms are distinguished; *direct discrimination* occurs when one person or group of people is treated less favourably than another on racial grounds; *indirect discrimination* occurs when a condition or requirement is applied where the effect is that a smaller proportion of people from one group than others can comply with it. Cases of direct or overt discrimination have been rare in the educational context, but indirect discrimination is less easy to eliminate (e.g. requirements re school headgear and uniform, entry requirements relating to language)...

Positive action

The term positive action is used in many contexts, including the Race Relations Act 1976 to describe policies which are initiated and implemented by public agencies and which attempt to counter the effect of past discrimination against ethnic minorities. Thus many local authorities have changed their job advertising policies to include advertisements placed in the minority press in order positively to encourage applications from black candidates. These measures, which are specifically permitted in the Race Relations Act, are seen as efforts to redress the lack of black employees in many categories of public and private employment, and have been widely adopted in Britain.

Continued...

The narrower term *positive discrimination* (or *affirmative action* as it is referred to in the United States) denotes a policy which reserves specific 'quotas' of jobs or educational awards for certain minority groups. The system has been in common use in the United States since the 1970s but has never achieved popularity in Britain.

Multicultural education

A redefinition of the ethnic approach, with an emphasis on the equal status of different cultures, became the dominant educational response to the presence of black communities in the late 1970s. It remains influential. There is a concern to provide opportunities for cultural and language maintenance among the black communities, to introduce ethnic and religious festivals into schools, to develop project work on ethnic communities and to develop links with ethnic minority parents and communities. Due recognition is given to the enrichment of British life by other communities and the ideal society is seen as one in which the different communities (including the dominant white community) hold each other in mutual respect. Multicultural strategies however tend to lay emphasis on the cultures and traditions of the countries of origin of those who initially settled in Britain in the 1950s and 1960s, the parents and grandparents of today's black young people and adults, rather than on the experiences of black people in this country. Multicultural strategies can therefore be seen as one element in any sensitive and appropriate curriculum for a multicultural society. Multicultural strategies have been criticised because they can be interpreted as directing attention away from the major issue of racism towards particular (and sometimes 'exotic') cultural features.

Anti-racist education

All the approaches mentioned in the previous four examples have been criticised by some because they were articulated and developed by educationists from the white community attempting to deal with the so-called problem of the presence of black people in schools and colleges. White British culture was seen as normal culture and the black cultures were to be defined by white initiatives. To most black people, the problem has been quite different; it has been what they regard as racism. The anti-racist approach to education has been articulated and developed by black educationists, arguing that the main problem for black children is not one of culture, but of racism, as exemplified in various ways in the education system. Before any hope of a multicultural society can be entertained (and as a matter of simple justice) racism must, they feel, be identified, exposed and eliminated. An anti-racist approach suggests that mainstream policy, practice and provision should be critically examined and evaluated in order to uncover the sources of racism in education and society, and that an anti-racist perspective and appropriate strategies should be developed in all educational institutions.

Black

The term black is now generally used in discussions of race relations to describe the British non-white population, whether of Asian, African or Caribbean origin. By extension it is often used to refer to other groups who have suffered racial discrimination or cultural subjugation in the colonial past or in the multiracial

Continued...

present. This usage has been generally (though not universally) adopted by such groups because it emphasises the commonality of their experience in relation to the European former colonial powers rather than the diversity of their cultural heritages. The term *white* is used to cover all groups within the dominant indigenous majority in Britain.

Coloured

This has been more or less abandoned as a descriptive term in race relations because of its euphemistic nature, and because of its use in South Africa where it denotes a particular category within the hierarchy of apartheid.

Ethnic minority

In current usage *ethnic minority* or *ethnic majority* (rather than racial minority or majority) are the most commonly used general descriptive terms employed to cover the variety of groups (e.g. Jamaican, Gujerati, Welsh) within wider categories such as black, white or British. In this project this usage is followed, and, in referring to individual communities, the most commonly used current form is adopted (e.g. Punjabi, rather than the technically more correct Panjabi), and where broader terms are useful as shorthand, Afro-Caribbean, African, Caribbean, Asian, South Asian and South East Asian are employed. Those whose ethnic heritage includes more than one group are referred to, again following the most common usage, as being of mixed race.

(FEU, 1988: 89–94)

A more specific definition of racism arises from a series of answers to the following question:

What do we mean by the word 'racism'?

1. Perpetuation of a belief that human races have distinctive characteristics that determine their respective cultures, usually involving the idea that one race is superior and has the right to dominate others; together with a policy of enforcing such asserted right and a system of government and society based upon such a policy.

2. Assertion of rights and interests of a particular racial group, who assume superiority, however unwittingly, and have power to enforce this, to the detriment of other racial groups.

3. The treatment of a minority, identified by racial background, as scapegoats for social stresses, injustices, or conflicts of interests affecting the whole society.

4. An inadequately acknowledged residue of the colonial encounter between white and black, in which personal attitudes and behaviour come second, and institutional power and pressures come first.

5. The conduct generated by the belief that some races, however identified, are inferior, not in this or that respect, but *as people,* and that, therefore, their interests and feelings do not deserve to be regarded as equally important or worthy of respect as those of any so-called superior race.

Continued...

45

6. Action that, regardless of the intentions involved, defends the advantages that whites have because of the subordinated position of black racial minorities, and based on, or fuelled by, culturally sanctioned beliefs, involving dehumanising stereotypes, and/or paternalism, and/or ethnocentrism.

7. A combination of prejudiced attitudes against black people and the power to implement action based on these, which leads, however unintentionally, to disproportionate under-privilege and disadvantage for black people in a white dominant society.

8. Justifying the relative disadvantaging of a group, through an attempt to 'biologise' social structures.

9. A way of rationalising a fear that the privileged position of one's own ethnic group in society might be eroded.

10. Racism, whether individual, cultural or institutional, is no less racism for being unintentional or unwitting: racism is defined by effects, not motives.

(Twitchin, 1988: 32)

The following extract – from the Introduction to Richard Skellington's book *'Race' in Britain today* – identifies the background to racism in modern Britain.

Racism in Britain

The CRE has argued for tougher laws to challenge entrenched forms of discrimination that still persist after 30 years of race relations legislation... The role and power of organisations such as the CRE may also require radical overhaul and proper funding.

The 1980s witnessed ... a deepening of the division in British society along the lines of 'race' and skin colour... Young people, and young black people in particular, have become increasingly vulnerable. In June 1991, Michael Day, then chair of the CRE, observed:

We have come a long way since 1966 but there are still too many token gestures. The achievements of many from the minority ethnic communities are impressive, but young black people in particular do not feel valued. Many of the social factors which contributed to inner city disturbances of 10 years ago are still apparent..

(Independent, 15 June 1991)

... The 1993 Policy Studies Institute (PSI) survey on minorities concluded that despite racial discrimination some minority ethnic groups had made progress since 1984, notably those of Indian origin, while others (those of Pakistani, Bangladeshi and Afro-Caribbean origin) had not. The PSI reported a growing gap in education, employment and socio-economic background between Indian and Chinese groups on the one hand and Pakistani, Bangladeshi and Afro-Caribbeans on the other. The survey also revealed sharp contrasts in relation to gender, with Pakistani and Bangladeshi women worst affected in terms of educational qualifications held compared with all other groups...

Continued...

... [Between 1991 and 1995] several factors have significantly affected minority ethnic groups.

- First, the recession deepened, exposing more black and Asian people, in particular the young, to unemployment, homelessness, hardship and disadvantage. The possible beginnings of a national recovery cannot disguise the high levels of unemployment and housing shortages that continue disproportionately to affect black people.

- Second, racial violence and racist attacks continue to rise and could be as high as 170,000 a year, according to the Home Office's 1994 British Crime Survey. The [then] Home Secretary, Michael Howard, insists that existing laws are adequate.

- Third, there is growing concern about the extent to which black and Asian households are suffering from acute levels of poverty.

- Fourth, more young Afro-Caribbean and Bangladeshi pupils are being subjected to exclusion from our educational institutions.

- Fifth, a disproportionate number of Afro-Caribbeans inhabit our prisons.

- Sixth, increasing evidence of police racism has emerged, amid growing concern about the vulnerability of black and Asian people in the criminal justice system. For example, Metropolitan Police Force (MPF) Commissioner Sir Paul Condon's claims in July 1995, supported by Home Secretary Michael Howard, that 80 per cent of recorded 'muggings' (street thefts and robberies) in high areas of black and Asian minority ethnic group concentration were committed by young 'black' (Afro-Caribbean) men, caused much debate, consternation and concern in Afro-Caribbean, Asian and African communities. By singling out 'black' communities, Sir Paul was accused of destabilising progress made in police-community relations (*Independent*, 8 July 1995, 14 July 1995; *Guardian*, 8 July 1995; *Independent on Sunday*, 9 July 1995). The Home Secretary's public support for Sir Paul's 'Eagle Eye' campaign was criticised by the United Nations Human Rights Committee: 'In a multi-racial state that Britain has become such comments do not contribute to a climate of racial harmony', the Committee observed (*Independent*, 21 July 1995).

- Seventh, disturbances in Birmingham, Bradford, in June 1995 witnessed the most significant urban unrest in the 1990s. British-born children of poor Pakistani migrants were involved in violent clashes with West Yorkshire Police. The disturbances raised further the extent to which black and Asian youth may be increasingly alienated by a range of cultural, economic and societal factors, especially if triggered by perceived insensitive policing.

- Finally, new calls for increased immigration and asylum controls, and a growing support for far right organisations especially among the working class, add to this complex picture of multi-ethnic Britain.

A PSI study on Britain's ethnic minorities has identified some improvement for some minorities and the growth in the black and Asian middle class..., whilst ... research into higher education revealed that some minorities were making significant progress (*The Times Higher Education Supplement*, 16 July 1993). But the persistent levels of racial discrimination in the labour market, and related high black and Asian unemployment, the squeeze on rights and benefits, the climate of resource

Continued...

underfunding and the substantial growth in relative poverty have, if anything, made the situations of many black and Asian people more vulnerable than they were at the end of the 1980s.

Further cuts in the urban programme and Section 11 funding (aimed specifically at meeting the special needs of minority ethnic groups), and more reductions in state welfare provision, will hit black and Asian minorities hard. Khurshid Ahmed, secretary of the National Association of Race Equality Advisors, commented:

It is a recipe for disaster that cuts are falling on the black community at a time when there is a rising tide of racism and fascism across Europe. These cuts are devastating.

(P Gosling 'Poor relations in race for government cash'
Independent, 10 December 1992)

Black and Asian minorities are still being denied a representative and influential political base, although there is evidence of increasing political awareness and participation at local level. Black and Asian people are increasingly recognising the need to establish their own political platforms, and to pressure for relevant shifts in legislative change.

In his inaugural address the first black chair of the CRE, Herman Ouseley, called for the eradication of racial intolerance and prejudice, and the freeing of our society from racial discrimination by the end of the century. His words were echoed by the new black chair of the Runnymede Trust, Trevor Phillips, who expressed his dismay at the divided, directionless and feeble response of those who say they want to improve 'race' relations in Britain. There is still, four years on, a very long way to go.

(Skellington, 1996: 13-16)

The extract that follows is from the conclusion to Skellington's book and points in the direction of radical reform to bring about change in modern Britain. It is interesting for us to note his speculation (in August 1995) as to the possible effects of a change of government in Westminster. Many would say that the effects have been less than anticipated.

The need for radical reform

The Home Affairs Committee concluded its third report on racial attacks and harassment with the following statement:

Racism, in whatever form, is an evil and destructive force in our undeniably multi-racial society. We are in no doubt that racial attacks and racial harassment, and the spread of literature which preaches racial hatred, are increasing and must be stopped. More can be done ... we re-emphasise the importance of all agencies and organisations working together... As racism is spreading so rapidly, time is short.

(Home Affairs Committee, 1994: vii)

Continued...

What is the nature of British society that has generated the litany of empirical evidence presented in this book? To what extent does it present too negative a picture of black and Asian inequality? How complex and inextricably interwoven are the dimensions of 'race', ethnicity, class and gender? To what degree are these patterns and trends the result of changes and developments in 'capitalist' society? How do these relate to our colonial history, and to contemporary cultural factors in multi-ethnic Britain? How will the diverse minority ethnic groups respond? Will the racialised inequalities and disadvantages be ameliorated in the next millennium? Is racism, as Gilroy has argued, 'a volatile presence at the very centre of British politics, actively shaping and determining the history not simply of blacks but this country as a whole' (Gilroy, 1990). Will European developments push Britain towards introducing more specific legislation directed at racism? To what extent will the political gains of far right parties in France, Belgium, Germany, Austria and Italy reinforce racism in Britain? What impact might a change in Government in Britain have on these issues?

We are living in a complex and rapidly changing multi-ethnic Britain, where there are no simple answers, but where old divisions seem resistant to change. We live in a society whose Governments, especially Conservative Governments since 1979, have lacked the political will to tackle inequalities, to transform rhetoric into action, and to confront British racism. There are real dangers of complacency as resources continue to contract: slippage in resolve and commitment may occur. We need to be increasingly vigilant and pro-active as a society, as communities and as individuals, to ensure that the positive changes that have occurred since 1992 are sustained and built upon, especially through legislation. The slowness of our progress, the persistence, and in some areas the increase, of social and economic disadvantage and racialised inequalities is testimony to past neglect, and the historical rootedness of British racist values. We need a Bill of Rights, but we need more than this to combat state, institutional and individual racism.

The VE Day celebrations in May 1995 provided an illuminating symbolic representation of just how blind Britain is to its multi-ethnic heritage. Of how, in Gilroy's terms, 'there ain't no black in the Union Jack'. Lost in the celebrations was any real acknowledgement or understanding of the contributions of black British and ex-colonial people to victory in 1945. Apart from one BBC East feature on the contribution of British Muslims, we were left with *The Dam Busters* and Guy Gibson's dog 'Nigger' to bear the burden of representation. Paul Gilroy has argued that we increasingly face more sophisticated forms of racism which, chameleon-like, avoid being recognised as such because they are able to hide behind a 'respectable' image of national culture. Is this racism becoming more established during the 1990s? Have we, as Gilroy suggests, produced a metaphysics of Britishness which has acquired racial referents (Gilroy, 1990)?

Racial attacks do not occur in a vacuum. They occur in a political system in which people from different cultures are said to constitute 'a problem'. What is needed is the political courage to emphasise the positive contributions that minority ethnic groups have made to the well-being of British society. The new millennium is surely

Continued...

49

a time to embrace this diversity, to recognise difference and to respond to change through understanding.

The 1990s have witnessed a gradual shift from rhetoric to action. There have been practical attempts throughout the past 30 years to tackle social inequalities, but they have been patchy and uncoordinated. Therefore there needs to be a radical programme of reform to tackle racism and the intrinsic divisions in British society, between rich and poor, to empower all the British people, irrespective of 'race', ethnicity, gender or class. The needs of multi-ethnic Britain may best be served by substantial reforms delivering social justice and increased life chances for all, but we must not fail to meet the challenge of the 'racism' within.

Reference

Gilroy P (1990) 'The end of anti-racism' in W Ball & J Solomos (eds) *Race and local politics* Macmillan

(Skellington, 1996: 246-247)

What, then, is known about the participation of ethnic minority groups in post-compulsory education and training? In terms of participation rates, most of what is known is the result of data-gathering activities by the colleges, and the collection of information on ethnicity is often a matter of great sensitivity. Only if there is a clear purpose in the compilation of such statistics, and the prospect of appropriate action resulting from it, will the subjects actively participate in the process.

Paul Gordon's chapter in Skellington provides a thorough and interesting discussion of the possibilities and problems associated with the collection of data on race and ethnicity. The following very brief extract outlines some of the arguments.

Equality monitoring: race and ethnicity

Statistical information can play an important role in identifying patterns of inequality and the processes that produce them. The data which will emerge, for example, from ethnic monitoring in education ought to point to any ways in which black people, whether pupils or teachers, are treated differently from their white counterparts...

Central to any discussion of statistics is, of course, the uses to which they are put. There is little value in collecting information simply for its own sake (undoubtedly a tendency in bureaucratic societies) and this is particularly true when the subjects of such data collection are human beings. [M]any people have objected to being the object of study, research or simply counting when they have been unable to see any benefits that might accrue. They have argued that a considerable amount of research has been conducted and a vast amount of data accumulated in the past 30 years, pointing to the existence of discrimination on a wide scale and to the continuing subordinate position of black people socially and economically, and that this has given rise to very little by way of action to alter the situation in any significant way.

Continued...

> The collection of ethnic data is not an end in itself but a means to an end: that of implementing equal opportunities and racial equality. The current support for ethnic monitoring in education, as well as in other areas, indicates a willingness to take at least the first steps in this process by identifying the ways in which minority ethnic groups may be discriminated against. But it must be remembered that these are first steps only. They will have to be followed, where the data show it to be necessary, by changes in policy and practice.
>
> (Gordon, 1996: 42)

The 1997 FEFC publication *How to widen participation – a guide to good practice* has collected data relating to students enrolled in further education colleges in England in the 1994/5 and 1995/6 teaching years. The Guide encourages colleges to make use of the data – including data on ethnicity – to plan, set targets, implement good practice and monitor progress in 'redressing educational inequality and injustice' (FEFC, 1997: vii).

Recruitment, retention and achievement
(reproduced with permission of the Further EducationFunding Council)

Data are derived from the individualised student record (ISR) returns made by colleges to the Council. A separate volume: *Widening Participation in Further Education: Statistical Evidence* (1997) explains in greater detail the methodology underlying the statistics (p40).

The ethnicity profile shows that nationally further education colleges are recruiting a higher proportion of students from ethnic minorities than the percentage in the population generally. There are, however, significant local variations. For colleges with a significant ethnic minority population in their local area it would be appropriate to disaggregate ... further by sex as well as by age group and to look in detail at the recruitment of individual minority ethnic groups (p41).

... Retention rates of students from different ethnic groups vary greatly, particularly for the 16 to 18 age group. Black Caribbean and black (other) students of all ages are harder to retain than other students, particularly Chinese and Indian students who have the lowest withdrawal rates. This is linked to the high proportion of black ethnic minority students on benefit, which is associated with lower retention...(p43).

Achievement rates of students from different ethnic groups vary significantly. As with retention rates, black African and black Caribbean students have lower achievement rates compared to other ethnic groups. Again, this is linked to the high proportion of black ethnic minority students on benefit, which is associated with lower achievement. White and Bangladeshi students tend to have higher achievement rates (p44).

(FEFC, 1997: 40–44)

The Council recommends that the Guide might usefully be used in conjunction with *Further education and equality – a manager's manual* (CRE/EOC, 1995). The industrial tribunal report which follows is taken from that publication.

Racial harassment

The CRE defines racial harassment as:

> *Violence which may be verbal, or physical, and which includes attacks on property as well as on the person, suffered by individuals or groups because of their colour, race, nationality and ethnic or national origins, when the victim believes that the perpetrator was acting on racial grounds and/or there is evidence of racism.*

The CRE points out that harassment in an educational institution may occur between students, between staff, from students to staff, or staff to students. It is hurtful to the victims and disrupts their learning or their teaching. Unlawful discrimination can arise not only from direct harassment but also from failure to act against it. The issues involved can perhaps best be understood through a consideration of the report of an industrial tribunal (names have been changed):

Simon Jones (Lecturer) vs Eastern Technical College

In 1994, an industrial tribunal ruled in favour of Simon Jones, a college lecturer, in *Simon Jones vs Eastern Technical College*. A letter sent by the CRE to all college principals following the judgement sets out the CRE's recommendations to colleges on how to deal with racial harassment.

> *I know you will agree with me that racial harassment is unacceptable behaviour in any circumstances, and perhaps especially in an educational establishment. The Commission is determined to use all its powers to ensure that potential victims of racial harassment, whatever their ethnic group, are fully protected from this behaviour.*

It should be noted that Eastern Technical College has acted on these recommendations, has reviewed its policies and procedures, and has started a programme of staff training.

The case: Simon Jones (lecturer) vs Eastern Technical College

Mr Jones, a full-time lecturer at Eastern Technical College since 1979, is of Asian origin, and was born in Zimbabwe.

In three tribunal applications he alleged that:
- he had been exposed to eight years of racial abuse and discrimination compounded by the failure of college management to take action;
- he had been victimised by having his teaching hours cut, and by the failure of college management to stop him being racially abused by students;
- he had been further victimised by the requirement to undertake teacher training and the threat of disciplinary action if he refused.

Mr Jones' main allegations were upheld.

Continued...

The tribunal found that:

He had been the victim of racist name calling ('sambo', 'nigger', 'kaffir') on many separate occasions, each reported to college management, but the employers did not approach the complaints with an open mind and fair attitude.

There had been a tendency to disbelieve Mr Jones' allegations, leading to suggestions that he had misheard the racist taunts directed at him, or misunderstood them due to alleged difficulty in understanding English.

This habitual treatment of Mr Jones as unreliable in his command of English, and unable to appreciate what was said to him by students, was irrational and unwarranted. It was racial prejudice.

Rather than acting on Mr Jones' complaints, the college acted in a way that could be construed as supporting the unfounded allegations of his harassers regarding his inability to teach and to communicate clearly.

The college failed to take formal disciplinary steps against the student who had been persistent in abusing Mr Jones.

The college's response to his complaints was to force him, under threat of disciplinary proceedings, to take a cut in teaching hours in order to undergo training. For him to be subject to these measures at a time when he had commenced proceedings against the college, and when hearings were pending, was victimisation.

Commission for Racial Equality recommendations

1. All colleges should adopt an equal opportunities policy to cover employment and service delivery... The Commission's *Codes of Practice* for education and employment, and our publication *Racial Discrimination and Grievance Procedures* provide essential guidance.

2. That policy should contain clear guidance on the unacceptability of racial harassment, and its inclusion in student and staff disciplinary codes, a description of the disciplinary penalties for racial harassment, and a method of recording and analysing all complaints of racial harassment and their resolution.

3. The case of Mr Jones was one of racial harassment of a lecturer by students. Policies and disciplinary codes should also cover the possibility of harassment of students by staff, of staff by other staff, and by students of other students. All are equally unacceptable.

4. All complaints of racial harassment should be taken seriously and acted on fairly. To act in a way which makes the complainant the primary subject of investigation and action is unacceptable.

5. The recommendations contained in the CRE's *Racial Discrimination and Grievance Procedures* should be discussed by senior management, and incorporated into the relevant personnel, disciplinary and grievance procedures.

6. It is advisable and desirable that the development of policies and procedures for dealing with racial harassment is undertaken in partnership with staff and student unions/representatives.

Continued...

---

7. A programme of training for all relevant staff in how to respond to racial harassment should be undertaken.

8. Colleges should ensure that allegations of under-performance of any sort are not confused with, or used in any way to justify, either racial harassment itself, or the failure to respond to it decisively. No lecturer, manager or student has to tolerate being racially harassed whatever other issues may be alleged to be present, or actually present...

Even if your college, like Eastern Technical College, has hardly any students or staff from ethnic minorities, the law still applies and the issue, as this case shows, can arise. We recommend strongly that all colleges adopt the recommendations above to ensure their compliance with the law...

(CRE/EOC, 1995: 8–10; 13–14)

A checklist for promoting race equality

We can go some way towards implementing such recommendations by routinely checking the strategies we employ and the materials we use. The following checklist may help us do this, under the three headings of: a) teaching and learning, b) materials and resources, and c) curriculum.

a. Teaching and learning strategies, classroom interaction and the 'hidden curriculum'

1. Is the teacher aware of the different racial/ethnic/religious/linguistic backgrounds of students, without making stereotyped assumptions about these?
2. Are student contributions to the curriculum from different cultural, class and gender perspectives acknowledged, used and valued in the teaching/learning process?
3. Are students' names remembered and pronounced correctly?
4. Does the teacher avoid language which is unnecessarily complex, obscure, jargonistic?
5. Is the bilingualism/multilingualism of students and staff used as a positive resource in teaching/learning?
6. Is the teacher aware of:
   ➢ patterns of classroom interaction and their effects on learners?
   ➢ overt or subtle differences in reaction to the contributions of different students?
   ➢ domination of teacher's time/attention by particular groups of students?
   ➢ any racial or other antagonisms within the group?
7. Does the teacher have a clear understanding of, and commitment to, race equality?
8. Is the teacher:
   ➢ able and willing to deal with racist comments or incidents immediately and appropriately?

  ➢ able and willing to discuss issues, where appropriate, when they arise through the curriculum or in classroom interaction?

9) What steps are taken to support staff in developing the approaches discussed above?

b. *Books, materials and other resources*

1. Are there strong role models with whom students from different ethnic/racial groups can identify positively? Are people from different ethnic/racial groups shown in a variety of roles?

2. Are materials and information presented in a way that enhances the self-image of students from all cultures?

3. Do illustrations realistically reflect the distinctive features of different ethnic/racial groups? Are they free from stereotyping?

4. Are customs, lifestyles and traditions of different countries and groups presented in a way which explains their value, meaning and role in the lives of the people?

5. Are the histories of different societies and the role of the people in developing their own society and institutions accurately presented, including their own perspectives?

6. Does the selection of facts, information and examples present a balanced view of the culture/society represented?

7. Is the role of women in the life, history and development of all societies adequately represented?

8. Is the content free from derogatory and insulting terminology?

9. Is the language of the people concerned treated with respect and presented accurately?

10. Is consideration similar to the above given to issues of disability, gender, sexuality and age, where appropriate, as well as race/ethnicity?

c. *Curriculum development, evaluation and review*

1. Has the content of the curriculum been carefully examined in terms of ethnocentricism/eurocentricism, i.e. white and/or European-biased approaches and the absence of black and 'third world' perspectives?

2. Does the curriculum reflect the multicultural nature of Britain and European and world contexts?

3. Is feedback sought from students on their reactions to content, materials and resources?

4. What steps have been taken in course teams or other relevant forums to make necessary changes in curricula, materials and resources and teaching/learning strategies with specific regard to:
  ➢ race equality criteria and performance indicators?
  ➢ curriculum review sessions
  ➢ workshops on materials and resources and developing assignments
  ➢ staff development in teaching/learning strategies, classroom interaction and language issues.

College code of practice

The following extract is an example of a code of practice operating in one college. It is reproduced from the Student Handbook.

Anti-racist code of practice

- The College is totally opposed to racism in all its forms. Racist behaviour, language and activities discriminate against and disadvantage black people and other ethnic minorities.

- Racism is also hurtful and damaging to individuals, the College and the community.

- Racism may be obvious or more disguised. Obvious (overt) racist acts include physical assaults, threats, comments, 'jokes', name calling, graffiti, wearing racist badges, bringing racist material into College and attempts to recruit students to racist groups.

- Any such offences against the Code may lead to suspension and exclusion from the College under the Disciplinary Procedures.

- Apart from more obvious racism, the actions of individuals and the practices and procedures of the College may be discriminatory towards black people and other ethnic minorities. Whether deliberate but disguised (covert), or unintentional, these forms of racism are equally damaging in their effects.

The purpose of our equality code is for all students and staff to work in an environment free of discrimination and harassment of any kind.

Where racism is built into the way Colleges work it is called 'institutional racism'. The College actively seeks to get rid of this form of racism by checking on student recruitment and progress by ethnic group, positively valuing all students' languages and cultures and by developing anti-racist approaches in subjects, tutorials, and other aspects of College life.

These issues are dealt with in more detail in the College *Race Equality Policy*, available in Site Offices and Libraries.

Equality procedures

What to do if you experience or witness behaviour or incidents which are against College equality codes and policies:

1. Report the incident to your course tutor, group tutor or any member of college staff, who will take the necessary immediate action to deal with the incident. (If you prefer, you can talk to a Student Services Officer or the College Equality Co-ordinator.)

2. Complete an incident form (equality policies) and send it to the Deputy Principal. These forms are available in Site Offices.

Following your verbal and/or written report, action will be taken to deal with the incident; you will be kept informed as to what is being done.

Continued...

Copies of the full procedures for reporting, dealing with, recording and monitoring behaviour and incidents which are against our equality policies and codes are also available in Site Offices.

References and further reading

Brandt G (1986) *The realization of anti-racist teaching* Falmer

Commission for Racial Equality/Equal Opportunities Commission (1995) *Further education and equality: a manager's manual* CRE/EOC

Drew D (1995) *Race, education and work: the statistics of inequality* Avebury

Fryer P (1984) *Staying power: the history of black people in Britain* Pluto

FEFC (1997) *How to widen participation: a guide to good practice* The Stationery Office

FEU (1985) *Black perspectives on FE provision* FEU

FEU (1988) *Staff development for a multicultural society (RP390)* FEU

FEU (1987) *FE in black & white* FEU

FEU (1989) *Black perspectives on adult education: identifying the needs* FEU

Gaine C (1987) *No problem here* Hutchison

Gaine C (1995) *Still no problem here* Trentham

Gill D & Levidow L (1987) *Anti-racist science teaching* Free Association Books

Gill D, Mayor B & Blair M (1992) *Racism and education* Sage/OUP

Gordon P (1996) 'The racialisation of statistics' in R Skellington *op cit*

Haralambos M & Holborn M (1995) *Sociology* 4th edn Collins

Klein G (1993) *Education towards race equality* Cassell

London Language and Literacy Unit (1990) *Language & power* Harcourt Brace Jovanovich

Luthra M (1997) *Britain's black population* Arena

Skellington R (1996) *'Race' in Britain today* 2nd edn Sage/OUP

Tizard B & Phoenix A (1993) *Black, white or mixed race?* Routledge

Twitchin J (ed) (1988) *The black and white media book* Trentham

Van Sertima I (ed) (1983) *Blacks in science, ancient and modern* Transaction Books

5.   Sex and Gender

Ann Lahiff

In this section, I will be referring to *gender* as well as to *sex* in the discussions that follow. This is because whilst the legal framework talks of Sex (as in *Sex Discrimination Act*) I find it helpful to keep the two concepts as distinct as possible in an exploration of dimensions of inequality. First, then, some definitions.

> *Sex: the division of human beings into male and female on the basis of chromosomal and reproductive differences...*
>
> (Bilton et al. 1996: 203)

Sex, then, is defined as a biological category and in this context we speak of *females* and *males*. Using the terms discussed in Section 1 of this Reader, females and males are clearly *not* equal in the *descriptive* sense of the term..

> *Gender: refers to the socially constructed ... categories of masculine and feminine...*
>
> (Bilton et al. 1996: 203)

Gender is defined as a social and cultural category and, in this context, we speak of *women* and *men*. When asked 'In what ways are women and men equal?', we put the focus immediately on the *social* environment rather than the biological. As will be seen, what is important for any discussion is the extent to which biology plays a part (if at all) in, for example, behaviours exhibited, successes achieved, careers chosen.

The following brief extract has been included to illustrate the difference between sex and gender, and to consider the various notions of femininity and masculinity that have emerged both historically and culturally.

'Ain't I a woman?'

In nineteenth century America ... the dominant femininity emphasised women's delicacy, and their need for male protection. This description may have seemed 'real' for some people, but of course it did not correspond to the experience of a great many women. The definition was challenged by Sojourner Truth, a feminist activist.

Truth was a former slave. She campaigned vigorously for extension of suffrage to black men and women. At a convention in Ohio in 1852 ... hostile men ... insisted that women needed protection, not the vote. Sojourner Truth strode to the platform to repudiate these claims. She declared :

That man over there says women need to be helped into carriages, and lifted over ditches, and to have the best place everywhere. Nobody ever helps me into

Continued...

---

carriages, or over mud-puddles, or gives me any best place! And ain't I a woman? Look at me! Look at my arms! I have ploughed and planted and gathered into barns, and no man could head me. And ain't I a woman? I could work as much and eat as much as a man – when I could get it – and bear the lash as well. And ain't I a woman? I have borne thirteen children, and seen most sold off to slavery, and when I cried out with my mother's grief, none but Jesus heard me. And ain't I a woman?

... Truth had never learned to read ... she demonstrated in her speech that an idea of 'woman' that appeared to reflect bodily reality was in fact a cultural construct, and relevant only to certain sections of the female population.

(Bilton *et al.* 1996: 202)

What inequality?

We have already made a distinction between individual inequality and social and economic inequality. Concern with social and economic inequality means identifying patterns of inequality and their sources. It is not possible here to provide a comprehensive overview of patterns of inequality in relation to gender in modern Britain, though the additional references at the end of this section would be a good place to begin a search for further information. However, a brief look at the employment market may begin to establish the point. Great changes have occurred in the employment field in relation to women and men. For instance, larger proportions of women now seek and obtain paid employment (56 percent in 1970s; 70 percent by the end of 1980s). Women now make up around 48 percent of the labour force, as opposed to 38 percent in the 1970s, and a greater percentage are working full-time. However, the employment market is still characterised by *gender segregation* – both horizontally and vertically.

Horizontal segregation means that women and men tend to be separated into different types of jobs and this has been a persistent feature of employment patterns in Britain. Vertical segregation means that women are concentrated at the lower levels of the occupational hierarchy in terms of wages or salaries, status and authority.

In spite of the popular image of women storming the citadels of male employment ... the labour force has not resulted in a fundamental challenge to demarcations or divisions of reward between men's and women's work.

(Bilton *et al.* 1996: 215)

Given that much of what goes on in colleges is related directly or indirectly to the occupational and employment market, its segregated nature is of particular relevance. We might wish to ask whether institutions of post-compulsory education and training simply *reproduce* these inequalities or help to *create* them.

As we turn the focus on to education and training, we need to link the concept of segregation with the issue of *achievement*. If modern Britain is based on the principle of meritocracy, then change in the segregated employment market ought to occur when women and men achieve similar results, both from their schooling and their post-compulsory education and training. If qualifications are required in order to enter employment, we need to examine the relative success of women and men in obtaining these.

The next reading in this section outlines the achievements of young women and men in 16-plus education – primarily in terms of GCSEs and A levels. It demonstrates that whilst women in society at large have fewer qualifications, are less-well paid and are not well represented in powerful positions, new generations of women are doing well at school/college in relation to their male counterparts. Indeed, the spotlight has now fallen on the 'underachievement' of boys and young men.

The underachievement of boys

There are marked differences between the sexes in education. Until the late 1980s, the major concern was with the underachievement of girls. This was because, while girls used to perform better than boys in the earlier stages of their education, from GCSE level they tended to fall behind, being less likely than boys to get the three A levels required for university entry and less likely to go into higher education.

However, in the early 1990s girls began to outperform boys in all areas and at all levels of the education system. The main problem today is with the under-achievement of boys, although there are still concerns about the different subjects studied by boys and girls. There are also concerns that girls could do even better if teachers spent as much time with girls as they are forced to do with boys.

The facts
Girls do better than boys at every stage in National Curriculum SAT (Standard Assessment Test) results in English, maths and science, and they are now more successful than boys at every level in GCSE, outperforming boys in every major subject (including traditional boys' subjects – design, technology, maths and chemistry) except physics. In 1995-96, 49.3% of girls got five or more GCSEs (grades A–C) compared to 39.8% of boys. In English at GCSE, the gender gap is huge, with nearly two thirds of girls getting a grade A–C, compared to less than half of boys.

A higher proportion of females stay on in post-16 sixth form and further education, and post-18 higher education. Female school leavers are now more likely than males to get three or more A level passes, and more females than males now get accepted for full-time university degree courses.

But problems still remain for girls...
Despite this general pattern of girls outperforming boys, problems do still remain for girls... Girls still tend to take different subjects from boys, which influences future career choices. Broadly, arts subjects are 'female', science and technology subjects 'male'. This is evident at GCSE-level, but becomes even more pronounced at A level and above. Girls are therefore less likely to participate after 16 in subjects leading to

Continued...

---

careers in science, engineering and technology. Girls tend to slip back between GCSE and A level, achieving fewer high-grade A levels than boys with the same GCSE results.

There is little evidence that the generally better results of girls at 16 and above lead to improved post-school opportunities in terms of training and employment. Women are still less likely than men with similar qualifications to achieve similar levels of success in paid employment, and men still hold the majority of the positions of power in society. In the 16-59 age group in the population as a whole who are in employment or are unemployed, men tend to be better qualified than women.

However, this gap has decreased among younger age groups, and can be expected to disappear if females keep on outperforming males in education.

Explaining gender differences in education

The change to girls outperforming boys is still a fairly recent development, and research to explain it is still at an early stage. There are some suggested explanations for the huge improvement in the performance of girls, the under-performance of boys and the subject choices that continue to separate males and females.

First, the *women's movement* and feminism have achieved considerable success in improving the rights and raising the expectations and self-esteem of women. They have challenged the traditional stereotype of women's roles as housewives and mothers, and this means that many women now look beyond the housewife/mother role as their main role in life.

Second, the work of sociologists in highlighting the educational under-performance of girls in the past led to a greater emphasis in schools on *equal opportunities* in order to enable girls to fulfil their potential more easily. These policies included, amongst others, monitoring teaching and teaching materials for sex bias to help schools to meet the needs of girls, by encouraging 'girl friendliness', not only in male-dominated subjects but across the whole range of the experience of girls in schools. Teachers are now much more sensitive about avoiding *gender-stereotyping* in the classroom; this may have overcome many of the former academic problems which girls faced in schools.

Third, the number of 'male' jobs, particularly in semi-skilled and unskilled manual work, has been declining in recent years, while there are growing *employment opportunities* for women in the service sector. As a consequence girls have become more ambitious and are less likely to see having a home and family as their main role in life. Many girls growing up today have mothers working in paid employment who provide positive role models for them. Many girls now recognise that the future involves paid employment, often combined with family responsibilities. Sue Sharpe found in *Just Like a Girl* in 1976 that girls' priorities were 'love, marriage, husbands, children, jobs and careers, more or less in that order'. When she repeated her research in 1994 she found that these priorities had changed to 'job, career and being able to support themselves'. These factors may all have provided more incentives for girls to gain qualifications.

Continued...

Fourth, there is mounting evidence that girls work harder, are more conscientious and are *better motivated* than boys. Girls put more effort into their work and spend more time on doing their homework properly. They take more care with the way their work is presented and they concentrate more in class. Research shows that the typical 14-year-old girl can concentrate for 3 or 4 times as long as her fellow male students. Girls are generally better organised: they bring the right equipment to school and meet deadlines for handing in work. It has been suggested that these factors may have helped girls to take more advantage of the increasing use of coursework in GCSE A level and GNVQ. Such work often requires good organisation and sustained application, and girls do better than boys in these respects.

Finally, by the age of **16** girls are estimated to be more mature than boys by up to two years. Put simply, this means that girls are more likely to view exams in a far more responsible way, recognise their seriousness and the importance of the academic and career choices that lie ahead of them.

Why do boys underachieve?

Many of the reasons given above also suggest why boys may be underachieving. However, there are some additional explanations. First there is some evidence that staff are not as strict with boys as with girls. They are more likely to extend deadlines for work, to have lower expectations of boys, to be more tolerant of disruptive, unruly behaviour from boys in the classroom and to accept poorly presented work.

Second, boys are generally more disruptive in classrooms than girls. They may lose classroom learning time because they are sent out of the room or sent home. Four out of every five permanent exclusions from schools are boys: most of these are for disobedience of various kinds and usually come at the end of a series of incidents.

Third, boys appear to gain 'street cred' and peer-group status by not working, and some develop almost an anti-education, anti-learning subculture, where schoolwork is seen as 'unmacho'. This may explain why they are less conscientious and lack the persistence and application required for exam success, particularly with the new coursework styles of assessment. This subculture was first discussed over **20** years ago by Paul Willis in *Learning to Labour* and was rediscovered by Stephen Byers, [then] the schools minister, in January 1998, when he said: 'We must challenge the laddish, anti-learning culture which has been allowed to develop over recent years and should not simply accept with a shrug of the shoulders that boys will be boys.'

Fourth, the *decline in traditional male* jobs is also a factor in explaining why many boys are under-performing in education. They may lack motivation and ambition because they may feel that they have only limited prospects and that getting qualifications won't get them anywhere anyway, so what's the point in bothering? These changing employment patterns and unemployment have resulted in a number of (predominantly white) boys and men having lowered expectations, a low self-image and a lack of self-esteem. This inevitably leads boys to attempt to construct a positive self-image away from achievement and towards 'laddish behaviour' and aggressive 'macho' posturing in attempts to draw attention to themselves.

Continued...

The interrelationship between the home, the community and schools becomes clear here. Beatrix Campbell showed in her book *Goliath* how, in the climate of underfunding and cutbacks in community provision in the early 1990s, funds are focused on the troublesome boys who destroy communities, rather than on the people who struggle to maintain those communities – who are mainly women. Educational research has shown the same pattern, where teachers' time is spent mostly on the troublesome boys, rather than on the girls who are keen to learn and to get on with their schooling. This suggests that girls may still be underachieving, even if they are not doing so in relation to the boys.

Feeling and behaving differently

Boys and girls feel differently about their own ability. Research by Michael Barber at Keele University's Centre for Successful Schools reveals that 'more boys than girls think that they are able or very able, and fewer boys than girls think they are "below average"'. Yet GCSE results show these perceptions to be the reverse of the truth. Boys feel that they are bright and capable but at the same time they keep stating that they don't like school and that they don't work hard. Girls, on the other hand, lack confidence in their ability, feel undervalued and see teachers spending more time with the boys than with them.

More research is coming to the conclusion that the differences in the achievement of girls and boys is due to the differing ways in which the genders behave and spend their spare time. To simplify and generalise: while boys run around kicking footballs, playing sports or computer games and engaging in other aspects of 'laddish' behaviour, girls are more likely to read or to stand around talking. Girls relate to one other by talking, while boys often relate to their peers by doing. The value of talking, even if it is about the heartthrob of Year II, is that it uses a key skill that is needed at school and in many non-manual, service-sector jobs: verbal reasoning. Peter Douglas argues: 'School is essentially a linguistic experience and most subjects require good levels of comprehension and writing skills.' Further research is revealing a picture of boys as viewing the crucial reading and linguistic skills as 'sissy'.

Boys don't like reading

Girls like reading while boys don't: boys see reading as a predominantly feminine activity, which is boring, not real work, a waste of time and to be avoided at all costs. The interrelationship between society and schooling is clear here. Reading is 'feminised' in our culture: women are not only the main consumers of reading in our society, but they also carry the responsibility for disseminating reading – it is women who read, talk about and 'spread the word' about books. The consequences of this are that there are very few positive role models for boys. Research has shown that boys tend to stop being interested in reading at about the age of eight.

Girls and boys also tend to read different things: girls read fiction while boys read for information. Schools tend to reproduce this gendered divide: fiction tends to be the main means of learning to read in the primary school years and this puts girls at an early advantage.

Continued...

Why do males and females still tend to do different subjects?

... There is still a difference between the subjects that males and females do at GCSE and above. Females are still more likely to take arts subjects, like English literature, history, foreign languages and sociology, and males are more likely to take scientific and technological subjects – particularly at A level and above (even though girls generally get better results when they do take them). This is despite the National Curriculum, which makes maths, English and science compulsory for all students. However, even within the National Curriculum, there are gender differences in option choices. For example, girls are more likely to take home economics, textiles and food technology, while boys are more likely to opt for electronics, woodwork or graphics. How can we explain these differences?

First, *gender socialisation* from an early age encourages boys and girls to play with different toys and do different activities around the home, and they very often grow up seeing their parents playing different roles in the home. Such socialisation may encourage boys to develop more interest in technical and scientific subjects and to discourage girls from taking them. In giving subject and career advice, teachers may be reflecting their own socialisation and expectations and reinforcing the different experiences of boys and girls by counselling them into different subject options, according to their own gender stereotypes of 'suitable subjects'.

Second, science and the science classroom is still seen as mainly *'masculine'*. Boys tend to dominate science classrooms – grabbing apparatus first, answering questions directed at girls and so on, which all undermine girls' confidence and intimidate them, so that they do not take these subjects. Gender stereotyping is still found in textbooks, with the 'invisibility' of females particularly obvious in maths and science textbooks. This reinforces the view that these are 'male' subjects.

The male identity crisis

In the face of girls' marked disadvantages, such as underrating themselves and lacking confidence in their ability, getting less of teachers' time and having to tolerate the dominance of boys in the classroom, it is perhaps surprising that they tend to do much better at school than boys. The reasons for boys' underachievement have to be placed firmly in the changing nature of men's position in society. The change has come about because of economic and political changes, but also because of a rise in women's expectations. This has brought on an *identity crisis* for men, who feel unsure about their role and position: this insecurity is reflected in schools, where boys don't see the point in working hard and trying to achieve. The future looks bleak and without clear purpose to them.

We must not forget, however, that it is still men who hold most of the highly paid, powerful positions in society – it is still mainly men who pull the strings and 'run' our society. Women go out to work more than they used to and they now make up about half the workforce. However, research has shown that in the home gender roles have not changed that much: women now not only go out to paid work a lot more, but they still have the majority of the burden of housework and childcare.

Continued...

We cannot predict what the future holds, but it is to be hoped that women will not continue with the triple burden of housework, childcare and jobs that increasingly reflect their high achievement at school, while working-class men continue with poor employment prospects or unemployment and while middle-class men continue to hold the majority of positions of power and control in society. 'Girl power' needs to go beyond the Spice Girls and media hype, with women achieving positions in society which are commensurate with their educational achievements.

References and further reading

Askew S & Ross C (1988) *Boys don't cry: boys and sexism in education* OUP
Browne K (1998) *An introduction to sociology* 2nd edn Polity Press
Equal Opportunities Commission and Ofsted (1996) *The gender divide* HMSO
Mitsos E (1995) 'Classroom voices' *The English and Media Magazine* 55 & 54 Autumn
Phillips A (1995) *The trouble with boys* Pandora
Spender D (1982) *Invisible women: the schooling scandal* Chameleon Books

(Mitsos & Browne, 1998: 27-31)

So whilst there is a range of explanations offered to account (at least partially) for the differential educational achievements of young men and women, there is also the pattern of *gendered segregation* in relation to subject choice to take into consideration. This is particularly noticeable in post-compulsory education and training when we look at the preferred vocational and academic areas which are chosen by those young people entering both further and higher education.

Gender segregated vocational curricula

In a recent publication on childcare courses (Owen *et al.* 1998) it was found that women make up nearly 99 percent of those who work in 'early years' childcare. According to the authors, this ranks the occupation alongside midwifery as the most heavily gendered of all occupations. Unlike the UK, the rights of children to experience male and female carers has led Nordic countries to adopt 'an unusually positive attitude towards the employment of men in childcare. The potential dangers of abuse are rightly acknowledged and tackled through risk assessment...' Charlie Owen, one of the three researchers who edited the book, suggests that in the UK such initiatives are a long way off, and it certainly seems at the moment that public opinion would not be very sympathetic to any such moves to employ men to work with very young children.

Science is another gender-segregated curriculum area – particularly after the age of 16. There have been various projects designed to encourage girls and young women into science and engineering and perhaps WISE (Women into Science and Engineering) is the best known (Kelly, 1985). In higher education something of the nature of the division as well as the policy intentions around it, can be seen from the following extract from a *Guardian* article:

Cash for female participation

British universities with the best policies for increasing female participation in science, engineering and technology could soon be rewarded with substantial cash grants... A number of initiatives to attract more women in science is being considered by the higher education funding councils, the Office of Science and Technology and the Commission for University and Career Opportunities. These are thought to include giving grants to institutions with specific initiatives such as mentoring or confidence-building schemes.

Despite much discussion and effort, women are still rare in the top ranks of science. Just 7 per cent of professors in Britain are women, compared with 18 per cent in the United States and 14 per cent in Australia. Only 3 per cent of British science professors and Royal Society fellows are female. In Brussels last week, a conference on women and science heard that despite initiatives to change the situation in many countries, the number of women entering science, engineering and technology is still low and women are very likely to drop off further up the academic hierarchy.

One delegate described the path of women undertaking a scientific career: 'At the beginning there is an iron gate, then a sticky floor. At the top there is a glass ceiling, and in between a hurdle race.'

(Hinde, 1998)

Sexual harassment

Women do, of course, enter into traditionally male-dominated occupations. However, it is not always recognised that their experiences as members of minorities are contributory factors in explaining why they leave employment or set up on their own (e.g. women-only companies in the construction industry, and increasing involvement in e-commerce).

In the previous section on Race and Ethnicity, we read of the case of a college lecturer who was the victim of racial harassment at work. The importance of the case, for me, was the way in which the *ethos of the organisation* was perpetuating a racist culture and how the power of the (white) majority was played out, at times, in very subtle ways.

In relation to gender, there are some striking parallels. We are all able to think of the more obvious forms of harassment – sexist taunts, wolf-whistles, the pages of the 'red-top' tabloids – that women face simply going about their everyday lives. However, harassment goes well beyond these. I have deliberately chosen to include the introductory section from a study on sexual harassment in a UK university, as it might be thought that the 'academic' setting of a university would project a more balanced and anti-discriminatory ethos than most other institutions. In this extract the authors present a summary of previous findings on harassment in universities; the definition with which they start reminds us that men can be subject to sexual harassment, too.

Sexual harassment in higher education

Sexual harassment means unwanted conduct of a sexual nature, or other conduct based on sex, affecting the dignity of women and men at work. This can include unwelcome physical, verbal or non-verbal conduct.

(Commission of the European Communities, 1992)

This behaviour is mostly 'towards people in less powerful positions or circumstances' and 'it may include an explicit or implicit threat of discriminatory action' (Herbert, 1992).

Although these definitions are written in gender-neutral language, sexual harassment is most often perpetrated by men against women. It is a problem faced almost exclusively by women (Benson & Thompson, 1982). A sizeable proportion of women surveyed in a wide variety of educational and work settings report sexual harassment (Riger, 1991).

It can be:

a. Physical, ranging from suggestive looks to indecent assault or rape.

b. Verbal, ranging from belittling or suggestive remarks and compromising invitations to aggressively foul language or unwanted demands for sex, or displays of sexually suggestive or degrading pictures in the work place...

The effect of such behaviour on the recipient is to create an intimidating, hostile, or offensive environment ... even if not intended.

(Herbert, 1991)

Christine Crawley, the Chair of the European Parliament Women's Rights Committee, states that sexual harassment is 'the most common and least discussed occupational health hazard for women. It makes millions of women miserable every day, causes work absenteeism, depression, underachievement, and poor motivation. Fifty-one percent of British women have suffered at some time in their working life' *(Guardian,* 2.11.1991).

Women workers have always been vulnerable to sexual abuse by male employees, but the key to its recognition has been the conceptualisation and the labelling of a broad class of behaviours as sexual harassment... It is the 'most recent form of victimisation of women to be redefined as a social rather than personal problem' (Riger, 1991: 497).

A summary of research

In theory, universities are supposedly occupational cultures of equal opportunity, even claiming to be meritocracies (Thomas, 1990). However, the pervasiveness of sexual harassment in US academic institutions is widely documented (Cammaert, 1985; Fitzgerald *et al.* 1988; Rubin & Borgers, 1990). Also, it has been shown that male dominated occupations and organisational environments, where women are in a minority, are more prone to the incidence of sexual harassment (Gruber, 1992).

Continued...

Perhaps the most important factor in reducing sexual harassment is an organisational culture that promotes equal opportunities for women... Workplaces low in perceived equality are the site of more frequent incidents of harassment... Sexual harassment both reflects and reinforces the underlying sexual inequality that produces a sex-segregated and sex-stratified occupational structure.

(Riger 1991: 503)

Universities are therefore particularly vulnerable. Women academics remain in a very small minority, a common problem across a range of countries (Acker, 1992). However, little is known and little has been written, about the extent of sexual harassment in UK universities.

In both the 'new' and 'old' universities women are under-represented at all levels. At present, they make up only 20 percent of the full-time academic staff in the 'old' UK universities, and similarly only 20 percent of 'new' university staff in 1990 (DES, 1992). The problem is illustrated more graphically when the proportions across the academic grades are considered. According to the latest figures available for 'new' universities, whilst 30 percent of lecturers are women this falls to 10 percent or less for grades above senior lecturer (DES, 1992). In the 'old' universities, only 3 percent of professors are women, and 6 percent of senior lecturers (Hart & Wilson, 1992).

Kanter (1977) demonstrates that structural characteristics of institutions, including power and authority, determine male and female behaviour, and the smaller a minority women find themselves to be in an organisation, the greater their chances of being isolated and marginalised. She points to the open and exaggerated discussion of sex among men as a mechanism to heighten the boundary between them and 'token' women.

Dudovitz (1983) has written on the difficulties and dilemmas for women academics attempting to survive in a hostile environment. The same is true for women students. Thomas (1990) demonstrates that they can succeed in higher education, but that they do so at a price. Benson & Thompson (1982) argue that 'because women can no longer be openly denied access to higher education, sexual harassment may remain an especially critical factor of more covert discrimination' (p240). An extensive survey undertaken by the National Union of Students (1987), in the UK, found that 95 percent of women respondents had experienced sexual harassment, with 65 percent of the incidents involving physical touching, pushing and grasping.

The 'homosocial theory of sex roles', offers a useful conceptualisation of the problem, where men are dominant in sex-segregated institutions and act to exclude women from participation (Lipman-Blumen, 1976). Universities are prime examples of homosocial institutions, being established and run by men who prefer people like them. They reward those most like them and exclude and marginalise women, who are different; 'by ignoring the existence of women outside the domestic, sexual and service realms, the male homosocial world relegates women to the sidelines of life' (p31).

Continued...

Universities value reputational status above all, which is heavily dependent upon one's integration into formal and informal networks in the academic community. This is obviously jeopardised when sexual harassment occurs.

Adams (1983) argues that:

> *... sexual politics, discrimination, anti-feminism, sexism, and the like are political niceties and civilised refinements, evasions and disguises that do not apply in academe. We are dealing with a primitive male society in which the presence of any women constitutes an invasion and threat of contamination, which must be carefully guarded against by the exercise of tribal pollution sanctions* (p136).

It has been argued that universities, with the relative autonomy of academics, lack of accountability, and shortage of women in positions of authority are ideal institutions to facilitate sexual harassment (Dzeich & Weiner, 1984). Ramazanoglu (1987) describes a patriarchal, competitive and hierarchical system which sets the context for male academic careers. She describes a rat race 'which "sorts out the men from the boys", and women start with considerable handicaps' (p69). Within this men are seen to use sexual harassment for the purposes of social control of women, where 'personal encounters are part of an institutional system of male domination' (p65). In Benson & Thompson's (1982) words, there is 'a nexus of power and sexual prerogative often enjoyed by men with formal authority over women' (p238).

[Some] years ago, Blackstone & Fulton (1975) presented statistical evidence of discrimination against women in British and American universities. More recently, the Committee of Vice-Chancellors and Principals issued a circular on sexual harassment (CVCP, 1990) and have acknowledged as a problem the imbalances in the proportion of women in universities, especially in senior positions (CVCP, 1991).

The social and institutional environment, which is responsible for women academics' lack of access and advancement in the academic profession, needs investigation... As Acker (1992) indicates, 'simply working in a mostly-male environment imposes different pressures on women' (p64).

References

Acker S (1992) 'New perspectives on an old problem: the position of women academics in British higher education' *Higher Education* 24, pp57-75

Adams HF (1983) 'Work in the interstices' in RL Dudovitch (ed) *Women in academe* Pergamon Press

Benson DJ & Thompson GE (1982) 'Sexual harassment on a university campus: the confluence of authority relations, sexual interest and gender stratification' *Social Problems* 29, pp237-251

Blackstone T & Fulton O (1975) 'Sex discrimination among university teachers: a British-American comparison' *British Journal of Sociology* 26 (30), pp261-275

Cammaert LP (1985) 'How widespread is sexual harassment on campus?' *International Journal of Women's Studies* 8, pp388–397

Continued...

Commission of the European Communities (1992) 'Commission recommendation of 27 November 1991 on the protection of the dignity of women and men at work' *Official Journal of the European Communities* L49, 39, 24 February, pp1-8

CVCP (1990) *Sexual and racial harassment: guidance for universities* Committee of Vice Chancellors and Principals

CVCP (1991) *Equal opportunies in employment in universities* Committee of Vice Chancellors and Principals

Department of Education and Science (1992) *Statistics of education: teachers in service, England and Wales, 1990* HMSO

Dudovitch RL (ed) (1983) *Women in academe* Pergamon Press

Dzeich BW & Weiner L (1984) *The lecherous professor on campus* Beacon Press

Fitzgerald LF, Shullman SL, Bailey N, Richards M, Swecker J, Gold Y, Omerod M & Weitzman L (1988) 'The incidence and dimensions of sexual harassment in academia and the workplace' *Journal of Vocational Behaviour* 32, pp152-175

Gruber JE (1992) 'A typology of personal and environmental sexual harassment: research and policy implications for the 1990s' *Sex Roles* 26, pp447-464

Hart A & Wilson T (1992) 'The politics of part-time staff' *AUT Bulletin* January, pp8-9

Herbert C (1991) Unpublished handout distributed at seminar at Loughborough University, March 1992

Herbert C (1992) *Sexual harrassment in schools: a guide for teachers* David Fulton

Kanter RM (1977) *Men and women of the corporations* Basic Books

Lipman-Blumen J (1976) 'Towards a homosocial theory of sex roles: an explanation of the sex-segregation of social institutions' *Signs* 3, pp15-22

National Union of Students (1987) *Sexual harassment survey: report of findings* NUS

Ramazanoglu C (1987) 'Sex and violence in academic life or you can't keep a good woman down' in J Hanmer & M Maynard (eds) *Women, violence and social control* Macmillan

Riger S (1991) 'Gender dilemmas in sexual harassment policies and procedures' *American Psychologist* 46, pp497-505

Rubin LJ & Borgers SB (1990) 'Sexual harassment in universities during the 1980s' *Sex Roles* 23, pp397-411

Thomas K (1990) *Gender and subject in higher education* Open University Press

(Bagilhole & Woodward, 1995: 37-40)

These extended examples serve to demonstrate two of the abiding issues relating to sex discrimination – the differential achievement of young women and young men at different stages in their educational careers, and the continuing unacceptable treatment of women even in institutions devoted to the education and training of the young.

They also reinforce the view that there are pernicious and obstructive social forces at work in the appointment and promotion of well-qualified women to posts in the public sector as well as in private businesses.

References and further reading

Abbott P & Wallace C (1997) *An introduction to sociology: feminist perspectives* 2nd edn Routledge (esp.Ch4)

Acker S (1994) *Gendered education* Open University Press

Arnot M (ed) (1985) *Race and gender: equal opportunities policies in education* Pergamon Press/Open University

Askew S & Ross C (1988) *Boys don't cry: boys and sexism in education* OUP

Bagilhole B & Woodward H (1995) 'An occupational hazard warning: academic life can seriously damage your health. An investigation of sexual harassment of women academics in a UK university' *British Journal of Sociology of Education* 16 (1)

Bilton T, Bonnett K, Jones P, Skinner D, Stanworth M & Webster A (1996) *Introductory sociology* 3rd edn Macmillan

Browne K (1998) *An introduction to sociology* 2nd edn Polity Press

Equal Opportunities Commission & Ofsted (1996) *The gender divide* HMSO

Hinde J (1998) 'Cash for female participation' *The Guardian* May 11th

Kelly A (1985) *Changing schools and changing society, some reflections on the girls into science and technology project* in Arnot M (ed) *op cit*

Mac An Ghaill (1994) *The making of men* Open University Press

Mitsos E (1995) 'Classroom voices' *The English and Media Magazine* 55 & 54, Autumn

Mitsos E & Browne K (1998) 'Gender differences in education: the underachievement of boys' *Sociology Review* 8 (1) September

Owen C, Cameron C & Moss P (eds) (1998) *Men as workers in services for young children: issues of a mixed gender workforce* Institute of Education

Phillips A (1995) *The trouble with boys* Pandora

Spender D (1982) *Invisible women: the schooling scandal* Chameleon Books

Weiner G (1994) *Feminisms in education* Open University Press

6.   Sexuality

Jane Andrews

If you are heterosexual you may well be wondering what sexuality has to do with your work as a teacher or trainer in PCET. Perhaps you think that these days being gay is not a problem. After all, there are gay characters in soaps on TV, there are several well known gay MPs, Michael Barrymore 'came out' a while back, Elton John sang in Westminster Abbey at Princess Diana's funeral.

The notion of inclusive learning implies that PCET institutions must develop a policy of responsiveness to each student's needs and make that policy implementation the responsibility of every member of staff. Inclusiveness is not usually extended to sexuality but it seems to me that it is a logical thing to do. Sexuality is an inclusiveness issue.

Young lesbians and gay men – experiences

The particular experiences of younger students are of concern to many teachers in colleges. In 1997, Lord Tope, one of the Liberal Democrats' education team, advertised in the gay press for young people to write to him about their experiences at school. Among the replies was:

> *My books were being defaced with filthy wording, or my file, folders and contents of my bag being emptied out of a first floor window as 'a punishment' for being gay.*

(Paul, aged 16, TES 16.10.98)

Regrettably this response is not unusual. In 1984 Lorraine Trenchard and Hugh Warren, of the London Gay Teenage Group, published the first major survey of young lesbians and gay men and found:

- 1 in 2 had experienced problems at school because they were lesbian or gay
- 1 in 5 had been beaten because they were lesbian or gay
- 6 in 10 had been verbally abused because they were lesbian or gay
- 1 in 5 had attempted suicide because they were lesbian or gay.

More recently Ian Rivers (1995) at the University of Luton, in a questionnaire involving 80 young lesbians and gay men, reported that:

- 80% had been subjected to namecalling
- 69% had faced open ridicule by pupils and occasionally by teachers
- 59% had been hit or kicked
- 49% had been teased
- 55% had had rumours or stories spread about them.

There has been no systematic research into the experiences of young lesbian, gay and bisexual students in further education and whether their experiences are similar to those at school. My own anecdotal evidence gathered from talking with young lesbians and gay men is that some say that the decision to come to college was partly to escape homophobic bullying at school. Unfortunately, they didn't necessarily find it easier at college.

Lesbians, gay men and bisexuals in PCET

There are also of course lesbians and gay men among the older students in all PCET institutions. Most surveys suggest that roughly 10% of the population is lesbian or gay, so a reasonable estimate is that in each class or group of 20 people one or two will be gay. Lesbians and gay men face prejudice and discrimination in all aspects of their lives: in education, in housing, in employment, in basic legal and human rights. For the lesbians and gay men in your classes this discrimination is a routine daily fact of life.

You will already know this if you are lesbian, gay or bisexual. You may, like the teacher quoted here, have chosen FE rather than school teaching because you think it will be easier:

> *I think when I talk to the staff at where I am now, I'm a lot more confident than I was in a school. I think you can be a lot more open in an FE College anyway.*

> (Epstein, 1994: 29)

Or perhaps as a gay trainee FE lecturer you are not 'out' to your tutors or to all your peers. You may still have to decide whether to be open in your teaching practice college. You may still be wondering what to say if a student asks you (usually out of the blue): 'Are you gay?' Or how to respond when there is some sniggering about a news story with potential gay interest.

Maybe your student or client groups change regularly, bringing new students each week. Do you dread that casual chatty conversation which strangers sometimes engage in? That question: 'And are you married?' Those of us who are lesbian, gay or bisexual know that the issue about being out or not is far from straightforward, and that, however open and confident we feel, we have to make numerous daily decisions about how 'out' to be.

If you are facing these dilemmas you will be interested that a 1997 survey by NATFHE of 42 lesbian and gay FE lecturers, found only 5% said they were 'out' to students. 21% said they were 'out' to 'close associates' only. A report about lesbian games teachers by Gill Clarke of the University of Southampton (Young, 1996) found that they were forced to conceal their sexuality for fear of being labelled as perverts and a danger to children.

It is unlikely that teachers will automatically know who are the gay students in their classes, or who their gay colleagues. One of the insidious ways in which homophobia operates is through self censorship and silence. If you are gay you can never be quite sure what will be the response to 'coming out' so many gay people are always cautious.

> *... concealment helps to avoid overt discrimination. However, the qualitative evidence suggests that the strain and indignity of keeping such an integral part of their lives secret is one of the most insidious forms of the discrimination that homosexual people experience.*
>
> (Snape, Thomson & Chetwynd, 1995: viii)

Patterns of discrimination

There are some similarities between patterns of homosexual discrimination and the kinds of discrimination experienced by other minority groups. Though most discrimination is the result of prejudice plus power, there are key differences in the nature of the discrimination faced by lesbians, gay men and bisexual people. One significant difference is that in the UK, as in most other countries, discrimination is reinforced by anomaly and legal inequality. (Only South Africa, interestingly, guarantees equality for gay people as part of their Constitution.) Though the age of sexual consent for gay men in the UK has now been lowered to 16, there is no corresponding age of consent for lesbians (Section 25 of the Public Order Act stops the incitement of gay male relationships). Only recently – under pressure from the European Court of Human Rights – did the Armed Forces Bill legalise homosexuality in the forces. Tax laws and inheritance restrictions at the present time fail to recognise gay relationships; there is no common law status for gay partners living together. In fact gay people have no legal protection against discrimination on the grounds of their sexuality.

As yet (July 2000) there is no Sexuality Discrimination Act. This means, for example, that it is still quite legal to turn down a gay applicant for a job, or to refuse a hotel room to a gay couple purely on the grounds of their sexuality. There are indications, though, that UK law falls foul of the European Convention on Human Rights. It was a judgement of the European Court of Human Rights in 1999 that caused the age of consent in the UK to be lowered, but only after great opposition, particularly in the House of Lords. In the Lords debate Lord Alli spoke passionately about the prejudice faced by gay people:

> *My Lords, many of your Lordships will know that I am openly gay. I am 34. I was gay when I was 24, when I was 21, when I was 20, when I was 19, when I was 18, when I was 17 and even when I was 16. I have never been confused about my sexuality. I have been confused about the way I am treated as a result of it. The only confusion lies in the prejudice shown... Many noble Lords probably cannot understand what it is like to be gay and young. It means that one can be called anything: 'sick'; 'abnormal'; 'unnatural'; 'ruined'. These words were used by colleagues tonight...*
>
> (Hansard: Sexual Offences(Amendment) Bill, 13 April 1999)

In 1999 and 2000 the Labour government took action to abolish Section 28 of the Thatcher government's 1988 Local Government Act. Section 28 made it illegal for local authorities intentionally to 'promote' homosexuality. This law never applied to FE or HE institutions, or indeed even directly to schools, but its existence has had a considerable self-censoring impact on teachers and lecturers. It has sent a clear signal that there is something wrong in talking about gay issues, or of addressing the needs of lesbian and gay students.

Attempts to abolish this discriminatory law have not been straightforward and there was considerable furore surrounding the repeal of Section 28; the proposal was twice defeated in the House of Lords, thus prejudicing an important Local Government Bill. Though MPs were flooded with letters opposing repeal, the Commons voted in favour. In Scotland a millionaire, Brian Souter, organised a private referendum – unsuccessful, as it turned out – to oppose repeal of the clause. The UK Government itself was persuaded to issue guidelines to schools emphasising the importance of marriage, urging schools to deal honestly and sensitively with sexual orientation issues, and offering support to deal with homophobic bullying. The climate in which repeal was discussed gives some indication of the unease with which lesbian and gay issues are still regarded, particularly where young people are concerned.

Legal inequalities in the UK are reinforced by widely held social perceptions about lesbians and gay men. While attitudes may perhaps appear to be changing quite rapidly, research still suggests marked instances of prejudice. A survey published in 1995 by SCPR (Snape *et al.* 1995) found that 41% of heterosexual respondents thought it was never or hardly ever acceptable for a gay man to be a secondary school teacher. 34% thought it was never or hardly ever acceptable for a lesbian to be a supervisor in a youth club. In the same survey 15% said that if they discovered that their 11-year-old son was being taught by a gay man then they would ask to have the child removed to another class. A further 30% said they would tell the headteacher or a school governor. 36% of the heterosexual respondents also said they would be less likely to employ a gay man if he had made his sexuality clear during a job interview. 58% said they would be less likely to rent a room to a lesbian couple than to a heterosexual couple if they had this choice. Such findings illustrate the levels of prejudice which are still commonplace in the UK.

Another way in which discrimination against lesbians, gay men and bisexuals is different from most other kinds of discrimination, is that the discrimination rests upon assumptions held by a significant proportion of the population that being gay is quite simply wrong or unnatural. The SCPR survey found that 41% of heterosexual respondents thought that sexual relations between two men were 'always wrong' (the figure was 37% for sexual relations between two women). A further example of this view occurred in the age of consent debate in the House of Commons in June 1998 when Patrick Cormack MP said he believed that homosexuals were 'not only different from heterosexuals but should not be regarded as equal or equivalent' (*Guardian* 23.6.98.). It is not possible to imagine that an MP could publicly make such a statement about any other group, about black people or women for example, without widespread public outcry.

Being gay in this society is not morally neutral. In the following extract, Warren Blumenfield and Diane Raymond explore this theme through an analogy between being gay and being left handed.

A discussion about difference: the left-handed analogy

What do left-handedness and homosexuality have in common? This prologue explores some of the similarities which do in fact exist between the two. Though comparing handedness and sexual orientation might seem akin to comparing artichokes and jet planes, as we do so, striking connections appear. Although this analogy is in no way meant to imply any statistical correlation between left-handedness and homosexuality, it does aim to show how society transforms the meanings of what appear to be value-neutral personal characteristics into morally significant facts.

Every analogy attempts to make a point. Whether one does so successfully depends on how much the items being compared really resemble each other. This one suggests that there are crucial ways in which handedness and sexual orientation are similar. What follows here is a thumbnail sketch of some of those similarities...

It is estimated that one out of every ten people is left-handed. In fact, this statistic probably holds true for all places and all times. That means there are approximately 25 million left-handed people in the United States alone; and, in a classroom of, say, thirty, at least three people are probably left-handed. Amazingly enough, the statistics are virtually the same for people who act on same-sex attractions.

Left-handed people have existed throughout all ages in all cultures, in all races, all social classes, and in every country. Even the earliest cave-drawings show left-handed figures. Similarly, same sex acts have probably always existed. Even some of our most ancient literary fragments contain references to love between members of the same sex.

Who is left-handed and lesbian and gay?

Though it may seem obvious, it is not always easy to determine who is left-handed. Some people, for example, use different hands for different activities. Former President Gerald Ford uses his left hand to write while sitting and his right hand to write on blackboards while standing. Some people can successfully manage with either hand. In fact, it is probably true that most people aren't exclusively right-handed or left-handed. We usually, however, define our handedness in terms of whichever hand we use the most, especially in writing. Nevertheless, people in general exhibit a great variety of hand skills, which covers a broad continuum between left-handedness and exclusive right-handedness.

The same difficulty exists when we try to apply labels referring to sexual orientation. Some people very early in their lives develop an awareness and acceptance of their attractions to members of their own sex. Others, though, may reach this stage later in life. Some people may be attracted to both sexes, defining themselves as 'bisexual'. In fact, it is probably true that most people aren't exclusively heterosexual or homosexual. Most of us, however, define our sexuality by the sex with which we feel more comfortable and to which we experience the stronger attraction. Nevertheless, people's sexuality is fairly flexible, covering a broad continuum between exclusive homosexuality and exclusive heterosexuality.

Continued...

So far, these facts might seem interesting, but not particularly noteworthy. But for those who are left-handed or lesbian or gay, it might be comforting to know that they are not alone. And for the majority, right-handed people and heterosexuals, it might be worth considering that not everyone is the same. What 'righties' usually take for granted – cutting with scissors, working with most tools, even writing from left to right – often involves awkward adjustment for 'lefties'. Similarly, what 'straights' usually take for granted – holding hands in public, going to school dances, introducing girlfriends or boyfriends to parents – also often involves awkward adjustments for lesbians and gays.

Prejudice and discrimination

Though you might not think your friend or mother or classmate is all that weird because she or he is left-handed, such tolerance has not always been the case. In fact, for centuries, left-handed people have been viewed with scorn and even, at times, with fear.

Such scorn was often justified with references to religious texts such as the Bible. Both the Old and New Testaments consider 'the left' to be the domain of the Devil, whereas 'the right' is the domain of God. For this reason, Jesus told his followers to 'not let thy left hand know what thy right hand doeth' (Matthew 6:3). Jesus also describes God's process for separating good from evil in the Last Judgment: '... the King (shall) say unto them on His right hand, "Come, ye blessed of my Father, inherit the Kingdom prepared for you from the foundation of the world..." Then shall He say unto them on the left hand, "Depart from me, ye cursed, into everlasting fire, prepared for the devil and his angels..."' (Matthew 25:32–41).

Early Christians applied these categories so strictly that they even held that the saints, while still infants, were so holy that they would not suck from the left breasts of their mothers!

It is not only the Bible that condemns left-handedness. This was also the case in some ancient societies. The ancient Greeks and Romans shared this attitude. For example, the philosopher Pythagoras argued that left-handedness was synonymous with 'dissolution' and evil, and Aristotle described good as 'what is on the right, above and in front, and bad what is on the left, below and behind'. The Romans further reinforced these beliefs by standardizing the right-handed handshake, and in Western countries alphabets favour right-handed people in being written from left to right.

Later, in the Middle Ages, left-handed people were sometimes accused of being witches or sorcerers. The present-day wedding custom of joining right hands and placing the gold ring on the third finger of the left hand began with the superstition that doing so would absorb the evil inherent in the left hand.

Though few people today condemn left-handedness, lesbians and gays continue to be feared and excluded. Such treatment is also often justified with references to religious texts such as the Bible.

Continued...

Though there is great disagreement over the interpretations of certain passages in the Bible, it is difficult to find anything positive in passages like the following: 'If a man also lie with mankind, as he lieth with a woman, both of them have committed an abomination: they shall surely be put to death; their blood shall be upon them' (Leviticus 20: 13).

Early Christians expanded this to include women when St. Paul condemned women 'who did change the natural use into that which is against nature' (Romans 1: 26).

Though homosexual relations were condoned for some males in Classical Greece, the Romans, beginning around the 4th century CE (Common Era), prescribed the death penalty for male homosexual behaviour. Though sentences were rarely carried out, these laws were later used as the foundation for both Canon Law (the law of the Catholic Church) and many civil laws throughout Europe. During the High Middle Ages, beginning in the late 12th century, a number of governments punished people accused of same-sex eroticism with banishment, mutilation, and death by fire. People discovered engaging in same-sex acts were sometimes accused of being witches or sorcerers. In fact, the present day term *faggot* is said by many to come from the practice of capturing gay men and tying them together as if they were a bundle (or 'faggot') of wood to ignite as kindling over which a woman suspected of being a 'witch' would be burned at the stake. Homosexuality was a crime punishable by death in colonial America, and in England until 1861. Following the American Revolution, Thomas Jefferson proposed that the penalty be reduced from death to castration. In the United States today, the Supreme Court has ruled that laws which prohibit private, consensual, adult sexual acts commonly associated with homosexuality are constitutional.

Even our terminology often reflects such biases. Words like *sinister* in Latin and *gauche* in French suggest a moral evil or physical awkwardness associated with left-handedness. (Note that their opposites, *dexter* in Latin and *droit* in French, mean 'skillful,' 'artful', 'clever', 'correct', or 'lawful'.) In fact, the English word *left* comes from an old Dutch word (*lyft*) meaning 'weak' or 'broken', whereas *right* derives from an Anglo-Saxon word (*right*) meaning 'straight', 'erect', or 'just'. The word 'ambidextrous' literally means' being right-handed on both sides'. Phrases like 'left-handed compliment' are insults to left-handed people.

Correspondingly, there exists a heterosexual bias in the language we use. There are no common words like *husband* or *wife* that refer to same sex partners. And words like *bachelor* and *spinster* often inaccurately label gay men and lesbians regardless of their relationship status. If a gay person is involved in a media story, newspapers, or the evening news commonly use phrases like 'avowed homosexual' or 'homosexual affair'; in contrast, no equivalent terminology is used to define the sexuality of a heterosexual person.

All right, you might respond, but what does this have to do with the treatment of left-handed people and lesbians and gays today? Regarding left-handers, most tools and utensils and most packaging of products are designed for the ease of right-handed

Continued...

people. These include phonograph arms, power saws, corkscrews, sewing machines, and even gum wrappers. Left-handed pilots are not allowed to sit on the right side of the cockpit to reach the controls in the centre, even though to do so would make it easier.

In the case of lesbians and gays, most laws and ordinances are made to protect the rights of heterosexuals, and , in most states in the United States, these protections do not extend to gays and lesbians. Homosexual relationships do not have legal status. No state recognizes lesbian and gay marriages, people can be denied employment and housing in most areas simply because they happen to be lesbian or gay, and gays and lesbians are often prevented from serving as adoptive or foster parents.

No one really knows why a little more strength in one hand over the other or preference for one sex over the other has been the basis of wide-scale persecution of a minority group of human beings.

How did such social preferences arise? Some people argue that the preference for right-handedness began with the military. If all soldiers were right-handed, they would all pass to the right of their enemy, keeping the enemy on their left side, where they held their shields, and enabling them to maintain a uniform defensive posture. This practice then extended to the rules of the road, except in countries such as England, where they drive on the left side of the road. But even there, the practice was established from a right-handed preference. Knights on horseback would keep their opponents to their right with their lances while jousting.

It is possible that the emphasis on heterosexuality began with the early Hebrews, who were under pressure from competing faiths and cultures. Male homosexuality was a religious practice of the holy men of the Canaanite cults and it was an accepted activity in the early years of the Greek empire. In order to ensure the survival of the Jewish faith, condemnations of many of the beliefs and practices of their neighbours, including that of homosexuality, were used to emphasize the differences between the Hebrews and their competition. Also, because their numbers were constantly depleted by drought, disease, and warfare with their neighbours, the early Hebrews placed restrictions on homosexual behaviour to promote an increase in their birthrate.

Nowadays, we tend to think of these practices as 'natural' and to overlook their origin in history and social necessity. Thus, what began as human diversity has been translated into moral pronouncements of all sorts.

Causes: Biology? Environment?

Any difference from the norm gets more attention from researchers. This is certainly the case with left-handedness and homosexuality. Few ask what causes right-handedness or hand orientation in general, or heterosexuality or sexual orientation in general.

Some theorists believe that the cause of left-handedness is biological, citing evidence that left-handed people are dominated by the right side (hemisphere) of the brain.

Continued...

Some researchers, though, dispute this view, arguing that the correlation does not hold true in many cases.

There is also evidence to suggest that left-handedness may be genetic — that it is inherited — since there is a higher statistical probability that two left-handed persons will have a left-handed child. Others maintain that left-handedness is a result of an imbalance in the mother's hormones while the foetus is developing *in utero*. Some theorists have suggested that a distinct preference for one side over the other is shown as early as the second day of life.

Some social scientists argue that left-handedness is environmentally determined and may be a form of mimicking or copying of the behaviour of another left-handed family member by the developing child. And some people argue that left-handedness is a choice as opposed to being biologically determined, while others maintain that hand orientation is influenced by both heredity and environment, citing possible genetic factors that are then modified by cultural influences. Some others say that left handedness is pathological, a result of trauma to the brain or stress to the mother during pregnancy.

Likewise, some people believe that the cause of homosexuality is biological, that some people are born with this orientation. Some researchers suggest that homosexuality is genetic, that there is a gay or lesbian gene. Others maintain that homosexuality is the result of a hormonal imbalance in the foetus of the pregnant woman. Some theorists have suggested that sexual orientation towards one's own sex over the other sex is determined as early as the fourth or fifth year of life.

Some researchers posit that homosexuality is environmentally determined as a result of certain family constellations. Some, though, argue that homosexuality is simply a choice a person makes, while others maintain that sexuality is influenced by both heredity and environment, citing possible genetic factors that are then modified by cultural influences. Still others say that homosexuality is a physical defect, perhaps a result of injury to the foetus or stress to the pregnant woman.

The fact remains that no one knows for sure the causal factors in the development of handedness or sexual orientation. The evidence that does exist tends to be inconsistent and often contradictory. It is therefore likely that there is no unitary explanation that applies in every instance.

Stereotypes abound in reference to both left-handed people and people with same-sex attractions. Left-handers are often labeled, for example, as willful or stubborn. Gays and lesbians are termed immature or sexually insatiable. Often, people have the notion that all left-handers are controlled by the right side of the brain, making then more visually oriented and artistic, while being less verbal and less inclined to grasp abstract concepts than right-handed people. In addition, some people even think that lefties are at a greater risk of committing criminal offenses. Likewise, some people have the notion that all gay men are overly effeminate and prey on young children, and lesbians are man-haters who secretly want to be men.

Continued...

Is it natural?

No one really knows why hand preference or sexual preference occurs. In nature, four-legged creatures do not seem to show a preference for a side. And more animals seem to have developed 'bilaterally', meaning that they have matching equal pairs which may be used interchangeably. There seems to be no solid evidence to support the idea of an animal preference of either the right or the left side, except for a few species of animals and plants, and sometimes a few individuals of different species. The honeysuckle is one of the few plants that twines to the left. The morning glory twines to the right, and others twist either way depending on other variables. Gorillas seem to exhibit a slight left-handed bias. But why humans prefer one side over the other remains a mystery even today. And in the universe overall, there seems to be no common law for inanimate objects in terms of motion or favouring sides.

With respect to sexuality, many varieties of insects and reptiles, almost every species of mammal, and many types of birds engage in some form of homosexual behaviour both in the wild and in captivity. Also, in some cultures, homosexual activity not only exists but is often encouraged. For example, the Azande and Mossi people of the Sudan in Africa and various tribes in New Guinea consider same-sex relations to be the norm. Adult lesbian relationships are quite common among the Azande, the Nupe, the Haussa, and the Nyakyusa people of Africa, as are adolescent lesbian activities among the Dahomeyan, the !Kung, and Australian aborigines.

Overall, there seems to be no common law for the attraction of inanimate objects, though some people have postulated that only opposites attract. Though this may hold true for positive and negative electric charges, this theory is contradicted time and time again. For example, in metallurgy, various metals which vary slightly chemically combine with little difficulty to form strong and stable unions. In addition, the concept of opposites is a subjective one, and males and females actually have quite a lot in common.

Why does this matter anyway? Well, it matters to some who believe that certain kinds of differences are innately unnatural. This attitude has led many theorists to propose strategies for changing an exhibited hand or sexual preference. They have urged parents to encourage young children to emphasise their right hands, especially in writing. In some schools, teachers have even tied the youngsters' left hands behind their backs or made them sit on their left hands to promote use of the right hand. Even noted baby doctor Benjamin Spock once urged mothers to discourage the use of the left hand in their infants.

This treatment often results in emotional outbursts, speech impairments such as stuttering, reading problems, and other learning disabilities. And some 'lefties' have tried to conceal their orientation, to 'pass' as right-handed in order to fit in with the dominant majority group.

Homosexuals have also been coerced into changing their sexuality. 'Experts' have urged parents to encourage young children to manifest behaviours and engage in activities which are considered 'appropriate' to their sex. Schools have traditionally

Continued...

withheld teaching about the positive contributions made by lesbians and gays in all areas of society. Most sex education either omits any mention of alternatives to heterosexuality or presents homosexuality as a form of deviance to be avoided. This often results, for those who are not heterosexual, in self-hatred and isolation. Like lefties, some gays and lesbians have tried to conceal their orientation, hoping to 'pass' as heterosexual in order to be accepted by the majority. These kinds of treatments have prompted some people to question the underlying assumptions of the superiority of the majority group. Some lefties have maintained that they are the same as righties and that there are as many different kinds of left-handed people as there are right. Similarly, some lesbians and gays have maintained that they too are the same as heterosexuals and that there are as many different kinds of homosexual people as there are heterosexuals – but that certain types tend to be more visible because they fit into our expectations.

Others, however, have maintained that 'being different' endows its possessors with exceptional qualities such as intuitiveness, creativity, and the like. In actuality, there seem to be some areas in which left-handed people do seem to have an advantage. Neurologists have shown that left-handed people adjust more readily to underwater vision, giving them an advantage in swimming. In the sport of baseball and tennis there is a significantly higher percentage of left-handed players. For instance, 40 percent of the top tennis professionals are left-handed, and 32 percent of all major league batters, 30 percent of pitchers, and 48 percent of all those who play first base are left-handed. In fact, the term 'southpaw' was coined to describe left-handed pitchers. In a typical major league ballpark they pitch from east to west with their south, or left arm (home plate being located to the west to keep the sun out of the batter's eyes).

Gay and lesbian people may also have certain advantages. For example, they are generally less bound to gender-based role expectations within a relationship, they don't constantly have to worry about birth control, and by not being fully accepted within society, they may be more tolerant of difference and so can objectively critique their cultures.

Politics

In a world which ignores or hinders expressions of diversity, some people are pushing for rights of minority groups. Many political activists reject mere 'tolerance', maintaining that such an attribute promotes invisibility and continues the discriminatory treatment of these groups. Some activists are demanding that society make more physical accommodations to left-handed people and reject all prejudices that prevent full support for the left-hander. Gay and lesbian activists, in like fashion, are demanding that society grant equality of treatment and an end to oppressive laws that prevent full inclusion of lesbians and gays.

An early left-handed activist of sorts was Michelangelo, himself a left-hander, who bucked convention in his Sistine Chapel mural by portraying God as granting the gift of life through Adam's left hand...

Continued...

Regardless of the diversity of political views among left-handed people, and among lesbians and gays, there seems to be agreement that there must be greater awareness of the needs of these minorities. Authors have formulated credos to help solidify these political movements. Here are excerpts from two of these essays.

From 'A Left-Handed Manifesto' (DeKay):

Be it resolved that all left-thinking citizens, mindful that their Birthleft has been denied them, shall henceforth stand up for their lefts. We call upon each one of them to support this Bill of Lefts, and specifically to buy left – purchase only left-handed products... Act left – don't knuckle under! You've made enough adjustments. Remember! There are at least 25 million left-handers in America. Singly, they can do nothing, but united they can change the world.

From 'A Gay Manifesto' (Wittman):

Where once there was frustration, alienation, and cynicism, there are new characteristics among us. We are full of love for each other and are showing it; we are full of anger at what has been done to us. And as we recall all our self-censorships and repression for so many years, a reservoir of tears pours out of our eyes. And we are euphoric, high, with the initial flourish of a movement.

(from Blumenfield WJ & Raymond D 1988: 23–33)

What teachers can do

By now I hope you realise that equality issues relating to sexuality are important in your work as a teacher or trainer because there are bound to be lesbian and gay students in your classes and groups. To acknowledge this in an open and comfortable way is an aspect of good equal opportunities practice. Some of the gay students in your groups may need your particular support and help if they are to benefit from their course, achieve good results and feel safe and secure in their learning.

Beyond this *all* students have a right to information about lesbian and gay issues, because lesbians and gay people are part of the community in which we all live, work and study. Being lesbian, gay or bisexual is only partly about sexual orientation, about *sex*. It is much more about respecting people's rights to choose who they have relationships with, who they choose to love and live with. All lecturers, teachers, trainers, facilitators have a responsibility for ensuring that the experiences of lesbians and gay people are made visible, and represented across all aspects of the curriculum. Just as it is not acceptable to exclude the experiences of say women or black people from the curriculum, so it is the case for gay people.

In describing the patterns of discrimination and harassment which can be faced by lesbians, gay men and bisexuals it is important not to portray lives negatively. There is a diversity of lesbian, gay and bisexual experience, much of it positive and very joyful as these quotations suggest:

My girlfriend and I always sleep together at my house and my mother wanders in and chats to us and even sometimes brings us morning tea in bed.

She is happy for me, for us. She commented on how she had never known me to be so happy before.

(Female 19, in Trenchard & Warren, 1984: 44)

When I met Richard we realised that we had more in common than just sex and it blossomed from there. We've lived together since then (over 32 years), and we've had a full and happy life. All our family and friends are accepting. We don't make a fuss about being gay, and everyone ensures that we're both included in family events.

(Chris, in Sanderson, 1991: 92)

Practical ideas

1. *Don't assume that everyone in your classes or groups is heterosexual*

   Assume instead that your groups are diverse. Among your students will be those who are married, have children, child free, divorced, celibate, separated, single, lesbian, gay, bisexual, undecided, unsure. Avoid referring exclusively to heterosexual relationships in your talk. Many teachers also casually refer to their own heterosexual partners even when they barely know students in their classes. This also is best avoided.

2. *Keep yourself informed about lesbian and gay issues*

   Do this by being aware of organisations such as Lesbian and Gay Switchboard (which offers advice and support to gay people), and Stonewall (the lobbying pressure group). Notice how the media respond to gay issues (particularly when they seem to involve scandals). If you see something which shocks you say something. Discuss it with colleagues.

3. *Be open to approaches from young lesbian, gay or bisexual students who want your help and support*

   A student who is questioning their sexuality will not be helped if you appear shocked or surprised. One of the worst things you could say to someone who is tentatively 'coming out' is to suggest that they 'are only going through a phase'. No one would dream of saying this to a young heterosexual man or woman thinking about a heterosexual relationship! Remember too that sexuality is fluid, and that people may be heterosexual and gay at different stages in their lives.

4. *Challenge homophobic and heterosexist remarks in the classroom*

   If you find yourself worrying whether people will think you might be gay if you do this, then imagine how a gay person feels!

5. *Promote positive images of lesbian, gay and bisexual relationships with younger students*

   If you are working with younger students, particularly in Sixth Form Colleges you may be asked to facilitate PSHE (Personal, Social, and Health Education). Make sure that this includes reference to sexuality and that lesbian and gay issues are referred to positively. In this context you may also be called upon to get involved in Aids education. You have a responsibility to keep informed about Aids, and of the particular HIV and Aids-related prevention and care needs of gay and bisexual students.

6. *Check your college/institution policy on sexuality issues*
   The NATFHE survey (NATFHE, 1997) found that 62% of further education colleges had an equal opportunities policy which included sexuality, but that most of such policies were not considered effective. Your college should have procedures in place for dealing with homophobic incidents, including bullying. It ought also to say something about curriculum issues (though only 24% of policies in the same survey covered the curriculum).

7. *Remember that lesbians, gay men and bisexuals are not an homogeneous group*
   There are lesbians and men in every social class, ethnic group, among older and younger people, among disabled and able-bodied groups. Lesbians and gay men may also be parents. Sometimes teachers argue that they cannot be open about lesbian and gay issues because they may offend particular racial or ethnic groups. This is an inaccurate and offensive assumption. Among Christians, Jews, Muslims, Hindus there are those who support lesbian and gay rights, and often groups who will lend specific support (e.g. Lesbian and Gay Christian Movement; SHAKTI – a group for young Asian lesbians).

8. *Use examples relating to lesbian, gay and bisexual lives in your teaching*
   This is possible in *all* curriculum areas, and all kinds of teaching and training scenarios.

A word about terminology

Sometimes the language used to describe lesbians and gay men may seem confusing. Acceptable patterns of language change quickly and, as with the language of race, sensitivity is important. It can be helpful to take a lead from the words which lesbians and gay men use about themselves.

Here are some current definitions and explanations:

- *Homosexual*
  A word first used in the nineteenth century to refer to people who are sexually and emotionally attracted to members of the same sex. It is usually used to describe gay men, and not often taken to include lesbians. The word has medical connotations and is not often one used by lesbians and gay men themselves now, though it was common in the first part of this century.

- *Gay men*
  The word 'gay' was adopted by gay people in the 1960s as a self-chosen term and a rejection of other negative words (e.g. poof, pervert). More recently the word 'gay' has tended to be associated specifically with men. As well as indicating a *sexual* preference by men of other men, being gay is also a wider description of emotional *relationships*.

- *Lesbians*
  The word is derived from the word meaning an inhabitant of Lesbos, the Greek island where Sappho, the lesbian poet lived. Lesbians have sexual and emotional relationships with other women. Not all lesbians feel comfortable using this word to describe themselves, and some prefer to say 'gay woman'.

- *Bisexuals*
Bisexuals are people who feel they are sexually attracted to both sexes.

- *Queer*
Until recently 'queer' was a term of abuse about gay people, often shouted as an insult. Some lesbians and gay men (mainly in big cities) have 'reclaimed' the word and use it positively about themselves.

- *Dyke*
Some lesbians use the word *dyke* to describe themselves. This is another example of a formerly insulting word being reclaimed and used in a positive way. (Heterosexuals may well be misunderstood if they use the words *dyke* and *queer* because they still carry strong negative messages.)

- *Homophobia*
Means literally 'fear of homosexuals'. This is the fear and prejudice felt by some people against lesbians and gay men. Homophobia has deep psychological roots which may be linked to what people were told (or not told) as children about lesbians and gay men.

- *Heterosexism*
This term emerged in the 1970s to describe the *institutional* prejudice and discrimination faced by lesbians and gay men. Heterosexism is a set of ideas and practices which assumes that heterosexual relationships are the only normal and natural kind of sexual relationships, and therefore that they are superior to lesbian and gay relationships. It is heterosexism which leads to discriminatory laws like the unequal age of consent. *Anti-heterosexism* means opposition to this prejudice: it doesn't mean being anti heterosexuals!

- *Sexuality*
This is a general term that covers all forms of sexual behaviour, and is not just about the gender of an individual's sexual partner.

- *Sexual orientation*
This is used to refer specifically to the gender preferred by an individual in the choice of sexual partner. (Sexual orientation refers to being heterosexual, bisexual, gay or lesbian.)

- *Transsexual*
A transsexual or *transgendered* person feels that their biological body is at odds with their real sex. Transsexuals may seek hormone treatment or surgery to change their body. Transsexuals, who have undergone this treatment may be heterosexual, or lesbian/gay.

- *Transvestites*
Transvestites are men or women who enjoy dressing in the clothes usually associated with the other sex. Transvestites may be heterosexual or homosexual.

References and further reading:

Blumenfield WJ & Raymond D (1988) 'A discussion about differences: the left-handed analogy' in *Looking at gay and lesbian life* Beacon Press

Cant B & Hemmings S (1988) *Radical records: 30 years of lesbian and gay history* Routledge

Douglas N, Warwick I, Kemp S & Whitty G (1997) *Playing it safe* Health and Education Research Unit, Institute of Education

Epstein D (1994) *Challenging lesbian and gay inequalities in education* Open University Press

Ghouri N (1998) 'Peer urges help for gay pupils' *Times Educational Supplement* 16.10.98

Hanscombe G & Humphries M (1987) *Heterosexuality* GMP Publishers

Harris S (1990) *Lesbian and gay issues in the English classroom* OUP

Jennings K (1994) *Becoming visible* Alyson Publications

Khayatt MD (1992) *Lesbian teachers: an invisible presence* State University of New York Press

NATFHE (1997) *Lesbian, gay and bisexual survey* NATFHE Equal Opportunities Unit

Plummer K (ed) (1992) *Modern homosexualities* Routledge

Rivers I (1995) 'The victimisation of gay teenagers in schools: homophobia in education' *Pastoral Care* March

Rivers I (1996) 'Young, gay and bullied' *Young People Now* January

Sanderson T (1991) *A stranger in the family: how to cope if your child is gay* The Other Way Press

Snape D, Thomson K, & Chetwynd M (1995) *Discrimination against gay men and lesbians* Social and Community Planning Research

Trenchard L & Warren H (1984) *Something to tell you* London Gay Teenage Group

Ward L (1998) 'Vote on gay consent age rouses Commons passions' *Guardian* 23.6.98

Weeks J (1991) *Against nature* Rivers Oram Press

Young S (1996) 'Lesbian teachers fear for their jobs' *Times Educational Supplement* 20.12.96

7.   Social Class

Ann Lahiff

The working classes form the majority of society (some 60% of males have manual occupations) and in 1991/92 some 25% of the population lived in households whose income was less than half that of the average income of households in Britain. Some 32% or 4.1 million children lived in this definition of poverty.

(Reid, 1997: 32)

Definitions

Ivan Reid offers the following definition of social levels (or strata):

Social strata are groupings defined in terms of their ownership of, or access to, social wealth. Social wealth refers to anything which is relatively scarce in society and which has a value, from wealth, property and income, power and influence, through health and health services, education and education services, to prestige and respect, values and self-image.

(Reid, 1996: 2)

He goes on to suggest that from his perspective social class is the fundamental form of social stratification in our society, providing a context for other forms of inequality (see also Reid, 1989; Reid & Stratta, 1989).

The exact nature of social class is at the centre of much debate in contemporary social theory, and further references are given at the end of this section for those who wish to take their study of such issues further than this brief introduction can provide. However, class is generally presented in terms of membership of an occupational grouping. The assumption underpinning this is that Professional and Managerial employees, for example, will have similar ownership of, or access to, social wealth (as defined by Reid, above) when compared to the lower levels of ownership experienced by Unskilled Manual workers.

Following this approach, then, one's ownership of, or access to, social wealth is the key to determining social class membership. In terms of addressing inequalities in relation to social class, some preliminary questions need to be addressed. For instance, what bearing does the family background and circumstances we are born into have on our educational success and the choices we make at 16? If so, does that matter? Indeed, should we who work in post-16 education and training be concerned about it?

Education and social class

Two indicators of the patterns that exist in relation to social class and education concern *qualifications achieved* and *length of time spent in further and higher education and training.* With respect to the former, information tends to be provided in relation to patterns between generations.

Reid (1997) reminds us that 'there is no national monitoring of social class and educational achievement, though something of the relationship is recorded in the continuous General Household survey'. The table that follows has been gathered by using such British government sources.

Group	Profess-ional	Employer & manager	Junior non-manual	Skilled manual	Semi-skilled manual service	Unskilled manual	Total %
Quals							
Degree	32	17	17	6	4	3	10
Other HE	19	15	18	10	7	5	11
A level	15	13	12	8	6	4	9
O level	19	24	24	21	19	15	21
CSE	4	9	7	12	12	10	10
Foreign	4	4	4	3	2	2	3
No quals	7	19	18	40	50	60	35
Total %	100	100	100	100	100	100	100

Highest qualification level attained by socio-economic group of father 1990-1: percentages.

(Adapted from Bilton *et al.* 1996: 342)

As can be seen from the table, the proportion of people with higher education, that is, above GCE A level, drops sharply across the social classes and this is mirrored by the rise in the percentage across the social classes of those without education qualifications. Studies which compare social class origins (the class into which we are born) with destinations (the class we achieve) confirm the pivotal role that social class background plays. Educational achievement is, then, still systematically related to social class and so too is the length of time spent in education.

It is perhaps surprising that at a time of expanding numbers of people entering higher education, the socio-economic profile of higher education students has not changed significantly (FEFC, 1997: 21; Dearing HE Report, 1997: Section 3).

What difference do educational qualifications make?

The Kennedy Report (FEFC, 1997) suggests that:

Studies consistently demonstrate that qualifications earned at 16 provide an excellent predictor of whether a young person will continue in full-time learning... Those who enter higher education as full-time students have already achieved academic success. Most will go on to achieve financial success too. On average, graduates earn over half as much again as those qualified to NVQ level 3, and nearly twice as much as those with no qualifications... Those with high levels of qualifications are more likely than those with low or no qualifications to receive job-related training from their employer.

(FEFC, 1997: 21)

These economic 'returns' on time spent in tertiary education and training were confirmed in a recently published report by the Organisation for Economic Cooperation and Development (OECD). The report, which covers 29 countries and includes the USA, Germany, Denmark, Greece, Netherlands as well as the UK, confirms:

By the time people are in their 30s and 40s they earn, on average, between 30 and 80 percent more than those who stopped at the end of upper secondary education... Gender differences emerge as well; a male Swedish university graduate can expect to earn 60 per cent more than a male school-leaver; the gap for women is closer to 40 per cent. Women with degrees from universities in the UK and Ireland enjoy the biggest 'educational premium' with earnings about twice those of women who do not go beyond upper secondary school.

(THES, 1998: 14)

For those from working class backgrounds who do enter post-compulsory education, evidence suggests that the financial hardships should not be underestimated (Bates, 1993). Evidence from the Dearing report into HE is relevant here:

Students from lower socio-economic groups have significantly higher levels of essential expenditure than most other groups. This is largely due to the additional costs of house and childcare for lower socio-economic group participants who will on average be older students, but also because some 'hidden' subsidies, such as cars or household goods, may be supplied by wealthier parents in a manner that is not available to financially constrained families.

(Dearing Report, 1997: para 2.29)

What can be done?

Clearly, there is a limit to the extent that practitioners can bring about social change. We cannot alter someone's material position, for instance. However, as has been identified in other sections of the Reader, policy decisions *can* influence both participation rates and levels of achievements (cf. gender). It has been seen that the government is committed to *widening participation* ('The government's most cherished higher education policy', THES 27.11.98). In this respect it could be argued that there may be a contradiction between the emphasis on wider participation and the reality of changes in the grants and fees awarded to students. As the Leader comment in the THES suggested:

[An] ... urgent issue is financial support for poorer students. The move to pilot grants for 16-19 year-olds is welcome. If it works, it should rapidly be implemented nationally. In due course the government may also need to revisit its decision to abolish grants for poorer higher education students.

(THES, 1998)

But sorting out the fees and grants system in itself will not change the participation rates or achievement levels. Nor, indeed, will 'quota' systems designed to increase the social mix of students. To alter the participation rates and achievement rates of students from working class backgrounds, an understanding of their educational experiences needs to be gained. Interestingly, social class was the first educational inequality to be addressed by theorists in education and the focus fell first on the home environment and cultural discontinuity; then the educational establishment; then the curriculum and forms of knowledge and classroom interaction.

What we can ensure is that our practices do not reproduce, unconsciously, stereotypes of social class membership, with its set horizons and limited expectations. In the following article, Ivan Reid presents an argument for developing an anti-classist checklist for literature and other media which enables practitioners to confront their practice. Reid also makes connections with other dimensions of social inequality, such as age and disability. In advocating the checklist, Reid suggests that an important value of such lists is the awareness which comes from both devising and using them.

An anti-classist checklist for literature and other media

There now exist a number of checklists for use in evaluating the suitability of books and materials in respect of gender and ethnicity. These are designed both to 'weed out' material which is sexist or racist and to identify material which is not and/or which is anti-sexist and anti-racist. These checklists are also useful in themselves for heightening our awareness of sexism and racism – implicit as well as explicit, unconscious as well as conscious – and sharpening our sensitivity towards these important social issues.

It is perhaps surprising that other forms of almost universal social stratification – social class, age and disability – have not received similar attention. On reflection it is self-evident that these other forms of social stratification characterise much of our society and its life, together with associated prejudices and discriminations.

The parallels are so close that they barely need spelling out, and the case for avoiding their reinforcement and for anti-classism, anti-disabilitism and anti-ageism, while much less commonly made, is similarly justifiable.

Such comprehensive considerations might well lead to the conclusion that a single checklist addressing all anti-social stratificationism (social class, gender, ethnicity, age and disability) is called for; so that inaccurate, misleading and offensive portrayals

Continued...

---

about all minority and disadvantaged groups in our society (or even all groups) might be recognised. However, views of this kind are so deeply ingrained at present, not only in our literature and other media, but also in our culture and social consciousness, that it is important to continue to examine them separately.

The evaluation checklist

The checklist that follows has been developed from a list for evaluating books for use in schools in multicultural society (Stibbs, 1987) and from one for identifying sexism in children's books (Stones, 1983). It is suitable in respect to all forms of social stratification. As Stibbs points out, an important value of such lists lies in the awareness (sensitivity) which comes both from devising and from using them. It would therefore be valuable for readers to attempt to produce their own versions or modifications.

Apart from developing sensitivity the list is designed to identify suitable/acceptable and unsuitable/unacceptable materials. The long history and cultural depth of ideas about social stratification in our society is such that very few books or other media products will pass the lists (or even one list!) with flying colours. Using the list in conjunction with media examples will heighten readers'/viewers'/users' sensitivity to social stratification and develop a critical awareness of social stereotyping, prejudice, discrimination, inequalities and conflicts. Some examples will stand out as being unacceptable, but this does not necessarily imply their removal or total avoidance, providing that awareness has been developed and that there are readily available alternatives which are both accurate and positive. Obviously, the lists are most useful in identifying suitable literature and materials, especially since most existing stocks will be in need of such input.

Categories

Except in the case of gender, the categories for checklists is problematic. Typically, unhelpful dichotomies are used, for example ethnic minority/majority, Asian etc., together with unidirectional views. In reality the situations are, of course, much more complex.

Although class in Britain is often, or even typically, portrayed simply as working and middle classes, this is an over-simplification (see Reid, 1989). In many cases the real differences exist between the extremes, for example, between the wealthy and the poor, the professional and the unskilled worker, and to an extent this difference may be disguised by the use of broad categories. Similarly, in the case of age, while the elderly are often recognised as being at a disadvantage in comparison with other age groups, it is also clear that the young share many aspects of that disadvantage – especially those of economic status and independence. Further, many of the values used to evaluate class and other social differences are essentially middle-class as opposed to working-class ones. Finally, it is obvious to many that social class is the fundamental social stratification which affects all others – being black, female, elderly or disabled and working-class is not the same as being black, female, disabled or elderly and middle-class. Clearly, combinations of strata give rise to a whole range of relative levels of advantage and disadvantage.

Continued...

An anti-classist checklist

Use this checklist in your own work:

1. Do working-class/manually occupied poor people feature in the text? Is their numerical representation similar to that in society at large, or are they 'token'?

2. Are working-class people shown as intelligent, independent and purposeful individuals, or as subservient to middle-class/professional people?

3. Are working-class people presented as stereotypes in stereotypical surroundings and situations? Is the stereotyping of the same order for middle-class people?

4. Does the text provide for any consideration or reflection on social inequality? Are there examples of how inequalities occur or are sustained, or are they presented as part of the 'natural' order of things?

5. Is the existence of class/snobbery/conflict appropriately recognised in the text?

6. Is history presented mainly as achievements by monarchs/aristocrats/ captains of industry/men of letters, and are the working classes disregarded or portrayed as troublesome?

7. Is the text designed to appeal to people from all social classes, or only one, or some?

8. Are different criteria used to evaluate working-class and middle-class characters. If yes, how appropriate are these? If not, are the criteria class based and/or biased?

9. Are middle-class characters portrayed as being superior to working-class ones in intelligence, manner, morals, worth to society, parenthood, language, cleanliness?

10. Are the representations of aspects of working-class and middle-class life, either (obviously, or subtly) patronising, derogatory, inaccurate or absurd?

Bibliography

Stibbs A (1987) 'Evaluating books' in *Teaching English and language in a multicultural society* National Association for the Teaching of English

Stones R (1983) 'Pour out the cocoa, Janet' in *Sexism in children's books* Longman for Schools' Council

(Reid, 1997: 32–33)

References and further reading

Bates I (1993) 'When I have my own studio' in I Bates & G Riseborough *Youth and inequality* Open University Press

Bernstein B (1970) 'Education cannot compensate for society' in E Butterworth & D Weir (eds) *The sociology of modern Britain* Fontana

Bernstein B (1971-7) *Class, codes and control* (3 volumes) Routledge & Kegan Paul

Bilton T, Bonnett K, Jones P, Skinner D, Stanworth M & Webster A (1996) *Introductory sociology* 3rd edn Macmillan

Bourdieu P (1976) 'The school as a conservative force' in R Dale *et al.* (eds) *Schooling and capitalism* Routledge & Kegan Paul

Bowles S & Gintis H (1976) *Schooling in capitalist America* Routledge & Kegan Paul

Dearing Report (1997) *HE in the learning society: report of the national committee of inquiry into higher education* Stationery Office

Further Education Funding Council (1997) *Learning works – widening participation in further education (Kennedy Report)* FEFC

Halsey AH (1980) *Origins and destinations: family, class and education in modern Britain* Clarendon Press

Reid I (1989) *Social class differences in Britain* Fontana Press

Reid I (1996) 'Education and inequality' in *Sociology Review* 6 (2) November, pp2–6

Reid I (1997) 'An anti-classist checklist for literature and other media' *Sociology Review* 6 (3) February, pp32–33

Reid I & Stratta E (1989) *Sex differences in Britain* Gower

Richardson R (1990) *Daring to be a teacher* Trentham Books

THES (1998) 'OECD report' *Times Higher Education Supplement* 27.11.98

Westergaard H (1991) 'Social stratification, culture and education' in *Sociology Review* November, pp26–30

Whitty G (1985) *Sociology and school knowledge* Methuen

Willis P (1977) *Learning to labour* Gower Publishing

8.   Age

Ann Lahiff

They said I couldn't go on the graduate trainee scheme because I was over 28 and already had social skills which couldn't be retrained. They said I wouldn't fit in.

(Sally Baker, aged 39, in *The Guardian,* 18th November 1998)

There are a number of connections to be made between social class and age in terms of participation rates in post-compulsory education and training. For instance, when students from lower socio-economic groups *do* enter higher education, according to the Dearing Report, 'they tend to be older than the average entrant, confirming the pattern of deferred entry or later qualification via "second chance" and similar routes' (Stationery Office, 1997 Section 3, 1.17). They also tend to study part-time. However, entering HE without traditional qualifications still remains a difficult task. The extracts, below, also from the Dearing Report into Higher Education, suggest that progress has been made in *some* institutions, but less in others.

Access to higher education

Considerable progress has been made in widening access to various groups of non-traditional students ..., whom [some] prefer to call 'alternative' students. The majority of HE entrants are now officially 'mature' i.e. over 21 years of age on entry and 30% are actually over 30... However ... mature students are still concentrated in the post-1992 universities... Just before the abolition of the binary line in 1993, the proportion of mature students in the post-1992 universities (34%) was twice the proportion in the pre-1992 university sector (17%)... A higher proportion of mature students study part-time and, conversely, the majority of part-time students are 21 years old or over. For instance, 63% of first degree students studying part-time are over the age of 30...

Entering HE without A Levels remains a difficult task. 61% of full-time undergraduates still enter via the traditional A Level route, 4% of students use Access courses and less than 1% have vocational entry qualifications... Non-A Level students are also over-represented in the post-1992 universities and there is wide intra- and inter-institutional variation in the acceptance of these students... To illustrate, in 1992 84% of students in pre-1992 universities had A Level qualifications whereas just 59% of students in the post-1992 universities did... Different subject areas also recruit varying proportions of non-A Level students and therefore some of the differences between higher education institutions reflect the balance of subjects offered by different institutions...

Admissions tutors retain considerable powers of discretion and appear to view students without A Levels as both problematic and resource-intensive in terms of

Continued...

---

recruitment and teaching... Factors identified as important determinants of institutions' acceptance of non-A Level students are: data collection and dissemination procedures, institutional mission priorities, whether prospective students perceive an application to that HEI in that subject as realistic, admissions practices, individual admission tutors and the development of franchising relationships...

(Stationery Office, 1997: Section 3)

Whilst participation rates for mature students are increasing (despite the obstacles) and achievement rates are high, the prospects after graduation vary. In the previous section on social class, increasing one's qualification base was seen to have a positive relationship with employment and salary. However, barriers to job opportunities are in evidence for older people:

... many [mature students] will face barriers when finding a suitable job because of discrimination over their age. And the discrimination increases with age.

(Tamsin Smith, *The Independent on Sunday,* 15.11.98)

The association of Graduate Careers Advisory Services (GCAS) have found that some sectors recruit from a much wider range than others. Social Work and other areas of the Public Sector tend to recruit from a very wide age range. Finance, commerce and manufacturing are less favourable. The reasons for this, according to the GCAS, are varied but, generally it is related to ageism.

... In our experience ageism is buried quite deep in the psyche of some graduate recruiters.

(*The Independent on Sunday,* 15.11.98)

Ageism

Ageism (discriminating against people because of their age), it seems, operates by people making decisions, judgements based on presumed characteristics associated with age. Age becomes the criterion, the variable around which other assumptions are made. With respect to the recruitment of mature graduates, it appears that some potential employers have a particular 'image' of who is suitable for graduate recruitment:

If you're in a more whizzy industry like IT, the sector is looking for a youthful image...

(Dianah Worman, of the Institute of Personnel and Development, *The Guardian* 18.11.98)

Legislation?

In November, 1998, the government unveiled its 'Action on Age' programme. This is a voluntary code, aimed at convincing employers that age discrimination makes bad business sense. The following newspaper article is critical of the current government's lack of commitment to legislation. It suggests that voluntary codes are not enough. Its author, Richard Worsley, is the director of the Carnegie Third Age Programme, which advocates against ageism.

Broken promises

It is hard to understand how a political party can make a clear pledge – on the record, through its official spokesperson and ratified by its leader – and then feel able to withdraw its commitment with impunity. And yet this is just what has happened with Labour's pre-election promise to introduce legislation against age discrimination...

It is part of the Government's patchy track record in addressing the needs of people in their third age – the active older members of our population – who should be of major concern to us all. Their numbers are growing, they are of major economic importance and they represent a vital source of wisdom and experience.

On the credit side – apart from the erstwhile commitment on legislation – we have had the welcome launch in June of the Better Government for Older People programme. This is seen as a flagship for 'joined-up government' and is working to achieve improvements in the delivery of services to older people, particularly at local level. And the Government has also announced the creation of an inter-ministerial group charged with developing a co-ordinated strategy on older people.

But it is in the area of employment that Labour's performance has proved particularly disappointing. The pre-election commitment to legislation, so warmly welcomed by all those older people excluded from work simply on grounds of their age, is no longer a commitment. What was once 'we will' is now 'we don't rule it out'.

Having given priority to unemployed younger people in its New Deal, the Government is now turning its attention to those over 25, working through pilot schemes, some of which include provision for unemployed people over 50. But they are addressed only to the registered unemployed and not to the much larger numbers of 'economically inactive' older people – 2.4 million between 50 and retirement age. The reasons why many of these are not claiming unemployment benefits are that they have become so disillusioned and discouraged with their failure to find work that they have given up – or are opting in alarming numbers for sickness benefit.

Andrew Smith, the minister responsible in these areas, has just published *Action On Age* – his conclusions from a consultation on age discrimination in employment.

Neither the consultation nor the report have presented an impression of urgency or conviction. There is no explanation of why the commitment to legislation has been abandoned. In a notably partisan section on the subject, all the evidence about the positive role of the law has been ignored – including the report I made to the minister on a recent visit to New Zealand, where there is a view that legislation has had a positive effect. The centrepiece, as he describes it, of the minister's report is the proposal of a voluntary code of practice, expected shortly – but it seems with no legislative base and no sanctions against employers who disregard it. Yet why should

Continued...

---

they do otherwise when government itself is giving such a clear message that discrimination on grounds of age warrants less rigorous treatment than all the other major causes of discrimination?

Of course legislation alone is not the answer, but, as Labour made clear in 1996, it is a necessary part of the package needed to persuade employers to mend their ways. Why raise hopes by promising it? Why back away now?

Action on Age is not convincing to real people out there who feel excluded and hopeless, worn down by repeated rejection of their skills and experience because of their age, and who were told that Labour was going to do something very specific about their plight. Perhaps Mr Smith will yet persuade us not only that he understands their situation but that he will take really effective action to improve it.

Three central questions remain unanswered. If there is good reason why 'we will legislate' has turned into 'we might', may we share it? Will he set out some real targets for reducing the extent of age discrimination, monitor performance against them and legislate if they are not met? Will he extend the New Deal not just to the registered unemployed but to all unemployed older people?

Without positive answers to these questions, older voters persuaded by Labour's pre-election promises may feel they have been taken for a ride.

(Worsley, 1998)

References and further reading

Age Concern (1995) *Just about coping* Age Concern
Bradley H (1995) *Fractured identities* Polity
Stationery Office (1997) *HE in the learning society: report of the national committee of inquiry into higher education (Dearing Report)*
Worsley R (1998) 'Broken promises' *The Guardian* 4.11.98

Part Three – The Development of Inclusive Provision

The sections in this Part are concerned with the exploration of two principal themes: the historical background to the development of current provision for students with learning difficulties and disabilities; and commentaries on more recent reports, policy initiatives and legislation.

The first extract, by David Johnstone, puts current arrangements and practices into the historical context of changing attitudes, precedents and earlier government activity. Although there have been significant developments in the past twenty or so years, both in the UK and overseas, provision in the PCET sector is neither uniform nor comprehensive. As you read, you may feel that there is still too little evidence of radical moves from segregated towards integrated or 'inclusive' provision. You are still not that much more likely to be working with colleagues with learning difficulties or disabilities than you would have been decades ago. Johnstone looks at the history of increasing provision and access for people with learning difficulty and disability in further education. Readers who work in other areas of the PCET sector will be able to find parallel developments.

Johnstone's second contribution explores one way in which support provision might be extended within the context of the European Union, through the establishment of a network of 'resource centres' at national, regional and local government levels.

The next five extracts consider some of the major reports, legislation and policies which are currently significant in relation to access to the PCET curriculum in the UK. The Warnock Report in 1978 was a comprehensive investigation into provision in England, and provided an interpretation of good practice from which later measures were launched. Warnock was not asked specifically to look at the post-school situation, but the committee found that colleges were already accepting students with disability and learning difficulty, and that post-16 provision was an important issue for both parents and young people. The relevant paragraphs are reprinted in Section 11. The decision of the Warnock Committee was to support integration but maintain some discrete provision in both schools and specialist colleges, and some of the recommendations were implemented through the 1981 Education Act.

The extract which follows in Section 12 is from the 1985 Fish Report (called *Equal Opportunities for All?* – the question mark in the title was significant) which represented the attempt of the former Inner London Education Authority (ILEA) to examine what needed to be done to promote equal opportunities in schools and colleges for students with learning difficulty and disability in London.

The Disability Discrimination Act 1995 has implications for all but a small number of excluded groups and has made a significant difference, for example, to arrangements to support the learning of students in further and higher education. Deborah Cooper's checklist, reprinted in the next extract, is an instrument which colleges have used to guide their response to the legislation.

The most recent official statement on the education and training of adults with learning difficulties and/or disabilities is the 1997 report of the Tomlinson committee, set up by the Further Education Funding Council to explore the implications of implementing the Disability Discrimination Act in the context of the expectations of the Further and Higher Education Act (1992), and the obligations which that placed on both the FEFC and FEFC-funded institutions. *Inclusive Learning* is a brief account of the work of the committee from the perspective of Professor Tomlinson himself. Lani Florian's contribution provides an informed interpretation and clarification of that report, the importance of which has been most recently emphasised in the Government White Paper introducing the new legislative and financial framework for post-16 education and training, taking effect from April 2001:

Funding and planning provision for people with special needs

4.13 Part of the Government's commitment to equality of opportunity is to ensure that planning and funding arrangements result in adequate support so that students with disabilities and special needs, from specific learning difficulties to severe and profound challenges, can achieve their full potential. The bringing together of post-16 education and training provides a unique opportunity to integrate different approaches and improve arrangements for the benefit of learners. This will build on and extend the progress made by further education colleges in recent years in provision for such students.

4.14 The Government will ensure that the new arrangements are based on the principles of the Tomlinson Committee's report to the FEFC, 'Inclusive Learning', and the examples of good practice in TEC-funded provision, particularly by a number of voluntary organisations.

(DfEE, 1999)

In the last contribution to this Part Liz Maudsley and Lesley Dee explore concepts that are used in the debates on access and participation. Their analysis clears away much of the confusion which surrounds some of the terms that we use, and provides a bridge to the final Part of this Reader.

Reference

Department for Education and Employment (1999) *White Paper: Learning to succeed – a new framework for post-16 learning* The Stationery Office

9. The Background to Furthering Opportunities in FE

David Johnstone

Whilst it is true that the rapid development of further education for students with learning difficulties and disabilities is a comparatively recent phenomenon it would be incorrect to ignore the pioneering work that had been gradually emerging since the end of the Second World War and in some cases even earlier. Bradley & Hegarty (1981) have asserted that 'until the mid-1970s there was little or no provision in the normal further education colleges for disabled young people'. This is not strictly true. There have always been some opportunities for students to attend courses in basic literacy, leisure courses or the like where the emphasis is upon self-motivation and personal improvement. Nevertheless, much of this early work took place in night schools and is more allied to adult education (Sutcliffe, 1992). It is also not easy to discover how many of the students on such courses came into the category of 'special education'.

As with so many other educational initiatives involving a group of people who have been marginalised, the beginnings of specialist provision for students with learning difficulties and disabilities are uncertain. It would inevitably have been sporadic and the numbers of students involved are unknown. However, there are sufficient examples of practice to suggest that concern for the development of vocational education and training is not new. It certainly does not mean that there had been no opportunities for the continuing education and training of people with learning difficulties and disabilities before the development of a recognised system of further education.

The emergence of further education for people with learning difficulties and disabilities can be traced using three broad and overlapping models. All three are associated with phases of political, historical and economic development. These phases are not really distinct, and there are traces of all of them still to be seen in current educational organisation, practices and discourses about the expansion of educational entitlement. They can, however, be traced in an historical linear progression as follows:

medical care ➔ needs and segregation ➔ rights and entitlements

Medical care model

... It is not difficult to see how, from the beginnings, special education has borrowed from and tended to be dominated by the medically defined construct. For students with learning difficulties and disabilities in further education, who have come through a school system that continues to pay great heed to the interpretations and wishes of the medical services, there is a tacit acceptance that medical interventions and interpretations of difference are part of their way of life. As Oliver (1986) has suggested, their education may have been disrupted by the inputs of a variety of paramedical professions: physiotherapy, speech therapy and the like. If children have left school and become adults believing, as a result of a range of such interventions, that they are ill, then it is no real surprise if they accept the passive role of being sick and dependent: receivers of care and expected to be grateful for it.

The evidence that disabled people are denied the full rights to citizenship as a result of the demands of the labour market is overwhelming. It would be unfair to suggest that, in such circumstances, colleges are deliberately colluding with the 'medical model'. However, it seems evident that despite political rhetoric to the contrary 'social disadvantage' has become associated with disability and learning difficulties and that young people with disabilities are cases to be treated rather than individuals with rights.

Needs and segregation

Just as we cannot really be surprised that students with disabilities take on the sick role, we should also not be surprised when we see students emerging from discrete special education courses considering themselves to be 'in need' and often as entitled to the benefits of charitable and statutory services. However, if students and people with disabilities see themselves as having 'needs' it is often because they have been socialised into accepting the definition of disability as a personal tragedy. Images of disabled people and child-care, together with the range of resource materials in both children's literature and adult horror magazines and videos, all of which are available to schools and colleges, have tended to continue to portray disabled people in a contradictory fashion. They are either pathetic victims, arch-villains or heroes. The stereotype of the disabled child is either that of the brave little lost boy/girl overcoming personal tragedy, or of the scheming malcontent determined to have revenge on society for the misfortune that has befallen him/her (e.g. Captain Hook, Quasimodo, Dr No, Freddy from *Nightmare on Elm Street)*. The other alternative is the hero overcoming personal loss but conquering all, for example Long John Silver or Douglas Bader.

The concept of 'need' had first emerged in education in 1946, in regulations that indicated how to implement the 1944 Education Act. These regulations led to the establishment of services and schools that acted on behalf of, rather than in consultation with, disabled people. This in turn has led, until recently, to a kind of passive citizenship on the part of disabled people within a fundamentally needs-based provision determined by professionals. The legal framework of the UK has consistently portrayed disabled people as a cost to the Exchequer rather than as individuals entitled to participate in the exercise of citizenship. Far from becoming involved in legislation that establishes the rights of disabled people, enabling them to determine their own needs, we have created a system that continues to exclude.

A feature of the 1944 Act was the creation of categories of handicap reflecting society's needs rather than individual considerations. Regulations in *Pamphlet 5*, following the Act, actually stated that some pupils may require special educational 'treatment', borrowing heavily from the medical model already referred to. For young people with handicaps and disabilities, leaving school meant a probable future in sheltered or closed employment. Even in 1968 it was estimated that there were approximately 70,000 severely mentally handicapped adults in England and Wales, approximately 24,500 of whom attended adult training centres (Whelan & Speake, 1977). The need to re-establish employment for returning members of the armed forces following the Second World War had the effect of excluding disabled individuals from open employment, even though some of them had fulfilled important work during the war years.

From needs to rights and entitlements

The examination of rights and entitlements moves the discourse of further opportunities for students with learning difficulties and disabilities into an exploration of the tensions between the private and public arenas of equal opportunities. It moves the debate from the narrowly private world of personal circumstances to the wider political examination of the publicly accountable provision made for and received by disabled people. This demand for civil rights, coming from various groups at the margins of an increasingly consumer-driven society, began to emerge as a phenomenon of the late 1950s and early 1960s in Western Europe and the United States.

Other major influences on the development of rights for disabled people are still currently emerging from the United States... The campaigns have all tended to come to successful fruition as a consequence of direct action and political activism. The Americans with Disabilities Act 1990 (ADA) (Morrissey, 1991) is an example of legislation that has come to be a powerful testimony to the campaigning zeal of disabled people. It is also a symbol of the potential strength of political activity in the development of civil rights for people with disabilities in other parts of the world.

In the United Kingdom legislation has been used to outlaw discrimination on the grounds of race and gender. These successful outcomes have encouraged disabled people to demand similar legislation with its major focus on 'rights' rather than 'needs'. By so doing, disabled people are arguing for legislation that challenges and stops the unfair discrimination that exists in society's attitudes and practices in both direct and indirect forms.

This shift towards addressing disability and learning difficulties within a political framework of rights and entitlements has been part of a process that has been given its head in the world of further education. As Corbett & Barton (1992) have pointed out, special education is in danger of being perceived as apolitical, focused on shallow judgements of individual needs as selected needs, and the business of access to buildings and the curriculum. Rather than this, it should be considered as an issue to be studied within the curriculum, with a proper examination of both the institutional and structural inequalities inherent in society. If by so doing we place the exploration of disability and special education in its proper context of equal opportunities, it then becomes part of a more fundamental discourse related to the wider distribution of opportunities and privileges in society.

Further education and training in the United Kingdom is now effectively a player in a larger political poker game or, perhaps more aptly, in attempts to pin the tail on the donkey. On the one hand it is being played by those seeking to recreate old certainties and 'family values'; on the other by those who consider that the requirement for wholesale change in education and employment is now irreversible. This has taken the form of an economic and class debate around poverty, 'family values' and 'back to basics'. It does not bode well for students with learning difficulties and disabilities. The structure of the National Curriculum and opting-out is acting as the driving force for curricular and managerial change in schools. This in turn is promoting initiatives that are being followed up in colleges and vocational training programmes. Whilst these circumstances include 'regard' for students with learning difficulties and disabilities, it is difficult to set the debate for educational change in terms of 'rights', 'entitlements' and 'citizenship'.

To many teachers and lecturers, such terms appear to carry little weight and may even be considered rather vague and naive. Any attempts to influence change in the funding of provision for students and young people with learning difficulties and disabilities now needs to recognise the additional responsibilities of engaging in political challenge, not simply seeking to affect legislation. The challenge is inherent in the language of debate, as well as participation in forming the agenda for action. In order to influence the structures of power and control in the education services the debates and judgements will have to be in terms of 'rights' rather than 'needs'. Corbett & Barton (1992) have pointed out that this can be alien to staff accustomed to working within the narrow focus of individual needs, isolated from wider political involvement.

Nevertheless, if services for students and young people with learning difficulties and disabilities are to emerge as a rights issue there is a need for all staff concerned to recognise their shared responsibility for the development of a new kind of political activism campaigning for civil rights. This may well involve the uncomfortable acknowledgement that there is still injustice towards disabled students in the education system.

This sense of inequity and injustice needs to touch the lives of the vast majority of British families if real changes are to occur, and if the consistent sources of funding to sustain them are to be secured. If this does not happen the responsibility for making provision and bringing about change will remain with a small group of people. As a result, the quality of the educational experience for students with learning difficulties and disabilities will be in danger of being reduced to little more than the charitable rump activity from which it emerged.

Summary

The background to the development of further education incorporates considerations of individual and institutional prejudice and suspicions, rather than toleration of individual difference. It also demands that we question our understanding of the tension between the role of education and the role of employment as the arena for equal opportunities... The rhetoric of equality of opportunity for students with learning difficulties and disabilities is emerging with the increasing influence of the Further Education Funding Council. It may, however, serve as a relatively hollow concept: to pay lip-service to the equality of people with severe and multiple disabilities may do little to meet their real needs.

References

Bradley J & Hegarty S (1981) *Students with special needs in further education: a review of current and completed research relating to young people in the 14–16 age range with special learning needs* Further Education Unit

Corbett J & Barton B (1992) *A struggle for choice: students with special needs in transition to adulthood* Routledge

Morrissey P (1991) *A primer for corporate America on civil rights for the disabled* LRP Publications

Oliver M (1986) 'Social policy and disability' *Disability, Handicap and Society* 1 (1)

Sutcliffe J (1992) *Integration for adults with learning difficulties: contexts and debates* NIACE

Whelan E & Speake B (1977) *Adult training centres in England and Wales* University of Manchester Press

10. The Role of Resource Centres in the Development of Inclusive Learning

David Johnstone

The development of the road to inclusive education has emerged at a European level over the last quarter century. It has changed the way in which people look at special education. At a European level, inclusive education has developed within wider considerations of social justice and human rights. At a national level, the individual countries that make up the Union have introduced educational legislation that has questioned the quality, cost effectiveness and pedagogical purpose of 'special' education within segregated schools. There is an expectation that all teachers have responsibility and should be equipped to teach all children and that the best place for this is the mainstream school. The overall effect of this change has been to refocus upon the strengths and weaknesses of the visible face of special education – the special school. If all teachers are the teachers of children with special needs, the additional resources allocated to special schools and units become more difficult to justify.

The philosophy of inclusive provision has been a fundamental factor contributing to the development of learning support services in the form of resource centres. Education systems throughout Europe have had to become more flexible and responsive to change; but schools as symbols of educational stability in the community have not always been able to respond as rapidly as required, or expected. Teachers continue to perform their difficult task of helping children with special needs and their families towards the uncertain future of adulthood and social integration. However, their success depends upon both the quality and the quantity of resources allocated to them. The creation of the resource centre is one response to this problem of resource distribution.

Teachers have often been unfairly criticised for appearing to be isolated and unwilling to change their practices in the classroom. Research in some European countries has suggested that the role of the teacher in schools and colleges is non-collaborative, focused on every day classroom activity and individual learners (EASE, 1995; Johnstone, 1995 & 1996). This conservatism, however, can be challenged by the changes in working habits that have taken place in some countries (e.g. Tove-Cajina, 1996). Where teachers in the Nordic countries had previously tended to avoid long-term planning and collaboration with their colleagues, there is now a shift towards a collaborative working involvement in the whole school, college and community decision making. In other words, teachers have begun to recognise that in order to make their own individual teaching circumstances easier it is more appropriate to plan together in the development of policy and practice. What a teacher thinks, believes or assumes is bound to have a powerful influence on the way in which he/she formulates a philosophy of teaching. This, in turn influences his or her organisation of learning and how it is translated into action.

The world of special education is often perceived as a small social system within the wider orbit of mainstream education. Status and the intensity of personal and professional interaction is by way of face-to-face contact rather than departmental memo. For some, this has created a confusion about the value of professional status. Status confusion has also coincided with the decline of the 'individual deficit model' explanations of learning difficulties, whereby the purpose of the teacher in the special education service was once to identify individual deficiency and remedy it, rather than to recognise proficiency and develop it. There is now a wider understanding amongst teachers in all phases of education that educational change is whole change and not merely individual change.

The range of need for support provision crosses all age ranges from pre-school to post-school and community oriented education. A belief that equality of educational opportunity and social justice is at the heart of inclusive education has highlighted the need to consider the ethical, moral and economic purpose of both educational opportunity and curriculum progression. These issues are of particular concern to teachers and managers considering the purpose and function of the traditional classroom at a time of reduced resource allocation. Within the more negotiated environment of the integrated class, the resource centre provides one of the more viable sources for teacher and curriculum support.

The beginnings of special education in Europe for children and students with disabilities, like the history of provision for disabled people in general, is surrounded in some mystery. It is hidden in official records, religious superstition and the accounts of charitable organisations. Nevertheless, from the outset it has involved the relationship between the demands of the labour market and the social costs of providing services:

> *For too long education in all sectors has colluded with the demands of the labour market to keep disabled people out of the workforce. Most disabled children leave school thinking they are unemployable and immediately have this reinforced by social education centres and colleges of further education with their offers of 'further on' courses and 'independence training'.*

> (Oliver, 1990: 6)

Social justice, associated with a concern for access to education and employment opportunities, has gradually assumed a key focus amongst the policy documents of many countries in the European Union. Equality of opportunity has become a policy priority within education and training for a range of disadvantaged and under-represented groups:

> *The economic costs to the community of the continuing existence of failure are certainly high; insufficient use by a country of its potential talents and skills, particularly at a time of emerging shortage in labour markets, is likely to prove to be an expensive waste... As important today are the cultural and democratic arguments for ensuring that all individuals, young and old, and all social groups, are given the opportunity to engage in the participation that education and training allows...*

> (OECD, 1992: 89)

This realignment behind the social and moral, rather than solely the economic arguments for developing and extending the concept of 'quality' education and training echoes Skilbeck (1990):

> There has been a tendency in the 1980s to submerge long-term concerns for access, opportunity, equity and fairness in education to economic imperatives. It would be dangerous and unprincipled to continue along this track... Significant educational disadvantage continues to occur. For curriculum and pedagogy, a next step is to seek a new synthesis which directly and concurrently addresses:
>
> 1. the policy drive towards economic restructuring;
>
> 2. the technological revolution;
>
> 3. the universalist principle embedded in the claim that every person has educational rights and freedom.
>
> (Skilbeck, 1990: 79)

Within a specifically European context Daunt (1993) traces the emergence of equal opportunities and social justice within the European Union and its impact on children with special educational needs. He has usefully identified how the essentially political interventions to develop European policy for the improvement of quality of life and employment for disabled people across the European Union have been patchy:

> Here the record has been disappointing. Far less has been attempted than was at one time hoped and little indeed has been achieved. The Commission's first proposal, on employment, was adopted in 1986; it took the form of a recommendation rather than the much stronger directive which the Commission's own legal service preferred.
>
> (Daunt, 1993: 4)

The various ideological commitments of different European governments to the maintenance of market forces is a recurring barrier to the expansion of opportunities for disabled people. This element of pessimism fails to acknowledge the potential of Europe for collaborative community activities designed to promote equal opportunities in education and employment for disabled people. European funding for programmes such as HELIOS and HORIZON are indicative of how change can sometimes be developed more successfully through collaborative links across national boundaries.

The concept of the resource centre shares many of these enthusiasms. The idea has grown in popularity as a method of providing learners with additional support since the 1960s. The initial idea of the 'resource-room' that originated in the USA has become more developed in both its purpose and its sophistication as ideas and knowledge have emerged about the whole purpose of learning support within integrated classrooms. Thus, in place of the focus on specialist teachers, with their particular expertise, the resource centre focuses on teaching and learning and the self-sustaining nature of an individual or shared learning activity.

Models of resource centres

The role of the resource centre carries with it a variety of definitions depending upon the context of each participating nation state. Most resource centres are part of national, regional or local government administration and each needs to identify the models which best suit the needs of their education system.

However, not all resource centres have this broad all-encompassing role and some fulfil one or two of the functions outlined in this paper. An important minority of resource centres are run by non-governmental organisations including many whose prime function is to support disabled people, their parents and families.

Some innovatory models of resource centres consist of a network, or a loose federation of members. These may be individuals, schools, colleges, universities, or community education providers (e.g. Skill: National Bureau for Students with Disabilities in the United Kingdom, is a national organisation whose resource strength is drawn almost entirely from its membership). Most of the activities of a resource centre are generated by a process of partnerships of 'core and cluster' personnel who have different skills and contributions to make. And thus, people come together flexibly forming and reforming depending upon the issues to be resolved or the support task that is required.

The resource centre is also an idea or organisational device based around a premise of inclusion. While it is undoubtedly the case that the concept of inclusive education has been embraced as an ultimate goal through the European Union, it is also evident that the quality of integrated provision varies across the participant countries.

What learning support actually means from the perspective of the English education system is the development and resourcing of appropriate levels of support for learners with special needs. However, this ideal has often been sacrificed on the battlefield of political interpretation between segregated and inclusive education.

Roles and functions of resource centres

Many resource centres have a limited range of specific functions whilst others fulfil a broader role. As this paper reveals there are some obvious commonalties, but also distinct differences of perception about purposes and functions of learning support. Members of a European working party (Warwick *et al.* 1997) brought with them a range of expectations that they attached to the learning support role provided by resource centres.

There tended to be general agreement that at a European level the most important type of support that was most need included:

- identification, assessment and planning
- advice, guidance and support
- evaluation and monitoring of the teaching quality in schools

- in-service training
- information and communication technologies
- research, development and dissemination of reports of innovative practice.

Identification, assessment and planning

Traditional approaches of mainstream support typically involve direct engagement with individual learners. Such interventions may include diagnostic assessment and a prescription of an individual learning programme which is often developed and delivered by support service personnel. The procedure of this model of support is usually divorced from the mainstream school or college curriculum. Interaction between support services and mainstream staff is often very limited.

Inclusive approaches to education mean that traditional 'medical' or 'individual deficit' approaches to learning are being replaced by interventions which aim to empower mainstream teachers to become the key providers of special education. More time and emphasis is being given to developing the commitment and expertise in relation to individual learners.

Advice, guidance and support

As mainstream schools and colleges replace special schools and broader concepts of special educational needs and disabilities become accepted, there is growing realisation that it is insufficient to only focus on the need of individual learners, and in some countries this process is well underway. Central to these reforms are issues relating to school and college and management and to the mainstream curriculum.

The role of resource centres needs to extend beyond case-work in relation to individual learners to encompass management issues. Resource centres need to be able to provide advice, guidance and support for all those involved in the education system.

Evaluation and monitoring

The implication of 'school-effectiveness' research is increasingly influencing decision-making within education. An analysis of what makes one school or college more effective than another in, for example, providing for learners with special educational needs points the way forward for school or college managers. In a few countries (such as the United Kingdom and Norway) there is a growing emphasis on evaluating the effectiveness of provision. The most productive forms of evaluation are those that provide constructive advice and guidance on how current practice can be improved. Resource centres can provide specialist expertise to evaluate and monitor integrated and inclusive education. This approach is beginning to operate in different phases of education (e.g. in the United Kingdom, the Higher Education Funding Council for England (HEFCE) has recently appointed three national co-ordinators to develop, lead and evaluate learning support systems for students with disabilities in universities and colleges.)

In-service training

A major function of resource centres is the provision of in-service training. There is a vital and continuing need to develop the professional skills and expertise of staff within the mainstream system. For example in Norway, some local authorities may experience severe handicap or disability once in every tenth school year. In such circumstances the resource centre is a place that the local authority or the school can approach with a view to receiving help in the development of a training programme for the individual child and/or teacher (Tove-Cajina, 1996). Special school teachers also need training to adapt to new duties and responsibilities linked to integrated education. There is a developing trend towards providing in-service training within schools and colleges, as this is more likely to lead to change and development of educational practice. Resource centres are often linked with institutions of higher education for the delivery of post-initial qualifications in special education.

Information and communication technologies

Resource centres have an important function in helping mainstream teachers make the best use of information and communication technologies. There are four main uses of new technologies in particular, which need to be highlighted:

- computers as a means of curriculum delivery
- devices and equipment as aids for individual learners
- computer communication networks linking schools, teachers and learners across Europe and world-wide
- computer communication networks as a means of delivering in-service training and consultancy services.

The resource centre is particularly important in relation to these functions (e.g. in one or two cases, such as ACCESS micro-electronic centres in the United Kingdom or in Bologna, Italy the network itself fulfils the function of becoming the resource centre).

Innovation, research and development

Many innovatory curriculum developments have emerged from special schools. These have led to increased expectations of achievement from learners with special educational needs. The momentum of research and development needs to at least be maintained. New challenges are raised through the pursuit of inclusive education, which requires innovatory approaches and techniques. The resource centre has an important role in initiating, supporting and co-ordinating action research.

Another vital function of the resource centre is that of dissemination. Information about identified good practice, the results and development in policy and practice need to be made available within mainstream education as well as in special education schools for discrete disabilities.

The existence of the resource centre as a source of learning support presents all who are involved in education with a series of challenges and new opportunities. All teachers carry with them some responsibility for creating the future for the learners in their care. However, it is an uncertain road to travel and it is often unwise to set out on the journey alone. Teachers working in a creative collaboration reinforce the fundamental principles of social justice that guide the philosophy behind resource centres and inclusive learning. If teachers work alone, they are liable to remain isolated from change; if they work unsystematically they will waste precious time and energy. If on the other hand they work together and share in the development of support, the process of supporting learners who have previously been excluded from mainstream schools can be better sustained.

Resource centres are intended to give learners with special needs a qualitatively better training and/or education programme. Resource centres also operate to support the teachers and managers in the institutions wherever learning takes place. Many models of resource centres and support services exist and it is evident that there is no preferred structure or model that can be advocated. Each country, and in some cases each region or local area, probably needs to develop its own structure for services built on trust and collaboration.

These are the fundamental principles of social justice and inclusive education for all learners.

References

Daunt P (1993) 'Changes abroad – a European overview' *Educare* 45, pp3-7, Skill: National Bureau for Students with Disabilities

EASE (1995) *Job possibilities and quality of life for disabled and handicapped people in Europe* European Association of Special Education

Johnstone D (1995) *Further opportunities: learning difficulties and disabilities in further education* Cassell

Johnstone D (1996) 'Inclusive education and community: integrating the special professional' Paper given to the European Forum, Lucerne, 13-18 May 1996

OECD (1992) *High quality education and training for all* OECD

Oliver M (1990) *The politics of disablement* Macmillan

Skilbeck M (1990) *Curriculum reform: an overview of trends* OECD/CERI

Tove-Cajina W (1996) *Report to HELIOS study group* London 22-26 May 1996

Warwick C, Janssen M, Johnstone D & Rodrigues D (eds) (1997) *The role of resource centres in the development of integrated education* HELIOS

11.   Students with Special Needs

Mary Warnock

(from the 1978 *Report of the Committee of Enquiry into the Education of Handicapped Children and Young Persons*)

10.25 For the great majority of young people with disabilities or significant difficulties the year in which they are 16 marks the end of formal education. In January 1977 only 5,945 16-year-olds and 1,069 17-year-olds were attending special schools in England and Wales compared with 15,019 15-year-olds. In Scotland in September 1976 758 16-year-olds and 168 17-year-olds were attending special schools compared with 1,447 15-year-olds. Moreover, of the 18-year-olds in the sample studied in the research project carried out for us by the National Children's Bureau, five times as many of the non-handicapped as of those ascertained as handicapped were still at school or in further education...

10.26 A considerable number of contributors to the evidence submitted to us stressed the need for education to be available to young people with disabilities or significant difficulties beyond the age of 16. It was argued that far more encouragement needs to be given to pupils to remain at school beyond 16, and a handful of contributors suggested a return to a higher statutory school leaving age for handicapped young people. There was very wide support for an expansion of opportunities for such young people in further education.

10.27 We recognise that relatively few young people with disabilities or significant difficulties have achieved by the age of 16 either their full educational potential or an adequate degree of maturity to make a smooth transition to adult life. Some young people with handicapping conditions will have experienced interruptions to their schooling for health or other reasons; some will be slow in developing personally as well as educationally. Educational provision must therefore be far more widely available to such young people beyond the age of 16. This is a principle of which we are firmly convinced. It applies to all young people with special educational needs, and particularly to those with language problems, including young people whose first language is not English, those with impaired hearing, those with specific speech problems and some of those with learning difficulties. Their needs obviously vary, but the importance of intelligible speech and adequate language skills as components of social competence cannot be over-emphasised. Parents must be strongly encouraged to seek continued education for their children and the children themselves strongly encouraged to undertake it, either in schools or in establishments of further education...

10.29 The need for continued education does not stop when young people with special needs enter work. In their case, however, opportunities need to be provided on a part-time basis. Evening study may be impracticable for many of these young employees, but day release from work could provide an ideal basis for continued education. The TUC has for many years urged the case for universal day release for further education for all young workers up to the age of 18 years and in their evidence to us both the TUC and Scottish TUC supported the case for compulsory day release, whether for continued general education or for vocationally orientated courses. We considered recommending compulsory day release for further education for young workers with special needs but concluded that compulsion would be likely to deter employers from engaging them. At present employers are willing to contemplate day release when the qualifications or training will benefit the firm, for example where the employees have entered apprenticeships or where improved qualifications will lead to their promotion. Many employers will, however, need a great deal of persuasion to release employees for continued general education. Any substantial improvement in the opportunities for young people with special needs to continue their education will depend on general developments in the provision of opportunities for further education, and an extension of the present arrangements for day release. In the meantime, we urge that a sustained effort should be made to convince employers in both the public and private sectors that courses of continued general education will significantly enhance the general competence of those young employees with special needs. To this end there should be much closer links between local industry and commerce and establishments of further education, and joint discussion of the courses provided for young workers with special needs.

Provision in school

10.30   Until the statutory school leaving age for children in ordinary schools was raised to 16 from the beginning of the school year 1972–73, the school leaving age for children in special schools was higher by a year than that for children in ordinary schools. We would not wish to see any such special provision re-introduced since it would have the unfortunate effects of reinforcing the division between the handicapped and the non-handicapped which we are determined to see eliminated and of making for rigidity in the arrangements for continued education beyond 16. At the same time we should like to see a much higher proportion of young people over 16 with special needs continuing in full-time education. We recognise that for some children with special needs a change of educational setting may be preferable at the age of 16, but there are others who will benefit from staying on at school, particularly where the school offers specially designed programmes for those over 16. *We therefore recommend that, where it is in their interests, children with special educational needs should be enabled to stay at school beyond the statutory school leaving age.* Since some parents may be deterred by financial considerations from encouraging their children to stay at school, it is important that local education authorities should look sympathetically on the families of pupils with special needs who remain at school beyond 16 in deciding whether to make an educational maintenance allowance...

10.31   Our comments in the previous section on the need for the inclusion in the final stages of the curriculum for pupils with special needs of elements of preparation for the next phase in life apply equally to the curriculum for young people over statutory school leaving age, whether in schools or in establishments of further education. There is considerable scope at this stage for the organisation of all forms of work preparation and, indeed, work experience in particular might be offered more appropriately at this stage than previously. We recognise that our recommendation that pupils with special needs should be enabled to stay at school where it is in their interests will have considerable implications for many special schools and special classes which at present cater only for pupils up to 16. They will need to extend the scope of their provision and ensure that suitable courses for young people over 16 are developed.

10.32   At present some pupils in special schools who would benefit from taking a sixth form course are precluded from doing so because their school does not have a sixth form. We believe that wherever possible arrangements should be made for them to pursue their studies with any necessary support in the sixth form of an ordinary school or a sixth form college in the vicinity. *We therefore recommend that, where it is in their interests and possible to arrange, pupils with special educational needs should have access to sixth forms or sixth form colleges.* We discuss the need for adaptation of examination syllabuses to suit pupils with particular disabilities, particularly impaired vision, in the next chapter.

Further education

10.33   A variety of arrangements is needed for young people with special educational needs in establishments of further education. In all cases it is essential that careers guidance should be readily available and that careers officers should participate in the construction of educational programmes. For many young people an establishment of further education will be a more appropriate setting than a school in which to continue their general education. The need for the provision of courses in further education directed towards helping school leavers of low educational achievement and social competence, many of them deficient in the basic skills of literacy and numeracy, was identified in the Holland Report and was emphasised in a Joint Circular by the Department of Education and Science and Welsh Office in September 1977 and a Circular by the Scottish Education Department in October 1977. Courses of this kind will clearly be of great value to many young people with special needs and we hope that they will be made widely available. As the Holland Report pointed out, young people tend to respond better when courses are related to the world of work, and we therefore hope that they will be planned with close reference to local industry and commerce.

10.34   We believe that a positive effort should be made by colleges of further education to develop day or block release courses suited to the requirements of young workers with special needs. We are pleased to know that young people with disabilities are able to take part in the pilot schemes of unified vocational preparation introduced by the government in 1976. These are designed to help those young people who leave school with few or no qualifications to assess their potential and think realistically about jobs and careers, to develop basic skills which will be needed in adult life, to understand their society and how it works, and to strengthen the foundation of skill and knowledge on which further education and training can be built.

10.35   For those young people who, for whatever reason, are unable to take advantage of such courses in further education, we note here the opportunity which exists for them to develop basic skills through adult literacy classes. We were interested to learn that, of the young people ascertained as handicapped in the sample studied in the National Children's Bureau's research project who had undertaken some form of further education since leaving school, over half were receiving tuition in adult literacy classes. The actual number of people concerned was small (13) but it included all ten of the young people classified as ESN(M) who had taken some form of further education. While we hope that curricular developments in schools will result in far fewer young people leaving school deficient in literacy and numeracy, we believe that more encouragement should be given to those who do so to attend adult literacy classes.

10.36   In addition to courses designed to help school leavers to acquire basic skills, a range of courses of a more vocational nature is required for young people with special educational needs in further education. In practice far more young people with special needs are likely to take such courses than to take courses of higher education. Existing provision in further education, however, has developed in a piecemeal and unco-ordinated fashion. We consider that opportunities in further education should be increased and a coherent pattern of provision developed. We describe below what this should be and examine the conditions for its effective development.

10.37   In line with the principle we have supported in schools of the development of common provision for all children. *We recommend that wherever possible young people with special needs should be given the necessary support to enable them to attend ordinary courses of further education.* The support required may take the form, for example, of adaptations to premises, special equipment or help from advisory teachers with specialist training. We recognise that not every establishment of further education will be able to provide the different forms of support necessary. Consultations will be needed between local education authorities within a region on the support which can be provided in individual establishments and on the sharing of special equipment and specialist staff between different establishments. Moreover, area health authorities and social services departments will need to be consulted on the supporting services required. In many cases, however, the most important factor will be the attitude of the staff. We are convinced that a deeper and more sympathetic understanding on the part of staff in colleges of further education could enable many more young people with special needs to take part in and benefit from ordinary courses without the requirement of substantial additional resources.

10.38   Some young people with special needs will be able to master the content and attain the standards of ordinary courses of further education if some modification is made in, say, their duration or presentation. It may be desirable, for example, to extend a course or alter the entrance requirements, say, for the benefit of students with learning difficulties. *We therefore recommend that some establishments of further education should experiment with modified versions of ordinary further education courses for young people with special needs.*

10.39   Some special courses for young people with special needs will also be required, particularly special vocational courses at operative level.   It is important that such courses should not be based on traditional school methods but should take advantage of the adult environment and the range of facilities available in a college of further education.   We also referred in paragraph 10.33 to the need for special courses designed to help school leavers of low educational achievement to attain basic skills of literacy and numeracy.   In the case of young people with disabilities or disorders, training may also be needed in social competence and independence.   *We therefore recommend that some establishments of further education should provide special vocational courses at operative level for students with special needs and special courses of training in social competence and independence.*

10.40   There is also a need for special courses designed more specifically for young people with moderate or severe learning difficulties or physical or sensory disabilities. These must be backed up by special facilities and support, if necessary of an intensive kind, from different services.   If specialist resources for this purpose are to be deployed as effectively as possible, they will need to be concentrated in a number of special units.   *We therefore recommend that within each region there should be at least one special unit providing special courses for young people with more severe disabilities or difficulties which would be based in an establishment of further education.*   The special unit would also act as a supporting base for handicapped students following ordinary courses of further education in the college.   Some special units already exist, but others will need to be established.   The criteria for selecting the colleges in which the units would be based should include the facilities available, the interests and experience of the staff, and the ease of access within a region.   In many parts of the country residential accommodation will be a crucial element of the special facilities which need to be provided.   This should be organised flexibly, with opportunities for students to return home at weekends if they wish.

10.41   A number of conditions will need to be fulfilled if the development of further education provision for young people with special needs is to be as effective as possible. First, such provision requires a higher status. At present the high level of understanding and skills required to teach students with special needs is not sufficiently recognised and work with such students has a low professional status in further education.   We believe that provision for young people with special needs should be clearly recognised as an integral and very important part of further education.   Secondly, all teaching staff in further education must be aware of and understand the special needs which many young people have; and those teachers specialising in work with them must have specialist training for this purpose.   We make proposals for the training of teachers in further education in Chapter 12. Thirdly, more attention needs to be given to curriculum development in further education, and we return to this in the following chapter.   Fourthly, any necessary adaptations to premises must be made and special equipment together with help from supporting services, including financial support, provided as required.

10.42   It will be important, if the necessary support is to be provided, that there should be a member of staff in every place of further education to whom students with special needs, whether they are taking ordinary, modified or special courses of further education, can turn for help and advice on any problem which they face. Moreover, this person should be able to advise other members of the teaching staff about the students' special needs. *We therefore recommend that every establishment of further education should designate a member of staff as responsible for the welfare of students with special needs in the college and for briefing other members of staff on their special needs.*

10.43   A fifth condition of the coherent development of provision for young people with special needs is a co-ordinated approach by local education authorities. We have already pointed to the need for local education authorities within a region to consult each other on the provision of the necessary facilities and to consult the area health authorities and social services departments on the supporting services required. *We recommend that a co-ordinated approach to further education provision for young people with special needs should be adopted and publicised by the local education authorities within each region against a long-term plan within which arrangements for individual institutions will take their place.*

Further, the institutions themselves should publicise their policy on the admission of students with special needs as well as the courses and special facilities which they provide for them.

10.44   There are some national colleges which at present provide further education and vocational training for young people with particular disabilities. With the exception of Hereward College at Coventry, they are run by voluntary bodies. They were intended to provide vocational training, and became engaged in further education only because prospective students could not acquire their minimum entrance qualifications. We consider that most of these colleges will eventually perform a more useful function as part of the pattern of further education provision in their region rather than as national centres catering for particular areas of disability.   Experience at Hereward College, for example, has shown that, after completing their foundation year, some 50% of its students continue at local colleges. Moreover, as we have already emphasised in Chapter 3, special educational needs are not necessarily determined by the particular disabilities of the young people.   It follows that more emphasis should be placed on making provision for common educational needs than for particular disabilities. *We therefore recommend that the national colleges which currently provide further education or training for young people with disabilities should in time all become part of their regional patterns of further education for students with special needs.* Indeed, we understand that one or two of the colleges are already moving in this direction. We recognise that, in the case of the colleges run by voluntary bodies, the extent to which changes can be made may depend on the terms of their trust deeds, as in the case of non-maintained special schools.

10.45   It is impossible at present to predict accurately the likely level of demand for further education on the part of young people with special needs, since there is little experience to go on and it may be expected that demand will grow with provision.

The best guide will be the experience of local education authorities and other bodies who provide places for such young people in further education, and we therefore suggest that they should monitor carefully the extent to which places are taken up and whether a waiting list is formed.

10.46   There is also scope for young people with special needs, particularly those with disabilities which restrict their mobility, to pursue courses of further as well as higher education through distance teaching, using the medium of broadcasting or correspondence. We have noted that the Scottish Business Education Council runs correspondence courses in business studies, with some tutorial sessions, which were originally intended for the Highlands and Islands, where the distance between establishments of further education makes day release schemes impracticable, but which now cater also for physically handicapped students. Distance teaching offers a useful way of extending further education opportunities to young people with disabilities who might be unable to continue their education by other means, provided that it is accompanied by a significant amount of group work and tutorial sessions, which can help to avoid the sense of isolation that the young people might otherwise feel.

Higher education

10.47   Some universities and polytechnics have taken steps to enable students with disabilities to pursue courses of higher education. The University of Sussex, for example, provides facilities for deaf students as well as a small purpose-built residential unit for physically handicapped students, with medical facilities and support staff. We welcome these initiatives and hope that other establishments will emulate them.

10.48   The Open University has always made special arrangements for disabled students. They have been exempted from the usual 'first come, first served' basis of admission and from the normal minimum age limit of 21 [now 18]. Some are excused summer school and receive extra tuition locally instead; some have taken examinations at home or in hospital. A Liaison Committee with the Disabled was set up in 1970 which includes representatives of national organisations and assessors from the Departments of Education and Science and Health and Social Security. In 1972, the University appointed a senior counsellor with specific responsibility for disabled students and we understand that it is planning to introduce improvements in assessment, counselling, special facilities and teaching methods when additional resources are available. The report of the Open University Committee on Continuing Education recommended that the University's concern for the special needs of disabled students should extend to those who enrol for new courses as part of a continuing education programme outside the University's undergraduate programme, and we hope that this recommendation will be implemented.

10.49   *We recommend that all universities and ... other establishments of higher education should formulate and publicise a policy on the admission of students with disabilities or significant difficulties and should make systematic arrangements to meet the welfare and special needs, including careers counselling, of those who are admitted.* Because of the relatively small numbers of students, it will be desirable to concentrate special facilities and skills. Where institutions have already developed a bias towards certain disabilities (such as the facilities for deaf and physically handicapped students at the University of Sussex) these should be strengthened; and similar centres should be established for other disabilities. On the other hand, we do not wish to see prospective students deprived of any choice between institutions because of their disability. While this may be difficult to avoid for students who suffer from a relatively rare or particularly complex disability, we wish to see as many institutions as possible equipped to deal with students who are less severely handicapped.

10.50 The National Bureau for Handicapped Students has taken a valuable initiative in encouraging all establishments of further and higher education to become more aware of the needs of handicapped students and in providing information on facilities available for such students throughout the United Kingdom. We hope that it will receive adequate financial support to continue its valuable work.

12. Equal Opportunities for All?

John Fish

(from the 1985 *Report for the Inner London Education Authority*)

Interim and subsidiary recommendations

3.20.8

(v) (a) All 'special' courses should be asked for information on likely destinations of the students. Where these involve a further course (i.e. a progression) resources needed to support such progression should be specified.

(b) At the end of the academic year and/or at the beginning of a new session, colleges should be invited to give details of all students with special educational needs not in category (a) who will be following general college courses. The estimated resources needed to support each student should be listed.

(c) Some mechanism for ensuring speedy delivery of resources should be devised.

(vi) Teaching hours allocated for special or foundation courses should reflect the need for small group work, team teaching and course team meetings.

(vii) The Authority should ensure that there are sufficient Foundation and Bridging courses throughout the Authority to cater for students with sensory and physical disabilities.

(viii) The Authority should examine ways in which the services offered by schools, colleges and adult education institutes can be used flexibly to meet individual needs, and should establish new systems for assessing fees and recording placements for resourcing purposes...

(x) The Authority should recognise that there may always be a need for residential placements for a few young people. Funding for such placements in non-ILEA establishments should only be reduced as appropriate alternative placements within the Authority become available.

(xi) Each college should be issued with guidelines on provision for students with special educational needs. These should include appropriate staffing ratios, the siting of courses, the equipment and aids available and support and advisory services which can be called upon.

(xii) Initial training for all further education teachers should include preparation for meeting special educational needs. This should be an integrated and coherent part of the whole course. All institutions at which teachers are trained should use current skills and expertise from relevant fields of practice.

(xiii)   The Authority should make in-service training relating to special educational needs for teachers in the post-16 sector an urgent priority; this should be of two types. Authority-run courses for teachers specialising in, or wishing to specialise in, provision for students with special educational needs; institution-based and designed in-service education programmes for all teachers who may have students with special needs in their classes. This latter type should form the core of staff development initiatives, and colleges mounting such programmes should be resourced with visiting teacher hours.

(xiv)   When Authority budgets are fixed a sum should be allocated for resourcing in-house, in-service education. The allocation of these resources to institutions should be based on provision made or planned, and evidence of staff development proposed.

(xv)   In-service education should involve both teaching and non-teaching staff in colleges...

(xviii) Each college should have a written policy on provision for students with special needs. This policy should make explicit selection procedures, the support systems available for staff and students and avenues for progression.

(xix)   In each institution a senior member of staff of at least vice-principal status should have overall responsibility for the development of provision for students with special educational needs. This responsibility should form a major area of work...

(xx)   Each college should have a member of staff of at least senior lecturer status whose responsibilities include the oversight and co-ordination of provision to meet special educational needs. This person should work to the vice principal with overall responsibility and act as a first point of reference for students, staff and outside agencies about this aspect of the college's work...

(xxiv) Departments biased towards pre-vocational and vocational education should be asked to review their curriculum offer with a view to creating increased opportunities for students with special educational needs.

(xxv)   Colleges' interview and selection procedures should be examined and if necessary re-designed to ensure that proper account can be taken of applicants' special educational needs.

(xxvi) Selection interviews should be used to establish what support, for example tutorial support, aids and equipment, will be needed for the applicant to study effectively.

Editor's Note:

The Inner London Education Authority was abolished by Section 162 of the 1988 Education Reform Act, and responsibility for the provision of educational services in London transferred to the individual boroughs.

13.   Checklist for Disability Statements

Deborah Cooper

As a result of the Disability Discrimination Act, further education colleges in England and Wales [were required to] publish disability statements by 1 December 1996... College staff are keen to make sure their statements follow recommended practice and a number of people have asked Skill for help with this. I have therefore prepared this checklist based on the DfEE guidance document on disability statements [DfEE, 1996]. Numbers in brackets refer to the paragraph in the DfEE guidance. Matters of good practice recommended by Skill and FEDA, including issues related to the processes for developing statements, which are not mentioned in the DfEE guidance are not referred to in this checklist...

The checklist is not an interpretation of the legislation nor of DfEE policy or guidance. It is merely designed as a tool for colleges to use in the final stages of preparing their disability statements.

The final disability statement

- has the approval of the governing body (23)
- emphasises that students should discuss their needs on an individual basis (25)
- refers to, and is referred to in, other relevant college documentation (25, 26, 28)
- is consistent with strategic plans (28)
- is readily available to prospective students and agencies or organisations supporting them (31, 33)
- is an accurate reflection of current facilities in the college (32, 33)
- includes all aspects of education, including higher education and collaborative work where relevant (34)
- possibly includes proposed developments(35).

Formats

The document
- is possibly available in alternative formats (e.g. Braille) (27).

Apart from the overall information suggested by each heading the statement includes:

Overall policy
- willingness to respond flexibly to individual needs of prospective students (36).

Staff contact names
- clear and explicit details about how to contact the named person (37).

Admission arrangements

- any specific arrangements for disabled applicants, including assessment of needs (38)
- availability of support during admissions (38)
- details of pre-entry guidance, assessment prior to enrolment and enrolment (38)
- details of advice at application stage (38)
- what the application process will entail (38)
- early assessment procedures for students who may need to be placed in the independent sector (39).

Educational facilities and support – Information about:

- curriculum support
- equipment and technological support
- staff expertise including any specialisms
- other educational support (e.g. interpreters, readers)
- availability of support listed above (40).

Complaints and appeals procedures – Information about:

- any special arrangements in place to assist students with disabilities in accessing the appeals process
- the link with other documents which contain details of complaints procedures
- the grounds on which students may complain about the disability statement (41).

Examination arrangements

- arrangements related to internal exams and to those operated by examining bodies (42).

Other support – Information about:

- personal care support
- medical support
- welfare and advice services including named contact
- links with external organisations
- careers guidance including named contact (43).

Physical accommodation and access – Information about:

- libraries
- learning support workshops
- other academic facilities
- residential accommodation and catering facilities
- sport and leisure facilities

- other student facilities
- ramps, hoists and lifts
- toilet facilities
- car parking arrangements
- willingness to relocate classes to accessible locations
- availability of any site plans or maps (44).

Reference

Department for Education and Employment (1996) *The Education (disability statements for further education institutions) Regulations 1996, SI no 1664; guidance for colleges in the further education sector in England* DfEE

Editor's Note:

The Further Education Development Agency has subsequently carried out a review of college responses to these regulations:

FEDA (2000) *FE college disability statements: an evaluation* FEDA

14. Inclusive Learning

John Tomlinson

[The 1997 FEFC Learning Difficulties and/or Disabilities Committee's report] is the first national enquiry into the education of adults with learning difficulties and/or disabilities. It stemmed from Parliament's wording of the 1992 Further and Higher Education Act, in which these students are the only group specifically mentioned, and the enlightened decision of the Further Education Funding Council (FEFC) to set up a major enquiry and give it adequate resources. I thank the members of the committee and the staff team for three years of hard and dedicated work. The results, *Inclusive Learning* [the 'Tomlinson' Report] and its associated publications, are being seen as a landmark in the development of the education system.

Evidence

Listening to the sector and students and collecting both qualitative and quantitative data has been a very important feature of the work. In particular the committee collected the evidence through the following:

- a review of existing research, published by NFER as 'Students with Disabilities and/or Learning Difficulties in Further Education: A Review of Research Carried out by the National Foundation for Educational Research'
- a call for evidence – over 1000 responses were received by the committee
- student voices – around 300 students with learning difficulties/disabilities attended workshops to give direct evidence, published by Skill as 'Student Voices'
- speaking engagements and conferences attended by me, committee members and the staff team
- the legal analysis indicating the duties and powers of different agencies – commissioned when it became evident that these were unclear and often misunderstood – published by HMSO as 'Duties and Powers'
- an exercise to map participation in further education of students with learning difficulties and/or disabilities, published by HMSO as 'Mapping Provision: The Provision of and Participation in Further Education by Students with Learning Difficulties and/or Disabilities'
- a practical guide to help colleges conduct their needs analyses (undertaken with the Widening Participation Committee)
- international visits
- an exercise to test the committee's approach to learning with colleges.

The volume of evidence taken by the committee and the continuous dialogue it established with the field meant that the report is as much a report from the sector to the Council as it is from the committee to the Council.

Other research

The world did not stand still while the committee was doing its work. Sir Ron Dearing carried out his review of post-16 qualifications. The committee gave evidence to this review. Its recommendations to recognise small steps of progress and to develop a Skills for Adult Life award appear in Sir Ron's report and are currently in the pilot stage of development.

The Mental Health Foundation carried out a review of services for people with learning difficulties and the FEFC established the Widening Participation Committee. I met the chairs and representative members of both these committees to discuss each of the reports and their findings.

Why include these students?

It is important to offer educational opportunities to people with learning difficulties and/or disabilities, not only for the humane reason of giving them power over their own lives but for economic reasons. Qualifications can lead to employment and economic independence, which in turn benefits productivity, may increase revenues from taxation and reduces dependency costs to the State.

Background

The Further and Higher Education Act 1992 stated that the Further Education Funding Council should have regard to the needs of students with learning difficulties and/or disabilities in all that it does. The Council established the committee to offer advice on:

- how it should best discharge its duties under the Act
- how far current provision was satisfactory
- what should be done about any shortcomings.

The committee's findings

The committee found that the Council is meeting its legal duties, if these are interpreted narrowly, in that those who want further education can generally gain access to it. That is, current provision is meeting expressed demand. However, there are those who are not participating in further education; in particular, those with profound and multiple disabilities, young people with emotional and behavioural difficulties and adults with mental health difficulties. There is therefore a problem about how to include these missing groups in education.

A further concern is the need to raise quality in this area of work. The committee recognised the hard work and commitment of teachers working with students with learning difficulties and/or disabilities, but inspection evidence indicates that the quality of the learning taking place is generally lower than in other aspects of further education. This is supported by what students themselves told the committee and what teachers said: they know they can do better, given better materials, conditions and management.

The committee's approach to learning

The committee is therefore suggesting a radically different approach which goes back to the basic principles of how people learn. If this learning is successful, then the teachers, the colleges and the Council are all doing their jobs. The approach is about finding the best match between the way the student learns best, their learning goals and the learning environment. The learning environment is individually tailored and includes such things as the physical environment, equipment, support for learning, teaching methods and the training and insight of teachers. This is called 'inclusive learning'. The approach can be described in five stages:

1. Find out how each individual learns best. This applies to all students but particularly to those with learning difficulties/disabilities who may have a history of good and bad educational experiences. This knowledge enables the teacher to determine the best teaching methods for that student and to share the approach with the student as part of raising confidence.

2. Negotiate the learning goals with the student to define the appropriate curriculum. This also gives the student ownership of their learning and so increases motivation.

3. Assess what the subject matter demands in terms of skills and knowledge and incorporate this into the learning programme.

4. Agree with the student what will constitute evidence of progress; use it to improve the learning process.

5. Empower the student to meet the demands of accreditation.

Because of a historical neglect of the work, all these processes are less well developed in relation to students with learning difficulties and/or disabilities than in further education generally. However, when these ideas were tested in some colleges they were strongly supported. Moreover, colleges have told the committee that this is what they were trying to achieve with all of their students.

Labels

The idea of inclusive learning also answers the question of whether students should or should not be labelled as having a learning difficulty or disability. It has become clear that for the purposes of education and teaching, labelling is not helpful. All labels imply that it is the student who has the problem or deficit, when the problem is in fact an educational one for the college, teachers, managers and indeed the country. It should be up to a national education system to provide for everyone.

However, there is still a need to be able to count students; firstly to measure the incidence of need and secondly – for audit purposes – to check that money is being spent where it was intended. This counting is completely separate from, and should not interfere in any way with, the educational process.

The committee's recommendations

To the Funding Council

The Council has four levers which it can use to promote inclusive learning and the committee has based many of its recommendations on these. The recommendations include:

Funding

- retain funding tied to the individual, but allow personal equipment and transport costs within the funding bands;
- allocate extra funds for entry;
- publish an accessible guide to the methodology – many people do not understand what it is capable of;
- revisit the Council's interpretation of Schedule 2 (j).

The committee does not want to go against the original intention of parliament but thinks the Council's definition of progress should be expanded. Details of how this could be done are given in the Report (pp143–146):

- survey and improve the capital stock of the sector;
- allocate new funds to start up new provision where there is evidence of a gap;
- allocate funds for a quality initiative to improve teaching and management skills for learning.

Strategic planning

- invite colleges to share with the Council the duty to have regard;
- improve regional planning by increasing collaboration;
- ask colleges to use the practical guide to improve their needs analyses and to explain where participation does not match their local population.

Inspection

- the approach to inclusive learning should be the basis for inspection;
- the approach needs to go on being developed; the Inspectorate are best placed to do this as they see working examples of good practice in colleges; the Inspectorate gave evidence to the committee on good practice, and this will be published shortly. (Now published as *Good Practice Report*, December 1996.)

Data collection

- the committee has recommended revisions to the Individualised Student Record (ISR) and Staff Individual Record (SIR); the SIR needs to provide a better record of staff training;
- longitudinal studies should be developed; we still know very little about the life educational experiences of people with learning difficulties and/or disabilities.

To the Government and those working in the field

Some recommendations are directed to Government, especially the need to have an interdepartmental circular on collaboration and a review of Schedule 2 (j) of the

Further and Higher Education Act 1992. Other recommendations can be considered immediately by teachers and managers in the colleges and other centres, and by other agencies and voluntary organisations. While the national staff development programme is essential, so much good practice is already evident in some places that all concerned should begin now to see how improvements can be made, following the principles set out in the Report. Such preliminary work will make the training and curriculum development programmes even more effective.

Next steps

The Council will be consulting on the recommendations. It will only implement them if there is widespread interest and broad agreement, so it is important that both individuals and organisations respond to the consultation.

Final word

Inclusive learning requires a corporate effort between governors, managers and teachers. It needs the efforts of all three to work. The organisation, its people and the curriculum need to be developed together to a common philosophy. The report is not a utopian dream. It is possible. Most things in it are already being done somewhere, in some colleges or other organisations. It is now up to us to convince others that it can and should be done everywhere.

The word 'inclusion' is now used a great deal in the discourse on social policy and many things are meant by it. In educational discussion it is sometimes used to mean integration. This is not what the committee means by inclusion as the description of 'Inclusive Learning' will have made clear. The report and its ideas belong in the notion of equity and equal opportunities. It is about enfranchising a group of people not previously able to take part in education, and about the political theory that all members of society should be able to have access to whatever society decides to provide in common. This education means that people can gain adult status, live as independently as possible and contribute as fully as possible both in their personal relationships and to the economy. It represents another important step towards the creation of a participative democracy.

References

Further Education Funding Council (1996a) *Inclusive learning: report of the learning difficulties and/or disabilities committee (the Tomlinson Report)* HMSO

Further Education Funding Council (1996b) *Inclusive learning: principles and recommendations: a summary of the findings of the learning difficulties and/or disabilities committee* FEFC

Further Education Funding Council (1996c) *Good practice report: provision for students with learning difficulties and/or disabilities* FEFC

HMSO (1996) *Duties and powers: the law governing the provision of further education to students with learning difficulties and/or disabilities: a report to the learning difficulties and/or disabilities committee* HMSO

Meagers N, Evans C & Dench S (1996) *Mapping provision: the provision of and participation in further education by students with learning difficulties and/or disabilities* HMSO

NFER (1996) *A review of research carried out by the NFER* National Foundation for Educational Research Stanleys

SCPR (1996) *Student voices: the views of further education students with learning difficulties and/or disabilities: a report to the learning difficulties and/or disabilities committee* Skill: National Bureau for Students with Disabilities

15.   The Tomlinson Committee

Lani Florian

Inclusion is more than integration. It is the notion of extending what most of us can have to marginalised groups

Professor John Tomlinson

Introduction

Laws governing the eligibility for, and availability of, post-school provision for people with learning difficulties and/or disabilities are complex and often misunderstood. Local education authorities, social services, health agencies and employers all have legal responsibilities to people with learning difficulties and/or disabilities.

Sometimes the duties of LEAs and other agencies overlap, with more than one having some responsibility for the provision of services. Such is the case with students who have statements of special educational needs but are over compulsory school age. Uncertainty about whether the responsibility for such services rests with the LEA or the Further Education Funding Council (FEFC) has led to gaps in provision... Recent reforms have not necessarily clarified this long-standing problem.

The *Further and Higher Education Act 1992* placed a duty upon the FEFC to 'have regard to the requirements of persons having learning difficulties'. Though flexible and open to interpretation, the duty 'to have regard to' is obligatory rather than discretionary and carries with it an implied responsibility for the provision of further education (FE) for all. Clearly the needs of a person with a learning difficulty and/or disability cannot be ignored. Yet the Act is silent regarding any requirement for special education provision. In addition, it has little to say about what constitutes a curriculum for FE. Instead the Act authorises the FEFC to fund specific courses listed within it. Schedule 2 (j) refers to courses that prepare people with learning difficulties and/or disabilities for entry into other funded courses...

The FEFC is required to fund sufficient and adequate facilities for FE in general, and to have regard to students with learning difficulties in particular. Under current arrangements, FE course offerings must meet certain requirements for funding, notably, courses must lead towards a recognised qualification. One exception, Schedule 2 (j), refers to programmes or courses for people with learning difficulties and/or disabilities, the primary objective of which is preparation for entry to a course leading to a vocational qualification. To be funded by the FEFC Schedule 2 (j), programmes must have college accreditation or show other evidence which enables the student to progress to another course. Griffiths (1994) noted that the content of these courses tends to be based on concepts of personal development and transition to adult life. They aim to promote adult status by teaching skills of self-care and employability, while also providing opportunities to develop adult self-concept and adult relationships. The extent to which these courses achieve their aims is not taken up directly in the (Tomlinson) Report. Rather the focus is on approaches to learning which encourage colleges to develop their own practice in working flexibly and with more heterogeneous populations of students to teach the skills of adult life. The Report describes these skills as:

- 'employability' (preparation for working life)
- understanding roles in the family, including parenting skills and relationships
- understanding the local community, including travel, leisure pursuits and voluntary work
- understanding the society in which we live, including the laws and the individual benefits and allowances (p147).

Thus, the approach to learning which has given the Report its name, *Inclusive Learning,* is central to the analysis and the recommendations embodied in it. Inclusive learning is referred to as 'a way of thinking about further education that uses a revitalised understanding of learning and the learner's requirements as its starting-point' (p25).

> *Put simply, we want to avoid a viewpoint which locates the difficulty or deficit with the student and focuses instead on the capacity of the educational institution to understand and respond to the individual learner's requirement. This means we must move away from labelling the student and towards creating an appropriate educational environment; concentrate on understanding better how people learn so that they can be better helped to learn; and see people with disabilities and/or learning difficulties first and foremost as learners (p4).*

What represents a departure from traditional thinking in this approach is the move away from extending current provision through the modification of existing courses to one that emphasises redesigning the provision itself. The focus is on the curriculum, and how it is taught, including a consideration of the students' pre-existing skills and knowledge, their aptitudes and interests as well as their current and future needs. The redesigned provision called for in the Report would match the requirements of the subject matter, materials and teaching methods to students' predispositions and developmental levels.

It is intended that this approach to FE would broaden its constituency and, in this way, render it more inclusive. Such a system, then, would have the capacity to provide for a more diverse group of people. *Inclusive Learning* can be seen as a blueprint for FE to increase the participation of all who come forward, rather than just those for whom existing courses are deemed to be appropriate. The magnitude of this task is not underestimated by the Report...

Recommendations

The Report contains over 50 recommendations based on the principles of inclusive learning. These are of three types: those which could be implemented at the level of the college; those that should be addressed through the work of the FEFC; and those which involve other agencies (p185). The main recommendations call for:

- colleges to develop long-term strategic plans to implement the principles of inclusive learning
- concerted efforts to increase participation by under-represented groups of persons with learning difficulties and/or disabilities
- the development of a new pre-foundation award within the national qualifications framework which is relevant to all students and focuses on preparation for adult life
- the development of relevant and comprehensive assessment and recording procedures
- the adoption of the principles of inclusive learning to underpin funding mechanisms and the inspection process
- a centrally co-ordinated programme of staff development
- the development of a joint departmental circular detailing the responsibilities of education, health and social services in the provision of services to people with learning difficulties and/or disabilities.

To date, the FEFC has broadly endorsed the Report and is seeking a response from the field through the consultation process currently underway. Cost implications for the recommendations contained in the Report are being determined (Lamb, 1996). It remains to be seen whether government funding will follow. In the meantime, mechanisms to hold colleges to the higher standards called for in the Report may be put in place. Such standards will be difficult to achieve without proper resources. Sophisticated levels of skill are required to implement the principles of inclusive learning and to achieve the quality of provision envisaged by the Tomlinson Committee. There is clearly a need for the long-term professional development called for in the Report if this is to occur.

Conclusion

Although the more progressive and inclusive educational opportunities currently available to school-age pupils with learning difficulties and/or disabilities will change the prior educational history of new generations of young adults, it will do so in ways that will continue to make great demands on colleges to ensure flexibility. Moreover, advances in medicine and technology will continue to change the nature of the population of students with learning difficulties and/or disabilities. The Tomlinson Report provides a blueprint for building the capacity of the FE sector in order that it can become more inclusive by providing a meaningful opportunity for all who wish to participate.

Inclusive Learning articulates a set of principles upon which new provision may be based. The redesigned provision, called for in the Report, is exemplified by recommendations for it to be extended in more than one direction. If implemented according to the principles of inclusive learning, the new pre-foundation award will not be a specialised course for people with learning difficulties and/or disabilities only; it will be accessible to all who need it. General inspection procedures will reflect the principles of inclusive learning in order that judgements of quality will be based, at least in part, on the extent to which the college provides learning which is inclusive.

Currently teachers in FE are not required to hold a professional qualification. If the principles of inclusive learning are to be based on a model of learning that matches students' predispositions and developmental level to the requirements of the subject-matter, then teachers will need explicit training in learning theory as well as special educational needs. The recommendation for a centrally co-ordinated programme of staff development along with the funding to implement it will be essential in order to improve access and quality. The Report notes the documented relationship between staff development and quality of provision, and calls for a serious investment in staff development and teacher education as a necessary condition to achieving the recommendations of the Report.

The Tomlinson Committee estimates that the number of students with learning difficulties and/or disabilities enrolled in FE colleges has tripled in ten years. However, when compared with their peers, students with learning difficulties and/or disabilities lag behind on key quality of life indicators like employment. Although they represent one-fifth of the population, two-fifths of people with learning difficulties and/or disabilities have no vocational qualification (Tomlinson, 1996). Surely, access to a vocational qualification is the key to improving the quality of life possible for people with learning difficulties and/or disabilities. The recommendation for a pre-foundation award within the national vocational qualifications framework creates an opportunity for more people with learning difficulties and/or disabilities to have such access to employment.

Whether *Inclusive Learning* becomes a blueprint for the future development of further education, depends less on its thoughtful recommendations, but more on whether the government has the political will to develop inclusive national policies, and to invest sufficient resources to enable colleges to undertake the necessary developmental work. The endorsement of the Report by the FEFC is reassuring to all concerned with the education of people with learning difficulties and/or disabilities. Action must now follow the words.

References

Further Education Funding Council (1996) *Inclusive learning: report of the learning difficulties and/or disabilities select committee* FEFC

Griffiths M (1994) *Transition to adulthood: the role of education for young people with severe learning difficulties* David Fulton

Lamb M (1996) *Inclusive learning: responses to the report*. Responding to Tomlinson: the report of the Further Education Funding Council Committee on Learning Difficulties and/or Disabilities. Conference held at the University of Cambridge Institute of Education, November

16.   Beyond the 'Inclusionist' Debate

Liz Maudsley & Lesley Dee

Introduction

Much recent discussion about provision for students with learning difficulties and disabilities has focused around the 'inclusionist debate'. As often happens the key words of this debate have tended to become slogans which are used without a real analysis of what they mean. Current discussion has often polarised into an assumption that an inclusive system in which all students can be accommodated within a mainstream offer is by nature 'good' – the Further Education Funding Council (FEFC) document *Funding Learning* speaks of how integrated provision is recognised as being more effective in meeting students' needs. In this paper we certainly do not wish to deny the importance of a vision which sees new ways of including students with learning difficulties and disabilities within the Further and Adult Education framework. We are also very ready to acknowledge the inadequacy of much current provision, both discrete and integrated, for students with learning difficulties and disabilities.

What we do want to do is to focus on two main issues. The first is to recognise the current practical limitations of including all students with learning difficulties and disabilities into mainstream provision without fundamental changes to that mainstream offer. While accepting the importance of the vision we feel it is irresponsible to assume that this goal can be achieved within the situation as it currently exists. Secondly, we feel that the vision itself requires certain redefinitions. The debate appears to have become locked into a skewed polarity between 'integration' and 'segregation' and what we hope to postulate in the second half of this paper is a model which goes beyond this polarity and instead looks at a framework for Further and Adult Education which allows for students with learning difficulties and disabilities to be able to follow patterns of learning which are most appropriate to their individual requirements.

The current context

It is worth reminding ourselves about the nature of the learners we are considering. The group includes both school leavers and adults. Many will have clearly identifiable learning difficulties or disabilities and, if at school over the last twelve years or so, will have had a Statement. Others will be part of a larger group of people who experienced learning or behavioural difficulties at school and who left with few or no qualifications and low levels of basic skills. Some may have had interrupted schooling because of illness, family or socio-economic reasons. Others are returning to live in the community after living in institutions for many years while some people may be recently disabled. Of course, not everyone wishes to receive further or continuing education and training. For those who do however the further education sector offers an important opportunity to enhance the quality of many aspects of people's lives including, but not only, their employment prospects. As McGinty & Fish (1992) put it 'education must be aimed at informed adulthood, lifelong learning and concern for others as well as vocational proficiency'.

Many students, particularly those from the mainstream school sector and those with more severe and complex needs, do not continue into further education either because they choose not to or because Further and Adult Education rejects them or cannot meet their needs They are in effect selected out. Some go on to youth training, others drift into low paid or unskilled work or are unemployed. Others may go to residential colleges.

The majority of students who attend colleges and are cognitively impaired are on so-called 'discrete' courses. The concept of discrete provision in Further and Adult Education implies that:

1. it is organisationally, administratively and possibly locationally separate;
2. the course is not accredited;
3. the curriculum is designed to meet individual needs;
4. there is a greater emphasis on the overt development of core skills and cross-curricular themes.

In fact none of these perceptions may be true. There are courses where one and two may be so but where individual needs are not addressed and where little learning or progress at any level is occurring. Equally some discrete courses are fully integrated organisationally, administratively and locationally and individual needs are being met with certain aspects of the course accredited. To what extent can the Further Education mainstream curriculum challenge the first two negative factors while still answering the individual and holistic needs addressed by three and four? ...

The changing further and adult education curriculum

The shape of the new post-16 curriculum is beginning to emerge and the change is not without difficulty. In reality many students are still taught in groups by largely didactic methods (MacFarlane, 1993) and follow one or two year courses of study. It is still relatively rare in most colleges for students to follow individual learning plans on modular programmes using a variety of learning methods with access to appropriate learning support. The 1991 White Paper 'Education and Training for the 21st Century' set down a series of National Education and Training Targets in an attempt to improve the quality of the workforce and bring the UK into line with standards in the rest of the developed world. New controls over the curriculum offer were introduced by funding only certain kinds of programmes and the government is urging the FEFC to fund only externally accredited courses by 1995. In line with other parts of the public sector a percentage of colleges' budgets will be linked to outcomes. To encourage competition between institutions league tables of exam results are being published. In the wake of the Dearing Report, schools are being encouraged to offer GNVQs from 14 plus.

The impact of many of these changes remains to be seen. There is a fear however that, combined with a squeeze on resources, schools and colleges will compete for those students with higher levels of attainment who are likely to complete courses faster thereby costing less and earning more. This pattern is already emerging in Youth Training where similar controls have been introduced.

The 1992 FHE Act included safeguards to protect the interests of more vulnerable groups of learners, including those with learning difficulties. Yet the relative, contextual nature of many learning difficulties has made arriving at clear definitions of this group of students difficult. The FEFC has taken its responsibilities towards students with learning difficulties very seriously. Differential funding mechanisms ensure that colleges are having to address the needs of these learners at a strategic planning level. Many learning support co-ordinators are for the first time feeling a degree of empowerment although concerns are being raised about the concept of banding and individually linked funding. The establishment of the Specialist Committee under the chairmanship of Professor Tomlinson has been greeted with enthusiasm and is another indication of the FEFC's commitment to this aspect of provision...

While questions are being raised about the quality of many discrete courses for students with learning difficulties, concerns are also being voiced about the nature of the 'new FE'. Criticisms by Michael Young (1993) and Alan Smithers in a recent television programme suggest that NVQs are too narrowly defined and job specific. They feel that the post-16 curriculum with its vocational/academic divide is failing to prepare young people for life in the [new] century. In a recent TES article Beryl Pratley sounds warning bells about GNVQs which were designed to address the educational core missing from NVQs. She asserts that the real purpose of GNVQs is in danger of being undermined because the DfE and the DoE have failed to agree a joint strategy and resources for their implementation. Schools will do the cheap bits and colleges the vocational, resource intensive aspects. Nowhere will students gain access to GNVQs as they were originally conceived.

Geoff Stanton (1992) suggests that the current curriculum offer needs to be enhanced, while not 'turning off' potential students by becoming too generalist. Separate provision for cross-curricular themes and core skills, such as in the French system, would enable core skills to be developed by all students no matter what programme they were following. This, then, begins to sound like the sort of curricular content that would address the learning needs of many students with learning difficulties or disabilities. But this still leaves us with questions about teaching methods as well as appropriate modes of delivery and we intend now to address these issues.

Redefining the future: learning support and access courses

The notion of 'learning support' can include help with core skills; additional resources; modified teaching and learning methods and materials and also different modes of learning. Recently there has been a shift towards seeing provision for students with learning difficulties and disabilities as a part of 'learning support'. This is a move we welcome as it recognises the specific needs of these students as forming part of a spectrum of learning support which any student might require at some stage of their education. In a recent FEU document 'Supporting Learning – Promoting Equity and Participation' the authors give a list of 'specific necessary variants' which certain individuals or groups might require in order to gain access to education. One of these variants is the provision of Access Courses. Access Courses are an essential part of a College's offer in that they allow learners who have often had an unconventional educational experience the chance to regain their place in an educational system. Adults who chose to follow Access Courses could also choose to follow a conventional route to Higher Education – for example A levels or BTec National/GNVQ. However, they often feel their particular learning needs require a programme of learning which will help them fill in the gaps they have missed and have the chance to receive extra support – for example through the explicit teaching of a variety of study skills; through an emphasis on individual tutorials; and through having the chance to share a period of education with other students who experience difficulties similar to their own.

Our contention is that so-called 'discrete' provision for certain groups of students, particularly those with severe learning difficulties, must be seen as a kind of Access Course. As we have already stated these students' educational background has often been different from that of other students – they may well have attended special schools; they may have had long periods in hospital or in a long-term institution; and they may experience particular cognitive difficulties which make certain aspects of learning particularly difficult for them. We believe that certain groups of students with cognitive difficulties do have distinct needs both in content and teaching methods which are at time most effectively addressed through their being taught in a distinct group. Too often the theoretical options for students with learning difficulties are seen as either provision which is totally segregated or that which is totally integrated. We maintain that what needs to be addressed is not a polarised integration/segregation debate but the specific needs of students with cognitive disabilities and what is the most effective practice which will lead to them experiencing an enhanced quality of life.

Identity and learning difficulties

We wish to focus on the right of particular groups of individuals to choose to have times when they can identify as a distinct group. To do this we wish to look very briefly at certain parallel experiences in the women's movement. In the early days of the women's movement there was often a pressure for women to prove themselves by gaining acceptance and status within a male dominated world. It is only as the movement developed that many women began to articulate that this was not necessarily the kind of success they actually wanted as, on its own, it often resulted in a denial of what they felt was important to their identity as women. Instead they began to challenge the assumptions and values which underpin that world. In order to do this many women have felt the need to have certain times when they chose to strengthen and confirm the reality of their own beliefs in a discrete group.

Our belief is that a model in which total inclusion is seen as the only way forward can deny the specific identity, and hence undermine the dignity, of people with learning difficulties and disabilities. Much has been stated about the importance of people with learning difficulties having the right to choose to integrate into the mainstream. This is a choice we would strongly advocate. However, less is articulated about the right of people to choose to spend time and receive education with a peer group of people with similar educational needs as themselves. We feel that if a choice is only one way it does not in fact constitute a real choice. We find that the model of integration currently formulated adheres to an individualistic philosophy which denies the option to spend time, and sometimes to learn, within a peer group environment.

An example from Denmark

We wish to conclude by looking at an example of a recent research project in Denmark – *Co-write Your Own Life: Quality of Life as Discussed in the Danish Context*, by Per Holm, Jesper Holst and Birger Perit. In a section of their paper entitled 'The Tyranny of the Normal' the authors speak of 'the real danger of falling into a natural fallacy' in which a perceived notion of 'what a normal life ought to be for a particular section of the population becomes what is right for them'. Instead they feel that what is needed is 'a discussion not so much about what is normal, but about quality of life, what determines the quality of life, and what conditions are necessary to enable people to follow their own convictions and shape their own lives'. They question 'whether it is right to integrate people with learning difficulties formally into local communities without providing them with meeting or activity centres' and state how 'such places can take the form of cafes, meetings rooms, or cultural arrangements where people with learning difficulties can be together on their own terms and develop patterns of mutual interaction where they feel they are both necessary and important to each other.'

Their work with people with learning difficulties is characterised by a recognition of the primary importance of personal history and identity. From this starting point. individuals are encouraged to articulate their own vision of their future and are supported in moving towards it. Their research led them to question the validity of a product-orientated approach for people with learning difficulties and also to challenge the automatic assumption of paid employment as a necessary measure of identity and self-respect. Instead they recognised the need for process-based, creative activities which would 'create real and coherent forms of co-operation and the stimulation of people with learning difficulties to form their own activities and seek new challenges'. Sometimes the skills learnt through these activities did lead on employment activities – for example in the case where a group of people with learning difficulties took over the running of a youth hostel which was threatened with closure. Their own centre was not only 'a place where they could come together, establish social contacts and build up a sub-culture in their own terms' but also a place which other people who wanted to use the facilities could attend, 'in other words, a community centre was established along untraditional lines'. Hence people with learning difficulties were seen as being an integral part of the community and as having their own essential contribution to make to it.

We believe that this model has much to teach Further and Adult Education in the UK. Its focus moves us away from a rigid dichotomy between integration and segregation towards a model which allows for 'grouping and re-grouping'. In this model, certain parts of the curriculum offer would allow students with learning difficulties to develop their own identity and express their own aims at the same time as developing the communication and self-advocacy skills necessary to articulate these aims. There would be other times when individuals might well choose to integrate into other vocational options and learn alongside other students. Aspects of their programme would be accredited. Finally, this integration would not be seen as a 'one-way traffic' as there would be other times, in common with the Danish example, when other students could opt to take part in certain classes which were specifically focused on students with learning difficulties.

We wish to end with two riders. The first is to stress that in this paper our main concern has been with provision for those students who have a distinct cognitive disability. We have not been writing here about students with sensory or physical disabilities or about the large numbers of students whose difficulty with learning has been created by social and educational factors. Secondly, we recognise that educational provision must conform to certain quality standards if it is to be effective for its students. Too often the excuse has been used that, because it is difficult to arrive at suitable performance indicators, it therefore somehow can escape any kind of evaluation. One is left either with a situation in which students are made to follow unsuitable provision because it can be evaluated, or one in which they follow a programme which has no quality standards and evaluation. We maintain it is possible to evaluate and bring quality to the kind of flexible programme we have outlined, and it is here that resources and energy need to be put.

References

DES (1991) *Education and training for the 21st Century* (White Paper) HMSO

DfE (1992) *Further and higher education act* HMSO

Holm P, Holst J & Perit B *Co-write your own life: quality of life as discussed in the Danish context* Undated

MacFarlane E (1993) *Education 16-19 in transition* Routledge

McGinty J & Fish J (1992) *Learning support for young people in transition* Open University Press

Stanton G (1992) 'Post-16 curriculum and qualifications. Confession and incoherence or diversity and choice?' in E Maudsley & L Dee (1995) *Redefining the future: perspectives on students with learning difficulties and disabilities in FE* Institute of Education

Young M (1993) 'A curriculum for the 21st century. Towards a new basis for overcoming academic/vocational divisions' *British Journal of Educational Studies*. August 1993.

Part Four – The Experience of Students and Teachers

Contributions to the final Part of this volume look at the impact which current policies are having on provision for students with learning difficulties and disabilities, and on the practical implications of these for their teachers and tutors.

One of the functions of policy is to reflect principle. When a new policy is formulated it is likely to represent the values of the majority of the members of the community adopting it, though there are many examples of policies and legislation which are deliberately adopted by government in advance of a general change in values. So practitioners have the task of implementing policy, and the contributions to the final Part of this volume describe approaches to the policy of inclusion. Institutions and individual teachers have had to adjust in a short period of time to the new concepts which this policy embodies.

Previous perceptions may have been that a subject being taught was the most significant factor in delivering the curriculum; even where the importance of 'process' has been accepted, this may not have influenced practice to the point of considering the individual learning needs of students. There is a significant difference between getting one's subject across in innovative and exciting ways and getting it across to everyone in ways they find helpful. With anxieties about 'covering' a curriculum, teachers may have valid concerns about how far inclusive practice might be possible. Many institutions will have in place arrangements for individual learning support which very effectively increase the students' chances of success. The policy of inclusion, however, demands more than that. It suggests that each teacher is responsible for inclusive practice. How do we define that? How do we manage it? What changes in methodology do we need to make? It is obvious that we need to adjust our practice so that learning in our classrooms is made possible for students with visual or hearing impairment, students in wheelchairs, students with learning difficulties and so on.

Institutions must have in place systems which identify these sorts of learning support needs well in advance of the first teaching session so that discussions can have taken place which identify the support required. Theoretically that ought to be the easy bit; we are after all skilled practitioners: we ought to be able to produce the right sort of handout on the right coloured paper; we ought to be able to teach as effectively as usual using a microphone; we ought to be able to organise our practical rooms in such a way that wheelchair bound students can participate as effectively as any in the group; we ought to be able to conduct our lessons so that our delivery, our questioning and our testing can encompass a variety of ability and previous achievement in our students.

Anecdotal evidence suggests that both institutions and individuals are still finding it a challenge to think of the needs of the individual at the same time as they are thinking 'bums on seats', 'quality', 'retention', etc.

The eight readings fall into two categories. The first four contribute to the debate about provision for groups with learning difficulties. The examples chosen look at courses specifically designed for people with learning difficulties as well as at those which offer support when students with learning difficulties are included on courses within the mainline college curriculum offer. You may wish to consider what is appropriate learning at post-16, and what is missing from the current provision.

You will find some conflicts in these readings. Deborah Weymont and John Lawton are writing about similar groups of people with profound and multiple learning disabilities, for example, but have different perceptions of how our institutions can provide appropriate learning experiences for them. Sensitive issues such as 'normalisation' are raised by Hilary Beverley, while Bryan Merton describes an attempt to express personal and social learning outcomes in terms of performance criteria. In deciding your attitude to these issues, you will be exploring the boundaries of the concepts of integration and inclusion, and your conclusions may be shaped by some of the research papers which are included in this section.

The final four readings describe principles and strategies for delivering inclusion in further and higher education, and give examples of a variety of practice in selected areas both in colleges and in universities. Joyce Harrison sets the scene by presenting an account of a piece of research in Hampshire which found out from students with learning difficulties and disabilities themselves what their expectations and experiences were of their further education colleges. Detailed guidance on the teaching of maths is provided by Nicola Martin, and Jenny Corbett and Sue Ralph describe an example of project work with students with learning disabilities at the University of Portsmouth. The final contribution to the Reader, by Viv Parker and Marion West, is an account of an access to higher education programme at the University of East London.

By analysing the examples of good practice reported here, and of others which you will read of elsewhere, we hope you will be able to abstract workable strategies and so evaluate your own experience in your own organisation.

17.   The Learning Age

John Lawton

It is imperative, however, that we consider the impact of all of this Green Paper's proposals on the lives of people with learning difficulties.

In his passionate and appealing introduction [to the Green Paper], David Blunkett, Secretary of State for Education and Employment, quotes President John F Kennedy: 'Liberty without learning is always in peril and learning without liberty is always in vain'.

On first reading one might be disappointed to find that virtually the only direct reference to people with learning difficulties is contained in one paragraph (DfEE, 1998: 4.36).   This talks about improving access to learning;   building on the Tomlinson Report, *Inclusive Learning,* and in particular the 'Quality Initiative';   the New Deal for disabled students, mostly in higher education;   and the importance of ensuring that all programmes for improving quality include people with disabilities and learning difficulties.   (The Green Paper, despite making reference to the implementation of the recommendations of the Tomlinson Report, 'Inclusive Learning', fails to cite it as one of the sources of inspiration for the Green Paper itself. This is a small omission, but a significant one.)

It is imperative, however, that we consider the impact of all of this Green Paper's proposals on the lives of people with learning difficulties, precisely because they are not specifically mentioned elsewhere.   People with learning difficulties must be included in the debates we have about the future role of learning in this country's growth.

People with all types and levels of learning difficulty should be included in our thinking as we frame responses to the consultative paper.   For example, how will the proposals affect the lives of people with profound and multiple learning difficulties, many of whom will never enter the labour market?   What supports will be available to enable people with challenging behaviours to access learning in local communities, which are promoted as good practice as part of *The Learning Age?*

We have to ensure that 'all' genuinely means all.   NIACE has recently concluded its project, 'All Things Being Equal', which looks at equal opportunities in learning for people with learning difficulties from Black and Asian communities, people with profound and multiple disabilities, and older learners This found that while there are isolated examples of innovative good practice, there is 'little equity' and such groups are still marginalised.

We are at a critical moment.   It would be very dangerous – but easy – to assume that because this country's wealth is likely to be built on the intellectual capital of its workforce, that this is not relevant to the lives of disadvantaged, learning-poor individuals, particularly those with learning difficulties. The Green Paper argues that quite the opposite is true.

Thriving in work

Many adults with learning difficulties are striving to enter the labour market, often for the first time. They want to work. They want paid jobs. They see learning as a way in which this aspiration can be realised.

People with learning difficulties want to thrive in work, not just survive there. The Green Paper makes the point clearly that the workforce that does not continually review and renew its skills and knowledge bases is vulnerable to the rapid fluctuations in economic cycles and changing markets. What does this say for the learning needs of those who, traditionally at least, have been perceived as lacking flexible and portable skills? We must ensure that people with learning difficulties in work have access to lifelong learning which enables them to keep up with these changes in the labour market.

The opportunities of IT

The proposals to establish a University for Industry, therefore, have potentially much to offer those with learning difficulties who are in or about to enter work. We have to ensure that the learning materials, particularly those using innovative technologies, are accessible to people with learning difficulties. It has been argued elsewhere that 'new' technology can be liberating for people with disabilities. It can, as long as people are given access to and taught how to use it. It is vital that people with learning difficulties are given access to the Internet. Voice e-mail, video-conferencing and distance learning technologies can all be made accessible to people with learning difficulties if sufficient creativity and imagination are used.

There are inspiring examples of people with learning difficulties using the emerging technologies to communicate with others. Northampton People First, a self-advocacy organisation, has its own Internet website. Students with learning difficulties have received support from the European-funded Leonardo da Vinci programme for promoting quality and innovation in vocational training to produce a video news-letter about different kinds of jobs. The project is called, 'Self-Advocacy Training Initiatives' and information about it is available on the Internet at:

http://www.modus.co.uk/mhm

I would like to see support for people with learning difficulties being set as one of the targets by industry, learning providers and the Government. Without support in using the University for Industry in its early developmental stages, history tells us that people with learning difficulties will struggle to shape its future growth and development.

Financial resources

Individual Learning Accounts should also be made accessible to people with learning difficulties if they are going to be the measure by which others assess an individual's commitment to their own personal development in educational terms. Many people with learning difficulties, even those in work, have limited financial resources. It would be all too easy to assume that people with learning difficulties need not bother about this issue. That would risk people with learning difficulties being excluded from contributing financially to their own learning, from benefiting when subsidies were available and from demonstrating their own commitment to their learning goals. Individual Learning Accounts must take into consideration the additional cost of disability and support individuals accordingly.

Guidance

High quality advice and guidance services will be required to enable people to make informed and meaningful choices, but people should have the opportunity and right to make those choices in the first place.

People with learning difficulties are challenging the low expectations that others have of them in the learning arena. In my experience, they are challenging themselves and each other to participate more effectively in learning. People have high expectations of themselves in learning and want to be involved in what is happening around them, particularly those young people who have been through a desegregated school system.

Broadcast media

The use of the broadcast media to promote learning is positive, so long as consideration is given to the support necessary for all viewers and listeners to make use of the programmes available. MENCAP is working with NIACE, CHANGE (a self-advocacy organisation for people with learning difficulties and additional disabilities) and the Norah Fry Research Centre to support BBC Education in developing some pilot packs to support access to its mainstream programming. On average, recent lifestyle research showed that people with learning difficulties spend over 40 per cent more time than average 'watching' television. How better could this time be used if people were engaged in facilitated learning?

The proposal to increase basic skills provision to 500,000 people by 2002 is welcome. However, we must ensure that this provision is open to people with learning difficulties and that the teaching they receive is of a good quality, effective and relevant. It is likely that much of this growth will come from work-related provision and include employability skills. This should not be used as another hoop people have to jump through before entering the labour market, if they can do jobs that have a lesser literacy or numeracy demand.

It is clear that to progress in the workplace of the future, sound basic skills and key skills such as communication with others, problem-solving skills and team working skills are going to become more important, rather than less so. We have to ensure that the ways in which such skills and knowledge are developed recognise each individual's learning styles and strengths and do not exclude people because of their differences.

Higher education

It has long been my view that some of the self-advocates I have worked with have been the most articulate and informed proponents of inclusive social policies. Why then, can they not study at university? The usual answer is something to do with a lack of literacy skills and the production of course-work. Both these issues can be addressed if providers of learning are imaginative and skilled in enabling learning to take place. The Open University is acknowledged in the Green Paper as having contributed considerably to widening participation, but it is a lead that few universities have followed.

Considering learners' needs

There are a million people with learning difficulties in the United Kingdom. For too long such people have existed on the margins of society and therefore learning. Their needs have not always been fully taken into consideration. It is true that many now want to work and therefore the Green Paper is of great significance to them. But we must also promote learning which is not directly related to the needs of the labour market and that is about individual freedoms, growth, pleasure and involvement with others.

I vividly recall working with a self-advocacy group in a long-stay hospital for people with learning difficulties. I had asked them what they wanted. They knew I worked for 'education'. I had in mind that they may ask me to organise a photography session, or to do some reminiscence work or perhaps support them in running their meetings. Their studied responses taught me one of the most salutary lessons of my life: 'We want to wear our own clothes ... have a lie-in on Saturday mornings and to have a choice of what to eat for breakfast'.

Reference

Department for Education and Employment (1998) *Green Paper: The learning age* The Stationery Office

18.   Towards Exclusion

Deborah Weymont

It is a year now since the publication of the Tomlinson report, *Inclusive Learning*. For those of us who teach adult education classes for people with profound and multiple learning difficulties the report was exciting and hopeful. Exciting because it was clear that Professor Tomlinson had actually listened carefully to students and teachers in post-school special education. Hopeful because it recommended ways forward that seemed both imaginative and meaningful.

The Tomlinson report identified people with profound and multiple learning difficulties as a group of people currently under-represented in the further and adult education sector and excluded from the benefits of Further Education Funding Council (FEFC) funding.

In relation to what are known as Schedule 2 (j) courses,[1] the report recommended firstly that the current definition of progression on these courses should be extended to include both maintenance of skills and 'lateral' progression. Secondly, there should be specified Schedule 2 courses providing progression for students with profound and multiple learning difficulties.

Finally, the concept of 'inclusive learning' itself has a particular relevance to students with profound and multiple learning difficulties. The shift in emphasis away from learners (and their implied deficits) to learning environments gives new meaning to the term 'student-centred'. Now, we can dismantle the apparent contradiction between our commitment to 'integration' and the fact that the courses we run do not typically attract 'main-stream' students. The 'sensory curriculum' and the emphasis tutors place on 1:1 work, multi-agency collaboration, relationship building and enabling our students to make sense of the world have arisen precisely because we have sought to provide learning programmes which (in Tomlinson's words) 'fit the objectives and learning styles of the students'. We have, it seems, been involved in 'redesigning the very processes of learning, assessment and organisation' for years!

In addition the report suggests the possibility of rationalising funding available from Health and Social Services with FEFC funding. While this is primarily aimed at minimising 'double-funding', in fact the more interesting outcome would be that of formalising joint-funding and multi-agency initiatives. This would give formal recognition to the relatively expensive support requirements of students whose learning takes place at the intersection of education, therapy, care and social services.

Issues and implications

In spite of the overwhelming response to the consultation exercise carried out in March, and wide support for the report's recommendations (FEFC, 1997), there has been little progress made regarding the position of students currently excluded by the funding mechanism. The FEFC seems confused about how to give direction on this issue. In particular, it is concerned about whether 'courses for students with very severe learning difficulties have the necessary rigour to demonstrate progression'. Similarly, it seems worried by the funding implications and is questioning whether the FEFC is the appropriate funding body[2].

The problem with this approach is that it places functional issues of curriculum design and delivery and financial management at the heart of the educational decision-making process, rather than values and human rights. This is disappointing. Questions of rigour and the responsible management of resources are important, but they should not be used as a means of by-passing engagement with broader social and political issues. If we are explicit about the social and political context in which our decisions are framed it becomes much clearer how we should proceed.

Never again

Perhaps we need to remind ourselves of the fact that prior to the 1970 Education (Handicapped Children) Act children and adults with learning difficulties were officially labelled as 'ineducable'[3]. They also mainly lived in large institutions, segregated from their families and their communities and led lives that were characterised by dehumanising and often abusive practices (Morris, 1969). Have we forgotten the ideological and historical context in which this shameful situation arose?

It arose in part because of the rise of the influence of eugenicist ideas about biological inheritance and the application of Darwin's theories to human society (social Darwinism) at the turn of the century. The rationale for the mass incarceration of people with learning difficulties and their exclusion from education through the Mental Deficiency Act of 1913 was based on a concern with genetic degeneracy and a belief that through selective breeding we could get rid of social problems as various as alcoholism, unemployment and crime (Woodhouse, 1982). These beliefs were further legitimated and given 'scientific' credibility through the rise of the influence of psychology and its claims to be able to measure intelligence; and that intelligence was both inherited and unalterable.

With the benefit of hindsight, we know the limits of both eugenicism and psychology. We know that Hitler was wrong. Similarly, we know that the IQ test by which psychologists set such store at the turn of the century has been discredited not just because it is culturally biased but also because, while it purports to measure intelligence, it in fact defines it[4].

The participation in education of people who have previously been denied access to learning cannot simply be reduced to a matter of rigour in curriculum design and delivery. It must also be seen as an issue that requires 'positive action' to redress systematic disadvantage. A societal debt perhaps, to be repaid in memory of, and with respect to, all those whose lives have been broken and devalued by the eugenicist assumptions that have under-pinned education and services for people with learning difficulties this century.

Where are we going?

The question of progression has been brilliantly posed in the plethora of euphemisms the post-school special education sector finds to describe its courses for young people and adults with learning difficulties: 'Next Step', 'What Next?', 'Further On', 'Moving On', 'New Futures', to name a few. The fact that in the staff room we are more likely to be asking the question 'Where the hell are we?' does not detract from our genuine commitment to facilitating learning.

However, we have been increasingly puzzled as to why progression in learning has come to be defined simply in terms of steps towards higher and more complex goals. This narrow and essentially hierarchical view of learning both denies and devalues the potential of low achievers to be educated.

Quite rightly, we understand that learning must be about change. For young people with learning difficulties this has tended to be expressed in the emphasis placed on the 'Transition to Adulthood' (see Hutchinson & Tennyson, 1986, for example). For adult learners it is reflected in the provision of a wide range of learning opportunities that have included the development and consolidation of basic skills as well as creative and personal development activities.

What we do not understand is why the multi-dimensional sets of progression routes on these courses are not recognised as educationally valid under the current funding system. We have worked hard to adapt the way we describe our courses so that they sound achievement-oriented in the narrow academic and vocational terms that the policy-makers like. But in fact we are devious: what we still know and value is that the learning on these courses is multi-dimensional. Teachers know that progression can be this way, that way, over and under, up, down, side to side, backwards, forwards, inside, outside and even round and round! This is human learning in all its diversity.

Maybe it is the policy-makers who are stuck, who need to progress? We do not have to cling to the restrictive market-led, competitive and narrow definitions of what learning has come to mean over the last 15 years. We could reclaim our priorities and reassert what teachers have always known and are still saying: learning is about process as well as product; it can be fun and leisure-based, as well as challenging; it can be social, academic or vocational; it should be meaningful, negotiated, learner-centred; and it may include widening horizons alongside the consolidation, maintenance and repetition of activities and skills.

Principles of inclusive learning cannot be implemented effectively without the definition of progression being radically revised to include a multi-dimensional model of achievement and progression in learning.

Towards exclusion

Let's not delude ourselves about what the continued exclusion of people with profound and multiple learning difficulties from the FEFC funding mechanism means. It means returning to a definition of this particularly marginalised and disadvantaged group as 'ineducable'.

If the FEFC decides not to fund post-school education for people with profound and multiple learning difficulties then it has completely misunderstood the Tomlinson report and the concept of inclusive learning. It will have failed to seize the opportunity to see through the recommendations of the most progressive report the post-school sector has ever had the chance to engage with. It will have palpably failed to put its money where its mouth is. It can make no claims to supporting inclusion. And it can certainly not expect any college to take seriously the idea of being inspected in relation to the extent to which it is providing inclusive education or not.

The real challenge for inclusive education, the real measure of the extent to which colleges might be measured as successfully inclusive, has to lie in how we provide for groups currently marginalised by the FEFC funding methodology. Issues of participation, progression and inclusion are first and foremost issues of equality, rights and access. If we understand that, we stand some chance of getting our priorities right when we have to make difficult decisions about the management of quality in the curriculum and implementing restricted budgets.

Postscript (by Jeannie Sutcliffe, NIACE Development Officer for Adults with Learning Difficulties and Disabilities)

NIACE fully supports access to continuing education for adults with profound and multiple learning difficulties. Our Joseph Rowntree Foundation-supported book *Still a chance to learn?* (1996) highlighted concerns that those with profound and multiple learning difficulties were starting to miss out on continuing education following the implementation of the Further and Higher Education Act 1992. Staff were worried that the emphasis on accreditation and progression would exclude this group of learners. Our Joseph Rowntree Foundation research *All things being equal?* has found a few examples of FEFC-funded provision: one college, for example, has three full-time courses for adults with profound and multiple learning difficulties. Provision at this level is rare.

We were therefore delighted when the FEFC issued a press release on 15 July 1997 which changed the status of Recommendation 37 in the FEFC circular 97/24. The recommendation 'Seek to have the list of courses under Schedule 2 amended to include specific courses which provide progression opportunities in life skills for students with profound and multiple learning difficulties' will now be implemented.

References

Further Education Funding Council (1997) *Results of the consultation on the implementation of Inclusive Learning* FEFC Circular 97/24

Hutchinson D & Tennyson C (1986) *Transition to adulthood* FEU

Morris P (1969) *Put away: a sociological study of institutions for the mentally retarded* RKP

Tomlinson J (1996) *Inclusive learning: principles and recommendations. A summary of the findings of the learning difficulties and/or disabilities committee* FEFC

Woodhouse I (1982) 'Eugenics and the feeble-minded: the parliamentary debates of 1912–14' *History of Education* Vol 11, No 2

Notes:

1) Schedule 2 (j) courses are defined under the Further and Higher Education Act 1992 as 'independent living and communication for those with learning difficulties which prepare them for entry to courses listed in (d) and (g)' – (that is elsewhere in the Schedule). The report is responding here to the difficulty that practitioners and students have had with defining progression in such narrow and hierarchical terms.

2) I am referring here to information given by Karen Fletcher-Wright (FEFC Assistant Director Education Programmes) to delegates at a joint SKILL/ Network Training Conference entitled 'Towards Inclusive Learning: Theory into Practice', Worcester 13/14 May 1997. Some of this information has been reported formally in FEFC Circular 97/24.

3) The Mental Deficiency Act of 1913 excluded children we would now label as having profound and multiple learning difficulties on grounds of their ineducability. The 1944 Act extended this principle to further exclude children with what we would now term severe learning difficulties. These exclusions were based on psychological and IQ testing procedures. In fact most of the children excluded from education by these two acts would clearly not have been able to begin to participate in the assessment process – how they registered scores of above or below 60, for example, is a mystery!

4) What I mean by this is that IQ testing has been developed to measure a very limited part of our potential over a normal distribution curve. The fact that a certain number of people have IQs at the lower end of the scale is intrinsic to the design of the test and not to the individuals who complete them. In this sense IQ tests and their derivatives do not actually measure intelligence or 'degree of learning difficulty'; they define it.

19. Adult Appropriateness and Students with Learning Difficulties

Hilary Beverley

Introduction

This article is based on research carried our in North Lincolnshire during 1996, in an attempt to consider what was 'adult appropriate' for students with learning difficulties within adult continuing education. Five main areas were considered: adult status, choices, evaluation, group management and materials. These were selected because each of them related to specific factors within the ethos of adult continuing education, where stress is placed on the desirability for each student to direct and take responsibility for his or her own leaning.

The nature of the research

Unstructured interviews were used in an attempt to ensure that students with limited or no literacy skills could still participate. It was also hoped that this method would enable the respondents to express their opinions truly. Three groups were interviewed, namely managers, tutors and students with learning difficulties. As the students were in the 30 plus age group, a control group of adult continuing education students, not identified as having learning difficulties, was also interviewed.

Why consider adult appropriateness?

It had seemed for some time that there were discrepancies in how different groups viewed being adult. This was confirmed by considering definitions of adult. For example Knowles (1990) defines adulthood in legal, social and psychological terms which are difficult to apply to adults with learning difficulties. Many such adults will perhaps not perform adult roles such as spouse, full-time worker or parent, or arrive at a concept of being responsible for their own lives. Knowles's definition is supported by others (Tomlinson, 1995; Squires, 1993) all of which seem very restrictive when applied to adults with learning difficulties. This leads to the question: is there merely one definition (Bradley *et al*. 1994), even though it is widely accepted? Alongside this, a conversation with a manager within adult continuing education highlighted the question of what materials are appropriate for adults, especially those for whom learning presents in some instances severe difficulties.

Models of 'adult'

The research findings highlighted one major difficulty; managers and tutors had a model of adult very much in line with Knowles and others. Adults with learning difficulties, however, had a very different perspective. Whilst acknowledging their adult status, the majority did not define adult in the same way as the tutors, managers and other students. The students with learning difficulties perceived being adult very much in terms of physical stature – adults are bigger than other people –

and the right to a degree of independence – what time to go to bed. Few defined their adult status in terms of interpersonal relationships or of economic self-sufficiency. These factors may well reflect the attitudes of others towards the students, but whatever the reasons it was clear that those who teach and manage were using a different model of 'adult' from those who are taught.

This fact raises some very pertinent issues. The first of these is, whose model of adult is used? In order to talk about adult appropriateness this is the first question which must be raised. The second is also very important for it touches on the whole purpose of education. Were tutors and managers there to 'normalise' those students whose model of adult differs from their own or are they there to empower students with learning difficulties to define their status for themselves? In other words, do tutors and managers accept that there is more than one model of adult? This also raises a further question: whether in education the aim should be to make all people conform to norms, or whether part of education should be to help society to accept difference.

Choices

The research further highlighted the problems which many students with learning difficulties had in making choices. This was compounded by the fact that for many of the students choices had always been made for them by others. Some students found it almost impossible to choose and this posed problems for tutors in a situation where students are expected to make choices about their learning. The major question was how far could people be expected to make choices about things which may be unfamiliar even to the point of choosing whether or not to attend an adult education group? Very often this choice was taken out of the students' hands and they were told 'to try it and leave if you don't like it'. The research indicated that such a taster experience was not really happening, and that once placed in a group students were not really given the option to leave even though in some cases the request to do so was supported by the group tutor (Sutcliffe, 1990). Such facts highlight the question of who chooses and who helps those who found learning difficult to make informed choices. If such choices are not made with understanding, then there is the danger that adult education groups become places where adults with learning difficulties are contained or entertained, but that the activities taking place can no longer be described as educational. For if an activity is to be educational one assumes that those adults taking part are willing participants in the learning process.

Group management

Another area which gave rise to difficulties was that of group management. This area of the research was centred around what the tutor would be expected to do if a student was being disruptive. Whilst tutors and managers were keen to ensure that a disruptive student was handled in an adult way by asking the person concerned to discuss the problem, this model was not understood by most of the students with learning difficulties. Students suggested that a person who was disruptive should be sent to the office or be made to sit in the corner until behaviour improved. One can only assume that in an educational setting the students were referring to a model of discipline they had been used to in school. On the other hand one student said that sitting in the corner was the way in which bad behaviour was addressed at home. What became increasingly clear was that few, if any, of the students with learning difficulties understood the tutors' method of discussing the problem. It was also clear that in some instances this was not the way problems experienced elsewhere were handled. This is not to suggest that the tutors' approach was wrong, but merely to highlight different expectations. If the points made above are in fact the case, then in many instances the tutors' attempts at dealing with disruptive behaviour in what they believed to be an adult appropriate manner, were at best misunderstood by the students with learning difficulties and at worst set up tensions within some of the students because behavioural problems were not dealt with in similar ways in all situations.

Materials

This was yet another area in which the views of tutors and managers and those students with learning difficulties were very different. When asked to select materials, the students almost invariably chose those rejected by tutors as being unsuitable for adults. The reasons given for rejection were almost always the same as those given for acceptance. For example, a tutor would reject a book or worksheet because the illustrations were not felt to be adult appropriate and students would select it because they liked the picture. These facts pose yet more questions. In the last resort if students are asked to choose, surely their choice is important. Even if all the materials regarded as inappropriate are not given to students, how do and how should tutors regard materials brought from home? Very often students bring books or magazines clearly designed for a chronologically younger age group. If, however, the student wishes to use these materials and has chosen to do so, where does that leave adult appropriateness and who should own the learning anyway? There is a danger that tutors will ask students to choose, but only if that choice fits a preconceived notion of what is appropriate for adults.

Conclusion

The research posed more dilemmas than it resolved. Whilst it is clearly desirable that adults with learning difficulties should be enabled to reach their full potential, this should not be at the expense of rejecting their models in favour of those which have majority acceptance. If it is realised that there is more than one model of adult, then some of the difficulties vanish. If, however, it is felt that the definition of adult must always be along the lines of Knowles's definition, even if this is not done consciously, there is a danger that people with learning difficulties may always be treated inappropriately from their perspective. Whose model is being used and whose choice is being accepted?

References

Bradley J, Dee L & Wilenius F (1994) *Students with disabilities and/or learning difficulties in further education* National Foundation for Educational Research
Knowles M (1990) *The adult learner: a neglected species* Gulf Press
Squires C (1993) 'Education for adults' in M Thorpe, R Edwards & A Hanson (eds) *Culture and processes of adult learning* Routledge

Sutcliffe J (1990) *Adults with learning difficulties: education for choice and empowerment* NIACE

Tomlinson J (1995) 'Disability, learning difficulties and further education: work in progress by the council's committee' in C Hewitson (ed) *Current developments in further education: the third John Baillie memorial conference* Skill

20. Only Connect: a Curriculum for Personal Development and Social Inclusion

Bryan Merton

Motivating disillusioned and underachieving young adults to take the first steps to becoming lifelong learners is a major challenge. The Young Adult Learners' Project has been set up by NIACE and the National Youth Agency to respond by identifying, encouraging, supporting, developing and disseminating effective interventions.

Many of these young adults are caught in a tangled web of social problems. Unless and until they are able to achieve a reasonable degree of emotional stability and a baseline level of self-esteem they will be unable to become effective learners and take advantage of initiatives such as the New Deal and New Start.

'Softer' outcomes

There is a growing consensus among those who contract, devise and deliver programmes aimed at underachieving and often reluctant learners, that many are not yet ready to achieve the kind of 'hard' academic and vocational outcomes customarily required by funding bodies. Instead these learners need a curriculum more sensitive to the social characteristics which shape their lives; and which contains learning outcomes and assessment criteria to equip them to become more skilled at interpersonal relations and better self-starters, team-workers, problem-solvers and independent learners.

The project is therefore designing a curriculum framework which has these characteristics and will give young adults recognition for achieving these kinds of outcome. Increasingly young people are demanding that their achievements have national currency and therefore the curriculum will include the option of assessment and accreditation.

This curriculum is distinctive in the following respects:
- *nature* – by specifying learning outcomes it moves personal development beyond the soft focus in which its goals tend to be expressed to much sharper definition;
- *purpose* – it will help young people reach the threshold of learning readiness, so that they can more easily take up the education, training and employment opportunities now available to them;
- *focus* – it concentrates as much on feelings, attitudes and behaviour, that is the domain of emotional literacy, as on skills knowledge and understanding; however, there are elements of underpinning knowledge which inform the learning outcomes; it also incorporates basic and key skills;
- *mode* – young adults can map their progression towards these outcomes through projects and activities in which they choose to take part and which provide the means of contextualising the learning outcomes;

163

- *control* – the selection of outcomes and the means of achieving them will be determined by the young person and a mentor; there will be diverse modes of assessment including self and peer assessment; progress towards the outcomes will be recorded through a portfolio which can be used alongside the new National Record of Achievement (Progress File);
- *context* – it can be applied in a range of contexts and is most suitable in non-institutional settings such as youth projects and community service schemes.

Mentoring

This curriculum is based on two premises. Firstly, that in any form of social learning it is important to recognise that young adults are unique individuals with different needs, interests, abilities and aspirations. Secondly that the young adult learners will each have a mentor with whom they will decide the nature of the project or activity and the combination of outcomes they will seek to achieve through it. Central to the implementation of this framework is a relationship of trust and mutual respect with time set aside to pay attention to individual needs, interests and aspirations.

Indeed, the use of a mentor as guide and assessor could add considerable value to the learning experience. The curriculum requires mentors to be *inventive* in setting up the activities through which achievements can be demonstrated; *observant* in recording them; and *sensitive* in assessing them. Mentors need to identify and exploit activities which are inherently enjoyable or useful, and design programmes in such a way that certain learning outcomes are planned for at key stages in the process and young people are given opportunities to come up with evidence of their achievements through an exercise or a project of their own choice.

Themes, outcomes and criteria

The curriculum comprises nine units based on themes identified in clusters in the three [areas] set out in Figure 1.

A	Managing Yourself	
B	Using Information	**Me and the Wider World**
C	Exercising Rights and Responsibilities	
K	Handling Relationships	
L	Finding Support	**Me, You and Them**
M	Exploring Risks	
X	Knowing Yourself	
Y	Coping with Feelings	**Me**
Z	Holding Beliefs	

Figure 1 Curriculum themes

It will be for the young person and mentor together to determine an appropriate entry point from among them. They may decide that it is prudent to start on the inner world (XYZ) and work outwards or vice versa; or they may decide that the best place to start is on the relationships at home where the young person wants to see some change. It is essential that the young person and mentor have complete discretion in determining how to proceed.

Figure 2 illustrates how one of these themes can be ascribed learning outcomes and performance criteria by which they are assessed. Again, the learning outcomes are best achieved and assessed when they are contextualised within a project or activity.

Unit: Using Information		
Learning Outcomes		**Performance Criteria**
1)	know where to go for information	1.1 formulate the questions to get the required information; 1.2 record the answers given; 1.3 plan how *you* will use the information; 1.4 record what happens when you use the information.
2)	use a range of information to make a choice	2.1 make a preferred choice using the available information; 2.2 record the consequences of your choice and how you felt about them; 2.3 review the extent to which the information retrieved helped you make that choice; 2.4 consider whether and how you might act differently in similar situations.
3)	use different forms of communication to convey information	3.1 communicate information in the manner chosen; 3.2 record the consequences of doing this and how you felt about them; 3.3 consider what you might do differently next time.
4)	present information about yourself to best advantage	4.1 plan and prepare a spoken and written presentation about yourself to a potential employer; 4.2 make a spoken and written presentation about yourself to a potential employer; 4.3 receive and discuss feedback; 4.4 consider what you might do differently next time.
		Continued...

Unit: Using Information *(Cont'd)*			
Learning Outcomes		**Performance Criteria**	
5)	recognise that gaining and using information can give you greater control over your life	5.1	plan how to collect useful information in order to solve a problem or achieve a goal;
		5.2	carry out the plan;
		5.3	record the outcomes and consider how successful the plan was

**Figure 2 Learning outcomes and performance criteria
for the unit on using information**

Challenge

The challenge facing all those working with young adults on the edge of education, training and employment, indeed of society itself, is to come up with quality programmes which are attractive, hold their interest and stimulate them to achieve and progress. These programmes have to extend beyond the narrow educational objectives of formal learning and vocational training in order to fulfil broader educational purposes and provide all young people with opportunities to develop in the round.

In this context, it is worth recalling the four pillars of lifelong learning described by Jacques Delors, chair of the UNESCO Commission on Education for the twenty-first century, himself quoted in the recent NAGCELL report, *Learning for the twenty-first century:*

- learning to live together
- learning to know
- learning to do
- learning to be.

It is time therefore to provide a curriculum which is seen by young people less as a burden and more as an entitlement; and as modern and forward-looking with regard to both their own individual futures and the kind of world in which they want to live. It needs to embody connectedness: between the young people's experience of exclusion and life in the mainstream; between youth and adult roles and responsibilities; between feeling, thinking and doing; between words and actions; between process and outcomes.

For those young adults who have started out in life with multiple disadvantages this entitlement is all the more important. We must do our best to motivate them to redeem it so that they can begin to see the importance of becoming lifelong learners and give themselves and their own children better prospects for a decent life.

21. Accessing Further Education: Views and Experiences of Students

Joyce Harrison

Introduction

Since the 1970s there has been a steady growth of support to encourage access to Further Education for students with special needs... The inclusion of students with learning difficulties/disabilities is part of a much greater movement to include students from ethnic and other minority groups, those unfamiliar with continuing education, returning learners and those needing variations in their pace and style of learning (McGinty & Fish, 1993). This growth has demanded a re-appraisal of traditional teaching and assessment methods, the provision of bridging activities, negotiation of individual learning programmes and the availability of learner support...

Student views and feelings

Various studies note a move towards a learner-led model. In *Vocational Preparation* (1981) the FEU states that the 'content and aims of vocational preparation are derived as much from the perceived needs of the young people themselves as from a predetermined range of disciplines'. In a study of assessment procedures for students with moderate learning difficulties Roberts, Norwich & Wedell (1982) highlighted the importance of social skills development and found that some colleges had included student self-assessment methods. ALBSU (1983) also emphasised the importance of basic education provision being based on student-centred approaches, noting that adults requiring these provisions were unlikely to voice their needs.

Hutchison & Tennyson (1986), in their interviews of 16-20-year-old physically disabled students, found them to have very little experience of being consulted about their needs and wishes. Boulton (1988) noted that it was easy to pay lip service to the principles of decision making for people with severe learning difficulties without enabling them to develop the necessary skills. 'The ability to make decisions with confidence is an important factor in creating a positive self-image for all of us.'

Curriculum development models in FE have continued to move towards a learner-led model which places more emphasis on assessment, curriculum design, managing student learning and developing competences, for all learners (FEU, 1988). FEU (1990) suggests that criteria for quality learning should include the need for learners to reflect on what they have learned, to demonstrate how a learning task is tackled, and to explain their way of doing the task. The FEU (1991) proposed that: 'Students should be given the opportunity at all stages of their learning to be involved in the assessment process. It should be made as flexible as possible to remove unnecessary barriers and optimise access to nationally recognised competence-based qualifications. Assessment should take place in the diagnostic, formative and summative stages.'

Inclusive education demands that more attention is given to enabling students to be involved in setting their own learning targets, in self-assessment and in evaluating teaching and learner support. However, Corbett (1993) emphasises that 'We tend to assess how it feels to us, not how it feels to the person being assessed, as we can only guess at that. Assessment is about feelings and values as well as about measurement.'

Recent legislation with regard to children has focused on the right of the child to make their 'wishes and feelings' known in any legal matters (Children Act, 1989). Education legislation (DES, 1989: Circular 22/89) emphasised that 'the feelings and perceptions of the child should be taken into account' in making decisions about provision for special educational needs, and youngsters in possession of a Statement of Special Educational Need are now encouraged to reflect on their learning, at least annually, as part of the process of reviewing their needs.

Teachers have explored ways of helping these pupils and those with milder learning difficulties in setting and reviewing their own targets and expressing their feelings and views (DfE, 1993). In compiling records of achievement all pupils are encouraged to reflect on their learning and note their views as part of the assessment process. These youngsters are now moving into Further Education (FE) colleges. Are they more experienced and better able to express their views than previous cohorts?

Consumer rights and entitlements

Many colleges have worked towards developing more inclusive provision with varied and flexible approaches to support, integrated across the whole college. Concern was raised by colleges when funding arrangements changed after incorporation in April 1993. The new Further Education Funding Council emphasised the market place and cost effectiveness in provision, and at the same time sought to ensure that the existing range of FE provision for students with learning difficulties and disabilities be maintained and improved.

In order to facilitate inclusion the council decided that 'it would be more appropriate to attach weightings for funding purposes to individual students rather than to treat learning difficulties as a subject' (FEFC, 1992). It also emphasised that 'wherever possible, learning difficulties should be no bar to access to further education' (FEFC, 1993).

However, Corbett & Myers (1993) found that 'some colleges were struggling with fewer resources and being pressured to rationalise their existing position'; in trying to find the balance between student needs and institutional limitations they concluded that entitlement was perhaps best addressed as responding to consumer rights rather than to 'special' needs. Consumer rights carries with it the concepts of exerting a choice and of having your views and wishes heard.

This creates a dilemma for lecturers who, on the one hand, may believe that the goals of education are to encourage students to be more self-directed, more self-motivated learners, to become responsible, caring, feeling adults, valuing co-operation, mutual respect and learning for its own sake. On the other hand they have to meet the requirements of recent legislation which is requiring schools and colleges to publish results based on external summative assessments. Emphasis on results and league tables fails to take account of the real differences between students and 'there is a danger that the concept of assessment is being distorted into a process of outcomes that are mechanistic, detached from personal need. Instead they appear to be determined by external pressures and prevailing financial and economic conditions' (Johnstone, 1994)...

Learning support

The range and model of support a college offers is influenced by its philosophical stance with regard to equal opportunities. The FEU has defined learning support as 'a college-wide approach to meeting the needs of a wide variety of learners, including those with disabilities and/or learning difficulties' (FEU, 1993). This document emphasised that learning support systems are there for the benefit of all students and are inclusive within the college environment. Corbett & Myers (1993) found a wide range of provision under a variety of names; however, most favoured a workshop type approach.

Bradley, Dee & Wilenius (1994) found that support was probably the least researched aspect of special needs in further education, there being then no research on what determines effective support, on student views or on whether support makes any difference. Kincer (1991) showed that centralised support services in the USA were a significant aid in helping youngsters adjust to post-secondary education and Boxer (1990) made a case for students to be involved in the design and development of support provision.

Bradley *et al.* (1994) conclude that it is only recently that the importance of students' own views on quality has been widely acknowledged. The extent to which self-advocacy is developed and supported by the curriculum, and the mechanisms colleges use to gather students' views, had still to be investigated.

The FEFC's Tomlinson committee, set up to review further education in England for students with disabilities and/or learning difficulties, met in September 1993. Taking account of all the emphasis on the importance of listening to the students views, it particularly set 'out to seek student views and encouraged these to be submitted as evidence to the Committee', which has now reported.

This study aimed to find out what FE students with learning difficulties and disabilities have to say about their learning needs, their evaluation of the support they receive and their views and feelings on whether access to FE has met their expectations.

Method

A random group of students with learning difficulties and/or disabilities were selected from eight FE colleges (five were previously Sixth Form Colleges) in Hampshire.

They were interviewed using a structured interview schedule with follow-up questions to clarify or elicit further information about their views and experiences of FE college. Questions focused on support for learning, their understanding of their own and others' disabilities, their social, emotional, academic and vocational goals and the extent to which they felt these had been achieved...

Results

The results will be presented in the same order as that of the structured interview. Questions were repeated, expanded upon or re-phrased as necessary to help the students understand, and follow-up questions used to gain more detail.

The range of courses followed by students...

Students were accessing courses from college foundation level through to A level: college foundation programmes (12 students) and NVQ level 1 courses (six students) focus on foundational skills and together cater for the largest group in the study (18 students); followed by GNVQ intermediate level studies (13) and then A level courses (seven students). Only one student was unable to give any indication of the course he was following; he had difficulty understanding and answering other questions.

Difficulties experienced with work in college

The question 'What do you find difficult in your lessons at college?' was orally presented and expanded to ensure that the student understood. In response to this question students tended to mention one or two areas initially and some extended their list in response to interviewer prompts or to later questions. This question was followed by 'How do your lecturers help you?', 'Do you have any special tuition or use the learning support centre?' and 'Is there any other help you would like?...'

The majority, 43 students (93%), said they had some difficulties with learning: of these, 20 students identified just one area of difficulty; nine identified two areas; and 14 identified between three and five areas of difficulty. Not surprisingly, the most frequently mentioned areas of difficulty were reading (18), understanding (18) and spelling (17). Problems with writing were mentioned by 11 students and a wide range of helpful support strategies were described. Problems of completing tasks within the given time arose for nine students and included: the lecturer speaking too fast; rubbing work off the board before the student had copied it; needing extra time to read text books; completing class, homework and examination papers.

Additional help received and wanted by students

The majority of students, 35 (76%), received additional support and/or used the learning support centre. However, 11 students (24%) said that they neither received additional support nor used the learning support centre. Of these, two had a physical disability and needed no help with learning; two students had access to learning support but did not use it; two adult students had been identified as needing support but it had not yet been provided; and five students attended a special course with favourable adult-to-student ratios and did not receive any additional help.

Learning support centre

Access to a learning support centre was the most common provision available, used by 23 students (50%). Two of the colleges did not offer this provision. Of the students using a learning support centre 18 were satisfied with the level of support they were receiving. The other five students felt that they needed other specific support: two felt they needed more individual help; one wanted to be taught word processing; one wanted help in class; two dyslexic students wanted lecturers to better understand their difficulties.

Individual tuition

The next most common provision identified was individual tuition and nine students received this. Of these, six were satisfied with the level of provision they were receiving; three felt they needed more time with the tutor; and two felt they also needed support in class. Five of these nine students were following A level or similar level courses; two were resitting GCSEs. The three students with profound hearing impairments had individualised packages of support which included individual weekly curriculum support from subject teachers and/or a teacher advisor of the hearing impaired, in-class support for additional explanations and note-taking and radio aid. Three of the students with dyslexia also used the learning support centre and special equipment.

Support in class

Five students said that they had support assistance in class. Two of the students were the hearing impaired students mentioned above where the support assistant was designated specifically for them; one felt she had sufficient help; and the other missed the social and academic support of a HI unit. The other three students were attending college foundation courses staffed by a lecturer and a support assistant: one was satisfied with the level of provision; one was not sure; and the third felt she needed priority attention in the class.

Specialist support staff

Specialist support staff from outside the colleges included: teacher advisers for hearing impaired; a specialist teacher for the dyslexic; a speech therapist and special school part-time provision. In addition one student regretted no longer receiving physiotherapy. The colleges had also identified six of the students being interviewed as needing further assessment from an educational psychologist.

Specialist equipment and resources

The two students with wheelchairs attended different colleges. One said he had good access whereas the other felt several adaptations needed to be made to make the college more accessible. A third physically disabled student did not need any equipment but did have problems with slippery and uneven floors. Three out of the four hearing impaired students used a radio aid and four of the eight students known to have dyslexia used special equipment...

Discussion

With regard to access to further education this survey sampled students with a wide range of learning difficulties and/or disabilities (LDD). The majority of students, 35 (76%), admitted having learning difficulties and/or disabilities; five were unsure and six felt they did not have any difficulties. Students most often described their difficulties in terms of the tasks they found difficult. Only four of the sample described disability in terms of abnormality or being different from others. Some felt they had overcome earlier difficulties and others stressed that everyone could have difficulty in learning at some stage. This emphasises the importance of learning support being fully embedded within and across the whole college, accessible to anyone who feels the need for support whether with regard to a short-term difficulty or on a regular basis.

The majority, 40 students (87%), were pleased that they had gone to college. Their main reasons for enjoying college were firstly making progress in the subjects studied and secondly making new friends. There is evidence (Wade & Moore, 1992) that school pupils feel isolated from their peers when they attend schools outside their local catchment area; six (11%) of the students in this study particularly mentioned that they had more friends or had enjoyed college because they were attending a college nearer home and/or were now able to travel to college independently. When asked what they felt they had gained from college, 22 students (48%) mentioned progress in the subject studied, 20 (43%) mentioned aspects of personal development. Hence, the students measured effectiveness in terms of their learning progress, feelings of inclusiveness and development of personal autonomy and independence.

The colleges provided differing ranges of support: the most flexible offering a learning support centre with drop-in and workshop sessions, individual tuition, support in class, access to specialist services for students and support for lecturers. Overall 43 students (93%) valued the support they received. But 13 of these students (28%) also identified needs that they felt were not being met in college. Whilst it was beyond the scope of this study to check how the students perceived themselves against college assessments, it was known that further assessment from an educational psychologist or other agency had been requested.

There was also evidence to suggest that students with more complex needs such as hearing impairment, dyslexia and physical disabilities needed a wider range of support to fully access their chosen courses. They did not always have access to the range of provision they felt they needed, e.g. physiotherapy, teaching or in-class support, equipment, lecturers who understood their difficulties, physical access to the building. Equally, individual tuition, the most expensive resource, did not always appear to be the most effective from some students' perspectives. However, students with mild to moderate learning difficulties generally felt their needs were well met through Learning Support Centres and courses with a good curriculum match, and favourable adult-to-student ratios. Hence there was evidence that some of the students were becoming increasingly able to judge their own performances and assess their satisfaction or dissatisfaction by applying their own standards.

Further research matching student self-assessment with lecturers' assessments and comparing the range of provision with student satisfaction would provide valuable insights into ways of improving learning support within available resources. Outcomes from this research should lead into college policy development to facilitate change. There are also implications for the training of all staff in understanding the difficulties and differing learning styles and needs of students and encouraging staff to re-visit the models on which they have based their teaching and assessment practices.

Overall, 40 students (87%) expected college courses to help them to get a job: several already had job offers which they had been unable to obtain before attending college; eight (17%) hoped to go on to more advanced education before seeking employment. Only three were unsure what they would do after college and three expected to attend a centre for the disabled. Despite the long-standing shortage of youth employment, the majority of these students had clear goals with regard to obtaining work and saw college as a means of achieving this goal. This presents a clear challenge to colleges, employers and politicians to develop not only access to college but also real access to work. It begs the question of whether every citizen has an entitlement to work or supported work which allows individual productivity targets.

This also highlights the importance of listening to the feelings and perceptions of the students both when they apply to the college and shortly after they start their courses. Colleges provide a very different context for learning and students need to be encouraged to evaluate their support after a period of usage. FEU (1993) *Supporting Learning, Promoting Equity and Participation* states as a guiding principle that 'the assessment processes and procedures should be carried out in partnership with learners. This should be an empowering process which builds on an individual's strengths and enables them to take responsibility for their own learning.'

Further research looking at joint student/teacher short-term target setting and long-term goals of students, in the year prior to transfer to college and following through each year in college, would be needed to map the development of student self-assessment and of its impact on teaching methods and learning outcomes; along with an assessment of the ways in which teachers were seeking to develop the students' skills in setting and reviewing long-term goals, identifying short-term targets and monitoring and reviewing progress.

Given the FEFC's current methods of funding this means that assessment at each stage: prior to entry; on-programme; and at exit, to use the FEFC terminology, becomes crucial in ensuring flexible support at each stage. In many instances this will involve inter-agency collaboration between college assessments and those from externally purchased support agencies such as specialist teacher advisers, educational psychologists, careers advisers and medical personnel. As yet, the FEFC funding formula is a rather crude instrument for ensuring consumer rights of access. Hopefully, the on-going work of the FEFC Tomlinson committee will provide effective funding and support mechanisms to ensure access and quality of learning.

However access to learning is only the beginning. Inclusion is more than mere access; inclusion embraces personal and social involvement; as well as the right to study together it also embraces the concepts of being a full member of society and having an entitlement to work which brings with it the opportunity of being an economic contributor to society. Achieving these goals requires the ongoing education of society in general with regard to developing a greater understanding of the needs and challenges faced by people with learning difficulties and/or disabilities, and of employers in particular, with regard to the contribution that people with learning difficulties and/or disabilities can bring to the workplace.

From the perspectives of the students surveyed, access to FE colleges should bring progression in learning, personal autonomy, social development and vocational training leading to real jobs or supported employment. This is the real challenge of the 21st century; not the mechanistic and constraining performance indicators of NVQ nor the college league tables, but increased awareness of every individual's competencies and the contribution that he or she can give to society at large.

References

Berliner W (1993) 'Further needs of the special student' *Observer* 31 Jan 1993, p59 cited in Corbett & Myers (1993)

Boulton A (1988) 'Decision making for students with severe learning difficulties in the FE context' *Educare* 30, pp15-20

Boxer M (1990) 'Adults with special needs: tutor awareness' *Adults Learning* 1(10)

Bradley J, Dee L & Wilenius F (1994) *Students with disabilities and/or learning difficulties in further education* NFER

Corbett J (1993) 'Entitlement and ownership: assessment in further and higher education and training' in S Wolfendale (ed) *Assessing special educational needs* Cassell

Corbett J & Myers L (1993) 'Support for learning in further education' *Support for Learning* 8 (4), pp151-156

Department of Education and Science (1978) *Special educational needs: report of the committee into the education of handicapped children and young people* (Warnock Report) HMSO

Department for Education (1993) *Code of practice: on the identification and assessment of special educational needs* HMSO

Further Education Funding Council (1992) *Funding learning* FEFC

Further Education Funding Council (1993) *Students with learning difficulties and disabilities* Circular 93/05 FEFC

Further Education Unit (1981) *Vocational preparation* FEU

Further Education Unit (1982) *Skills for living* FEU

Further Education Unit (1988) *Flexible learning opportunities and special educational needs* FEU

Further Education Unit (1990) *Individuality in learning* FEU

Further Education Unit (1991) *Transition into employment* FEU

Further Education Unit (1993) *Supporting learning, promoting equity and participation* FEU

Further Education Unit (1994) *Supporting learning, promoting equity and participation. Part 3. 'Assessing learning support needs'* FEU

Hampshire County Council (1989) *Special educational needs post-16: a guide to good practice* HCC

Hutchinson D & Tennyson C (1986) *Transition to adulthood* FEU

Johnstone D (1994) *Further opportunities: learning difficulties and disabilities in further education* Cassell

Kincer K (1991) *Factors that influence adjustment to post-secondary institutions as perceived by students with learning disabilities in Virginia* Virginia Polytechnic Institute and University

McGinty J & Fish J (1993) *Further education in the market place* Routledge

Roberts J, Norwich B & Wedell K (1982) *Making progress: the function of assessment for students with moderate learning difficulties* FEU

22.   Specific Learning Difficulties in Maths: a Guide for Teachers and Tutors

Nicola Martin

Introduction

Teachers are becoming increasingly familiar with the term specific learning difficulties in relation to literacy (dyslexia). Learners of any age may also be affected by specific learning difficulties which cause them problems in the acquisition of mathematical skills. This could be because the language of maths presents a barrier, or as a result of a range of underlying difficulties which will be explored in this paper. The term *dyscalculia* is sometimes used to describe people with severe specific difficulties in mathematics.

This paper describes 'dyslexic' difficulties which may affect maths performance at any age, during school and at college. Information about possible school-based intervention is supplied to give a background on the type of assessments and teaching which may have taken place before a student reaches further education. Strategies for learning support are described.

Assessment: a note on statementing

A tiny minority (about 2%) of students have severe difficulties in school and undergo a statutory assessment which involves a multi-disciplinary team and leads to an annually reviewed individual learning programme. This 2% includes general and specific learning difficulties as well as a range of disabilities. Of the minority statemented for special learning difficulties most of those will have an individual learning programme which focuses on their literacy difficulties. If a student was statemented at school their assessment report will yield valuable information for the college tutor. It must not be assumed however that non-statemented students will have no difficulties, as about 20% of the school population require some extra help at some time. At High Peak College we support about 2% of the students with one-to-one teaching mainly in literacy and numeracy but find that the 20% figure applies in that about this percentage require additional input in numeracy and/or literacy at some stage...

The ALBSU (Basic Skills Agency) numeracy test is used in colleges together with subject-based assessments which assess against the requirements of a particular course.

Features of a specific learning difficulties profile and why they result in difficulties in maths

Sequencing – Chinn (1992) describes the 'ability to hold in mind successive items in a series of numbers' as an essential mathematical skill often compromised in students with specific learning difficulties. Following a sequence of instructions, counting and multiplication tables and place-value concepts also require sequencing, so difficulty in this area can affect more than the ability to read and spell or recite the months of the year in order.

Directionality – Operating a number line and plus and minus concepts requires an understanding of the directional progression of digits. Mixing 13 and 31 for example may indicate directional confusion. Single digits can also be reversed. Just as students reverse the letters b and d, numbers 6 and 9 may cause similar difficulties. Left to right progression as for reading does not apply to all mathematical processes and difficulties may arise with place-value and shifting to working from right to left for some processes. Map reading also requires directional understanding.

Orientation – Just as 6 and 9 may pose problems, symbols like + and x are actually the same shape presented in a slightly altered spatial orientation.

Memory – difficulties with long and short term memory feature in the profile of many students with specific learning difficulties. Tables have to be committed to long term memory and retrieved automatically. Multi-faceted problems requiring step by step working require short term (sequential) memory. Processes and formulas may not be retained easily. Problem solving strategies requiring memory and retrieval of different formulas for different occasions may be difficult.

Clumsiness – The practicalities of geometry for example may cause difficulties for a student whose manual dexterity is underdeveloped as with many people experiencing specific learning difficulties. Neatness of presentation and accuracy of number formation could also be affected.

Symbolic representation: language – Symbolic representation, whether of letters to represent sounds or numbers to represent amounts, is difficult for the student with specific learning difficulties. When problems are described in language which is beyond the reading and comprehension level of the student this in itself will cause a barrier to numeracy development. Chinn (1992) points out that symbols have to be arranged in sequence, thus drawing on two areas of difficulty simultaneously for many.

Intervention

Learner style – Chinn (1992) describes 'The Grasshopper' and 'The Inchworm'. The former looks at the whole picture while the latter takes a step by step approach. The ability to reduce the whole picture to its component parts and work through in sequence to solve the problem, or the process of 'holding in mind' successive items in a series of numbers, may be challenging to the student with specific learning difficulties. Miles (1992) reminds us that it is essential to work out how a student is tackling a problem and their preferred learner style. Those with spatial perceptual difficulties would probably not appreciate a diagram but would prefer clear step by step instructions, for example, at an appropriate language level. Cluttered worksheets with speech balloons and cartoon style boxes may look more attractive but could add an unnecessary layer of confusion.

Multi-sensory teaching – Dienes (1992) advocates the use of apparatus used in conjunction with oral language in order to facilitate 'linkages' as the language mediates the manual process. Number symbols may make sense to a student functioning at a stage where concrete representation of symbols is still required. Just as a picture can give a clue to the sound of a letter, six piles of three coloured counters may be needed to illustrate 6 x 3 for example. Structured practice will be needed in order to teach mathematics; estimation of an approximate answer should be encouraged as part of the process as an aid to self monitoring. Activities should be built in to facilitate generalisation as the transfer to concepts across contexts can be difficult for a student with specific learning difficulties.

Crombie (1994) reminds the teacher that the student may need to manipulate objects, talk through the process, listen to instructions and record information in a structured way in order to make use of all the senses. Sequencing of numbers may need to be practised using multi-sensory activities to develop auditory and visual sequential memory as described in Hickey (1992).

Consideration

Miles (1992) talks about 'a long history of failure' which children experience if they have struggled through several years with specific learning difficulties. Adults may have been hiding their perceived inadequacies for years and will not want them highlighted. Simple strategies like providing squared paper to aid place value will not draw attention to the learner (particularly if squared paper is used by the whole class). Crombie (1994) advocates enabling older students to develop *strategies to circumvent the problem* whenever possible. Again, an understanding of the learners' style and the nature of their difficulties is necessary and different strategies will work for different individuals, e.g. using mnemonics, colour coding. It is essential also to remember that students with literacy difficulties will need maths problems presented at an appropriate reading level.

References

Chinn S (1992) 'Individual diagnosis and cognitive style' in TR Miles & E Miles *Dyslexia and mathematics* Routledge
Crombie M (1994) *Dyslexia: a teacher's handbook* Open University
Dienes M (1992) *Mathematics and dyslexia* Whurr
Hickey K (1992) *Multi-Sensory language course* Whurr
Miles TR & Miles E (1992) *Dyslexia and mathematics* Routledge

23. Inclusive Practices in Higher Education

Jenny Corbett & Sue Ralph

Introduction

In this paper we describe the work of the Multi-Media project in the Learning Support Unit which is part of the Centre for Continuing and Community Education in the Faculty of Humanities at the University of Portsmouth. The key issues raised are those of: inclusive provision; learner empowerment; the development of critical reflection and decision making; using imaginative approaches to communication within a competencies based economy. This provision is offered as an example of the new initiatives which the changing higher education context in Britain can now include as part of its broadening access responding to diverse needs. It illustrates how inclusion works most effectively within a flexible and imaginative framework.

A brief history of this specific provision establishes the context in which current developments occur. This provision cannot be called typical within Britain as the amalgamation of further and higher education which it involved has not been a national pattern to date. However, it does reflect elements commonly found in American undergraduate programmes which tend to include a far more diverse range of learners than those accepted into British universities. In this respect, what is happening at Portsmouth gives us an insight into future possibilities in national higher education initiatives.

Background to the Portsmouth Project

The Multi-Media Scheme began in 1982 with a partnership between the local City Council and the then Portsmouth College of Art, Design and Further Education. It aimed to offer an alternative to the often demoralising experience of many young people with disabilities who had been 'handicapped' by their experiences. They knew that labels such as 'unemployable' were insults to their latent or less marketable abilities. Their inability to perform certain tasks under certain conditions was no index of their worth as individuals or of their ability, for example, to make an animation film, to devise or perform drama, to work sensitively with others or to discuss complex philosophical issues.

Evidence of ability by the first students on the scheme – some profoundly deaf, others with learning and mobility difficulties – was manifest in a public exhibition called 'Fresh Images'. A wide range of media was employed which included film, animation, video, tape/slide, art and photography, and provided opportunities for the students to reveal skills and vision which surprised both the public and themselves. For several of the students, full- or part-time employment soon followed. Others developed a taste for reading, painting, filming or the pleasure of learning for its own sake. Several went on to pursue certificated courses in further or higher education.

Over its fifteen years there have been changes in approach and emphasis. These have been conditioned by such factors as increasing numbers and greater diversity of students, problems of accommodation (finding accessible and well resourced sites in the university or city), the uncertainties of continued funding, efforts to secure appropriate staff and supports to meet student needs and response to greater self-advocacy (Olesker, 1992). Increased demands by students and funding bodies for more accreditation, the politcs of change, as the university absorbed the scheme in its take-over of further education, and the opportunities offered by the new location of the scheme within an institute of higher education, are all recent challenges for the late 1990s.

This last development has been particularly significant. Suddenly university resources such as the television centre or a drama studio were available to students who for much of their academic and non-academic life had resigned themselves to accepting improvised, barely adequate accommodation as apt reflections of their marginal status in educational institution or society. The students on the programme now began to see themselves as others were beginning to see and value them: as students in a university. Staff at the television centre were surprised and impressed by the students' ability to rise to the new conditions and occasions presented to them. They found the students' direct and natural approach to video projects often a refreshing contrast to many of the more intellectual and modish exercises by undergraduates. These students had something to offer. In drama they began to work alongside second year undergraduates in English, creating an imaginative production that effectively illustrated the many social and academic advantages of 'mixed ability' learning. Each group learned much from the other; perceptions and preoccupations were modified; differences were truly celebrated.

Learner empowerment

The unique situation at Portsmouth has allowed for a level of creativity in course design which has been to the advantage of students coming in via the learning support unit. The experience is empowering for them in a variety of ways. The inclusion of mainstream drama and arts students working jointly on film, theatre and photography projects offers a rich opportunity to learn and share from each other. It seems particularly significant that the mainstream students working alongside students with learning disabilities are not being prepared for caring professions, whilst some earlier post-school integration initiatives predominantly involved students who were training to be nurses, social workers or teachers of children with special needs... In this respect, this was an example of unequal power relationships where one group was learning caring skills for the other. The fact that these arts students are not preparing for roles as carers allows for a more balanced level of collaboration in the projects which the unit fosters.

Another way in which this experience is empowering is that it offers opportunities for progression whilst at the same time providing group cohesion. There are many advantages for the students being in a university rather than in a day centre or in a segregated further education course. For some of them this entails the possibility of moving from the multi-media course into other courses offered by the university. For others it may simply involve the value of sharing canteen and bar facilities with other university students. The level of group support is such that vulnerable individuals are nurtured by others who share their common experience of lack of confidence. The practice of negotiating joint programmes by listening to all the participants' views encourages mutual esteem building and a recognition of the politics of difference.

Group work, critical reflection and decision making

How can a dozen students, each at a different level of skill, academic, development or maturity, communally 'own' a project? They must first be excited by a theme which touches their imaginations. Myths, legends, dreams, music, masks, puppets: any of these might serve as stimulus for a film, play, animation, story or debate. A recent discussion about early Hebrew myths dealing with the precursors of Eve engaged the whole group and led to a passionate argument about the nature of religion, feminism, truth and heresy. Several of the 'slow learners' were clearly delighted to be part of an exchange that was being conducted on an adult and unpatronising level. The dialectics of debates soon shaped themselves into a play with script writer (a student who will be moving on to a degree course), director (a student applying to join a drama course), actors and back stage crew.

In all of this the role of tutor is a delicate but crucial one. The tutor establishes the terms from the outset: all contributions will be valued; all contributions can be modified or improved. The accent is on 'error permitted learning', effectively the 'trial and error' approach, so that students fully absorb the lessons learned. Yet, there are occasions when guidance and intervention, 'error free learning', are necessary either to pass on basic skills or to ensure that a performance is ready for a public presentation. Rehearsals are generally widened and students become increasingly, but not inhibitingly, self critical. They discuss together in a mutually supportive way how they could improve... As this individual and group autonomy develops, in which even the 'warm ups' are led by the students, so individual and group confidence increases. In improvisations students learn not to 'block', that is not to deny the terms of the situation or role with which they are presented. This seems to develop in the students a more open imagination in which they learn to play with hypotheses and see the world from other perspectives. Several staff have commented on the impact of the drama sessions on specific individuals and their newly acquired initiative or ability to articulate. Students themselves say things like:

> *How much I've changed! I organised a trip for the year group the other day.*
> *I'd never have had confidence to do that before I came to drama.*

Communication and competencies

Some of the most natural and effective communication occurs away from sessions labelled 'Communication Skills'. In film or drama the communication is unselfconscious and about something other than itself. Students communicate because they want to and because they have something to say. Ideas are discussed, storyboards drafted, scripts written, film edited, dialogue spoken, voice-overs improvised and recorded, performances given and the whole process evaluated. All of these activities can be, and are being, translated into appropriate key skills units so that not only can students gain accreditation but actually see the value of these subjects in supporting their literacy, numeracy or IT skills. However, key skills acquisition is a consequence rather than an initial aim of a process which should enrich and extend the students' general education.

Opportunities are constantly sought to include in any project a wide range of cultural references: historical, literary, scientific and aesthetic. This is particularly important with students who may previously have only experienced a programme of basic social survival skills. Again the environment of an institution of higher education, offering open lectures to the widest range of students, can be of enormous advantage to students discovering the delights of exploring new subjects, themes and ideas beyond the realms of 'training' or NVQs. The Portsmouth experience suggests that the presence of students with a wide range of learning styles and needs in an institution of higher education can enrich both students and institution alike.

Concluding reflections

Higher education in Britain is in a process of fundamental change which demands new ways of developing course provision, responding to consumer need and competing with other providers – beyond university institutions (Gokulsing & DaCosta, 1997). This has been greeted by traditionalists with alarm and anxiety. However, it is seen by others who have always worked within the most innovative areas of post-school provision as an opportunity to widen participation, as Sir Ron Dearing so aptly put it. American undergraduate provision has for some time provided course modification and assessment procedures which encourage students with learning disabilities... They have been seen as entitled to participate in this inclusive provision. Sceptics in British universities will readily suggest that such a development merely leads to an overall diminishing in status and standards in the currency of first degrees. Undoubtedly the inclusion of students with learning disabilities calls for a more flexible range of courses including those which may not lead to a conventional degree. Universities in Britain could take their lead from the Open University which, with courses like Equal People (Open University, People First and Mencap, 1996) has involved students with learning disabilities for a number of years. Where Portsmouth is offering another dimension is in including these students on campus rather than in outreach provision.

References

Gokulsing K & DaCosta C (eds) (1997) *Usable knowledge as the goal of university education* Edwin Meller Press

Olesker S (1992) 'Setting the agenda: students participation on a multi-media learning scheme' in T Booth, W Swann, M Masterton & P Potts (eds) *Curricula for diversity in education* Routledge

24. Improving Transition for Students with Disabilities and Dyslexia from Further Education to Higher Education

Viv Parker & Marion West

Introduction

The 'invisibility' of students with disabilities has been identified and analysed by Brock (1990) and the need to improve access for such students was recognised during 1993/94 and 1994/95 by the Higher Education Funding Council for England (HEFCE, 1994) in its offer to the higher education sector of £3 million for projects to widen access to students with disabilities and learning difficulties. The University of East London was funded, in 1994/95, for such a project which included an exploration of transition planning as it applied to progression into higher education for students with disabilities and learning difficulties.   This article will discuss transition planning for students with disabilities and learning difficulties and identify some of the key issues for further and higher education. The term students with disabilities will be used throughout to include students with specific learning difficulties (dyslexia).

What is transition planning?

The Code of Practice on the Identification and Assessment of Special Educational Needs (DfE, 1994) describes the 'Transition Plan' as an opportunity for everyone to plan together for young people leaving school. The annual review after the young person's fourteenth birthday and any subsequent annual reviews until the young person leaves school draw together information from 'within and beyond the school in order to plan coherently for the young person's transition to adult life' (DfE, 1994: para.6:45: 117). The Code covers the transition from school to further education but it is equally important to provide for the needs of the many mature students with disabilities seeking entry to higher education. The possibility of transition planning for mature students with disabilities is complicated as they enter higher education via many different routes so it is difficult to know what transition preparation may be offered, by whom, when and where and who will fund the costs.

The concept of transition to higher education and the need to prepare students for the very different learning and institutional culture they will enter has been well documented and fully discussed in the literature on Access for at least the last five years (e.g. see Blackmore *et al.* 1991). If the student has a disability, the move from Access/further education into higher education can be devastating and potentially unachievable in the absence of appropriate preparation for this transition. Preparation for successful transition into higher education for students with disabilities involves many of the considerations identified as important for all Access students (by Blackmore *et al.* 1991) with some additional factors.

The University of East London study of transition

There were three aims of this project:

1) to find out what transition planning for students with disabilities was taking place in further education;

2) to identify what information further education colleges had about the facilities for students with disabilities and learning difficulties in higher education;

3) to get an overview of the facilities and policies in further education for students with disabilities.

Between January and June 1995 twelve special needs co-ordinators from the local catchment area of the university were interviewed by one of the authors of this paper, Marion West. They represented a small sample from a variety of settings in the south east. Some of the special needs co-ordinators were involved in developing policies while others saw their jobs as fire fighters, called in only when things go wrong.

All 12 of the colleges had a policy for students with disabilities and learning difficulties which came under their equal opportunities policies. Policies on equal opportunities have had a much higher profile in former Inner London Education Authority (ILEA) colleges than in some of the rural or suburban colleges. This was reflected in the prominent equal opportunities policy in which disability was just one component. Within such a mechanism, discrimination can be pursued as a civil rights issue and disability placed alongside race, gender and sexuality. The issue of where special needs fits into equal opportunities appears to depend on the specific history of the institution, its location and political influences. Four of the colleges were updating their policies and their co-ordinators were very much involved with the decision making.

All the institutions have a named co-ordinator for students with special educational needs. Eight of the co-ordinators are members of the academic staff and teach on other courses in the colleges; three have different titles for their jobs: for example one is a curriculum development and quality control manager, one was a learning support and basic skills manager and another was the head of the department for learning support and discrete courses. These jobs reflect the co-ordinator's position within the college. Three of the co-ordinators were an integral part of management, with decision making powers. Over the last five years provision for students with disabilities in further education has altered; whilst many of the changes have come about through external legislation and economic pressures, others have come about through a philosophy of integration. The differences between the co-ordinators was related to the degree to which they felt an ownership of these changes. One Borough has a transition planning team involving a range of professionals and individuals with the aim of planning for the effective transition for individuals from further to higher education and this was set up through a commitment to integration.

Ten of the colleges have discrete courses, two being fully integrated. Four of the colleges assess all their students when they first start and this means that they have a greater awareness of students' learning difficulties and disabilities. The official policy of most colleges is to offer students with disabilities open access to all courses, on the same basis as other students. However, where there are few resources to provide the study support needed by the student this often cannot be taken up. Some colleges provide more resources for support services than others and some specialise in certain kinds of support. Two colleges had excellent services for students with hearing impairment, offering communicator/notetaker support across the whole range of courses – one college had 35-40 students with hearing impairments. One of the colleges has a counselling service for students with mental health difficulties. Two others supported 12 and 21 dyslexic students respectively.

Questions about services for disabled students usually prompt reactions in terms of students with physical, mental and sensory impairments and (more recently) dyslexia. The range of 'invisible' disabilities is considerable and many conditions which are disabling may be overlooked if the co-ordinator has no direct experience of them. All 12 co-ordinators supported students with conditions such as dyslexia, epilepsy, arthritis, mental health difficulties and diabetes and 11 mentioned students with visual and hearing impairments. For less well known conditions such as ME (myalgic encephalomyelitis) and Sickle Cell Anaemia, six co-ordinators had no knowledge and for Repetitive Strain Injury (RSI) the figure was eight. All co-ordinators indicated that all physical and mental impairments that may affect a student's studies would be considered for learning support and all the colleges had resource centres and workshops to provide study skills and various kinds of study support such as notetakers and large print. However several co-ordinators indicated that students would have to make their needs known to the co-ordinator before support would be forthcoming as there was no internal college publicity about the service.

The number of students seeking and finding support is likely to be limited by the amount and nature of the information available to them about services. Only six of the college prospectuses specifically mention that students with disabilities are welcome and internal information is often limited. It is therefore likely that only the more well informed and assertive students and those with the most apparent impairments will self-identify or be identified by staff. Students with 'invisible' disabilities such as RSI and ME may well not see themselves eligible for support and not be identified by staff as disabled and therefore eligible.

The colleges had arrangements for examinations but most depended on the Examination Boards to specify appropriate conditions. Seven mentioned that students needed an up-to-date assessment of their needs. This seems to be most problematic with dyslexic students as the assessment is costly unless the college employs its own staff (usually an educational psychologist) for this purpose. Screening for dyslexia was provided and funded by six colleges, formal assessment by two colleges, and four were able only to provide information on external specialists. Sixth form colleges were more likely to provide screening or assessments.

Assessment is increasingly perceived as the key to access to further education for students with disabilities. Yet there is a mixed response to concepts of what constitutes dyslexia; for instance, one co-ordinator asked if 'dyslexia was not just a spelling problem?'. Another indicated that if they did have students with dyslexia the careers department was very good at getting them fixed up with a Youth Training Scheme. She said 'Dyslexics don't go on to higher education, do they?'. Young people and mature students without a statement may find that their needs are not assessed because the cost is prohibitive.

Dyslexia is traditionally associated with written language skills and may manifest itself in many ways such as: slow reading; poor reading comprehension; faulty spelling; poor phonic skills. However, difficulties of this kind may not be due to dyslexia; they may arise from a number of educational, cultural and social sources. This means that further education colleges have problems in deciding who to put forward for assessment. Without an assessment it is very hard to identify who is dyslexic. The complexity and cost can be a contentious issue; one co-ordinator stated:

> *It costs two hundred pounds to have an assessment done; this is fine if that person is dyslexic as we can get the money back from the Further Education Funding Council but if they are not dyslexic we can't. Therefore before I make that decision I need to be certain that it is a dyslexic problem and not an educational, social or cultural one.*

Consequently many young people and mature dyslexic students come into higher education without assessment. The University of East London (UEL) has seen 120 dyslexic students this year (1994/5) and most of these are first identified and assessed only after they join the university. Over recent years, as our systems for identifying and assessing such students have improved, the numbers of students being assessed as dyslexic has increased sharply.

Most co-ordinators did not know how many students with disabilities were eligible for entry to higher education, but five were able to say how many were attending their college. Numbers were available from four colleges for students with dyslexia (21, 12, 6, 22) and for those with hearing impairments (35/40, 4, 4, 2) and from two for those with physical impairments (4, 6) but rarely for other (invisible) disabilities. All the colleges provide educational guidance and support and six have a higher education adviser. However, 10 indicated that work on transition was not included in this guidance, although two are planning to include it from next year.

Some colleges provided an information talk, or day, for A level or Access students on higher education, but no reference was made to the Disabled Student Allowances (DSA). As the support offered by the DSA is key in enabling many students with disabilities to study in higher education, the absence of information on this seems likely to circumscribe a student's decision to enter higher education. At UEL we have encountered students with disabilities who have been advised by Access and other college staff to take a part-time rather than full-time course of study because of the nature of their disability. The staff were apparently unaware that students would then become ineligible for the DSA.

Only three colleges provide guidance notes for students progressing to higher education. Information from universities on the support offered to students with disabilities was held by seven of the co-ordinators; five indicated that students with disabilities do make visits to the universities but only one indicated that such information would be sought on a student's behalf.

Most of the co-ordinators indicated that the number of students with disabilities going on to higher education was small, so they were able to work with those students on an individual basis. The co-ordinators seemed to employ *ad hoc* responses to these individual needs rather than an institutional strategy for identifying and meeting them. For example, below are the comments of different co-ordinators:

If a student comes to me about higher education I would find information for them. (staff A)

I only see students if they have a problem. (staff B)

I work with students on an individual basis. (staff C)

It depends on the university, I sometimes go with the students to visit the university to see their facilities. (staff D)

The co-ordinators seemed to be largely reactive to student demand and to identified 'high profile' need. They provided support to those students identified as having 'obvious' or visible impairments and those students who were sufficiently informed about the possibility of support and assertive enough to seek it out. If students did not self identify as disabled and seek out the co-ordinator, there was little pro-active publicity or targeting of information to encourage and enable students with 'invisible' disabilities and low awareness of support possibilities to become informed about and secure the support they needed.

All the special needs co-ordinators said they would be aware if students with disabilities or learning difficulties were applying to higher education. However, only three of the colleges had *Higher Education and Disability* (Hobsons, 1994), which gives information about all the universities and higher education colleges in Britain and their provision for students with disabilities. Only two of the further education colleges were drafting a transitional plan for students going on to higher education, training or employment.

Issues in assessment and labelling

The link between the assessment of educational need and official labelling as disabled is important in giving access to resources and therefore to study support. Funding for students with disabilities is given to those already identified as disabled. It is not available to enable institutions to identify students who may be disabled. To gain access to extra support for study two different kinds of evidence are usually required. The first is for the existence of the disability and the second for existence of the need for the specified support to study.

Any policy move away from the medical model which labels and categorises individuals as disabled according to their physical and mental impairments is often undermined in practice by the requirement that access to study support depends on being labelled as 'disabled'. When the need arises from a student's physical or sensory impairment those responsible for providing resources will usually require evidence from a medical source which is usually available with little difficulty or expense. This contrasts sharply with the cost of a dyslexia assessment (see above).

Funding and assessment of needs have to be worked out. At the moment it is too bureaucratic with too many agencies that can cause considerable tension between the desire to be client-led and finite resources. This study indicates how complex the various Education and Care in the Community Acts are. Most of the professionals who work with people with disabilities are aware of the legislation as it affects their own service but not of the whole range of legislation relevant to the support of an individual. There is a need for the co-ordination of the support for a given individual across all the agencies which provide the funding and services needed. One way that has been suggested (Maychell & Bradley, 1991) is that LEAs and Social Services, working in conjunction with local colleges, could combine non-Schedule 2 and Community Care funding to produce a single pool of resources which is not service specific. Vested interests in how the money is spent may then be reduced and criteria for its use would then be governed by the needs of the individual.

Wehman (1992) recommends the development of individual transition plans which place the learner at the centre of the process and are supported by shared policies, procedures and resources. The likelihood of all institutions developing transition plans for individual students with disabilities seems to be some way off. There is scope for developing systems and services to enhance the transition process and the remainder of this article will identify some of the issues affecting transition and suggest good practice.

Issues affecting transition into higher education

The style and ethos of higher education is often experienced by students as a culture shock after further education. It is becoming commonplace to note the effects of:

- the move from an elite to a mass system of higher education
- the far greater size and scale of institutions
- the requirement that the student must organise most of the support required as there may be no member of university staff with the time or responsibility allocated to this
- the absence of any, or very poor provision of, support staff
- the semesterised and modularised form of study
- escalating numbers of part-time, hourly paid staff
- the breakdown of personal tutoring support.

These factors sharply accentuate the pressures and stresses on all students and particularly those with disabilities who, almost by definition, need additional support. The formal and informal sources of support from staff and students available in further education are reduced by these factors. Personal contacts and friendships with fellow students and tutors are more difficult to develop. Students with a variety of physical and mental impairments, while quite able to meet course requirements, often have to expend more time and energy in doing this than other students. Just getting about the corridors, accessing and using library, computer, refectory and other facilities is harder when the number of other users is so great. The institutional culture is less supportive: the predominant ethos in higher education is that individuals manage their own learning and lives. Institutions of higher education are given no resources by HEFCE specifically to meet the costs of supporting students through this process, although some institutions have chosen to top-slice their budgets and fund advisory or support services (for a study of the co-ordinators' role see Parker, 1995).

As all these factors may seem overwhelmingly negative it is important to stress that students with all sorts of disabilities can enter higher education and study successfully and have been doing so in increasing numbers over recent years. It will enhance a student's chances of success in higher education if these factors can be identified and prepared for before they enter higher education.

Promoting transition for students with disabilities

We have identified some points which may help staff in further and higher education prepare students with disabilities for the transition to higher education. They are based on:

- our experience at UEL of developing a service for students with disabilities
- regular interview and questionnaire consultations with students in direct contact with the service over the last three years
- the outcome at the transition planning project
- the comments of 25 colleagues from further and higher education at a workshop on transition for students with disabilities (held at UEL on March 1 1995).

1. *Early contact and self-identification.* Students need to be enabled and encouraged to identify themselves as disabled or dyslexic as early as possible in their study career. This will then allow maximum time to identify and provide the equipment, systems and personal support best suited to their needs. A recent telephone enquirer to UEL indicated that her Access tutor had advised her against indicating her disability on the application form as she may be refused a place. At UEL those who do indicate a disability on the application form are contacted and offered extra advice and a visit to the site. The prospective student would have been disadvantaged had she followed this advice. If an institution is likely to discriminate against a student who indicates a disability on application it is probably as well that the student knows this in advance. There are many institutions now which do have positive policies and encourage applications from students with disabilities. Nationally collated information is available via Skill, Hobson's Guide (1994) and ECCTIS.

Student self-identification will be encouraged by publicity which goes to all students, not just those thought by staff to be disabled. Wide publicity is essential to raise awareness of many forms of disabling condition which may not be apparent to others

191

– e.g. mental health difficulties, epilepsy and diabetes. The publicity must indicate a purpose or point in self-identification: e.g. the possibility of modification to exams or special funds such as the DSA. There also needs to be system by means of which the student can identify him or herself and a person to whom he/she may speak about his/her needs.

2. *Personal skills for successful study.* Access courses have long played a very significant and successful role in preparing students for higher education. The personal skills traditionally developed through Access courses are of great importance for students with disabilities. These include time and stress management, basic word processing, planning and production of written work, familiarity with libraries, reading and notetaking and storage and retrieval of text material. For students with a disability self-knowledge and self-management skills will be particularly important, as will assertiveness and the skills of working with others. Where students have not achieved a satisfactory level of these skills they may be best advised to defer entry to higher education until they have.

3. *Knowledge, advice and guidance pre-higher education.* Knowledge of the requirements of different courses (especially of less obvious requirements such as the study of a foreign language as part of European Studies or field courses as part of Land Surveying) and of the suitability/accessibility of different universities is important to ensure a viable choice of course. Personal contact between staff at further education and higher education level may be one of the best means of ensuring an applicant chooses a suitable course and is given appropriate support through entry processes: e.g. a communicator or scribe for interview/written tasks and discussions. It is important to note here that there is no funding given to institutions of higher education to meet the cost of any special equipment, or personal support, that an applicant with a disability may need during any admissions/entry tests or procedures. Only registered students, not applicants, are eligible for the disability allowances.

Conclusion

The main finding of the project is that transition planning for students with disabilities and learning difficulties is not taking place within further education and the concept is not being addressed in higher education. The Code of Practice came into effect on 1st September 1994 and has not yet been taken up by further education colleges in planning for higher education. Planning for transition is not yet an established pattern. There are several examples of collaborative planning between schools and colleges and between social services at a local level. Yet local agreements cannot replace a planned professional framework (Maychell & Bradley, 1991). The fragmentation of services which confronts people with disabilities and learning difficulties has been well documented over the years (McGinty & Fish, 1992; HMI, 1991). Not only do difficulties exist between services, e.g. education and social services, but also within services, e.g. school and further education colleges. Just one example of such difficulties is in the division of responsibility for transport for students in further and higher education between LEAs, colleges, social services or social work departments and health services. In a recent study of transport, 29 out of 35 respondents indicated problems and 19 suggested the need for one body to have a clear responsibility. The need for increased co-ordination was frequently mentioned and this appears to be a necessity for improved transition planning.

Theoretically, emphasis on a needs driven, customer-led provision should encourage the development of student-centred programmes and lead to a shift away from service-led provision. However assessment is the basis of resource allocation. The danger in making assessment the gateway to further education is that it may reinforce the medical model of disability. This is a problematic area of funding. The central purpose of all assessment should be an objective appraisal of an individual's needs. Often funding and resources are linked to the assessment of needs; there is a danger that if a student is likely to be ineligible for funding there will appear to be no point in undertaking an assessment. Certain groups of student are excluded from certain sources of support; for example part-time, self-funded and overseas students are not eligible for disabled student allowances. Such students may not be assessed and then miss out on special support.

The resource available to support a student's studies is not open-ended and unlimited. The disability allowances for example are not sufficient to enable a student with a hearing impairment to be provided with a notetaker or communicator for all contact hours – the student has to choose those situations in which s/he will and will not be supported. A student who needs personal support to study is not likely to be funded for this support during extra curricular activities. The service is driven only by those needs which can be assessed and qualify for the label of disabled and are very strictly defined as educational. It is customer-led only where the student qualifies as customer and the assessment yields sufficient funding to enable the student to be provided with all the resources s/he needs for all aspects of studies.

Improvements to services usually require an incentive. One initiative which may provide this incentive for improvements in provision for students with disabilities in further and higher education is the Disability Discrimination Act 1995. The Act will enable the Further Education Funding Council to: '... require the governing body to publish disability statements at such intervals as may be prescribed, and may include conditions relating to the provision made, or to be made, by the institutions with respect to disabled persons' (Part IV, section 30, p25).

HEFCE will have similar powers at the higher education level and institutions must provide Disability Statements before February 1997. This requirement seems likely to prompt institutions to audit and review their facilities, systems and provision for students with disabilities. The process of producing the Statement is likely to improve knowledge and awareness amongst staff across an institution, promote some improvement to services and improve publicity about provision for staff and students. It should also raise the expectations of students, applicants and potential applicants and promote the demand for education from individuals with disabilities. Such changes would then provide some of the essential ingredients for improving the transition between further education and higher education.

References

Blackmore R, Bridgewood A, Chiswick L, Clark S & Cody C (1991) 'The transition from access courses: a student-centred approach' *Journal of Access Studies* 6 (2), pp221-226

Brock S (1990) 'The invisibility of disability' *Journal of Access Studies* 5 (2), pp214-217

Department for Education (1994) *Code of practice on the identification and assessment of special needs* HMSO

Higher Education Funding Council for England (1994) *Special initiatives to widen participation: Circular 8/94* HEFCE

Her Majesty's Inspectorate (1991) *Education for people with learning difficulties* HMSO

Hobsons (1994) *Higher education and disability: the 1995 guide to higher education for people with disabilities* Hobsons in conjunction with Skill

Maychell K & Bradley J (1991) *Preparing for partnership: multi-agency support for special needs* National Foundation for Educational Research

McGinty J & Fish J (1992) *Learning support for young people in transition* Open University Press

Parker V (1995) 'The role of the co-ordinator for students with special needs/disabilities in higher education' *The Skill Journal* 53, 15–23

Wehman P (1992) 'Life beyond the classroom: transition strategies for young people with disabilities' *Brookers* TB35